NET
GAINS

NET GAINS

Inside the Beautiful Game's
Analytics Revolution

RYAN O'HANLON

ABRAMS PRESS, NEW YORK

Library of Congress Control Number: 2022933713

ISBN: 978-1-4197-5891-1
eISBN: 978-1-64700-555-9

Printed and bound in the United States

10 9 8 7 6 5 4 3 2 1

Abrams books are available at special discounts when purchased in quantity
for premiums and promotions as well as fundraising or educational use.
Special editions can also be created to specification. For details, contact
specialsales@abramsbooks.com or the address below.

Abrams Press® is a registered trademark of Harry N. Abrams, Inc.

ABRAMS The Art of Books
195 Broadway, New York, NY 10007
abramsbooks.com

To Wally and Kathleen,
You got me started.

CONTENTS

INTRODUCTION

Playing football is very simple, but playing simple football is the hardest thing there is.
—JOHAN CRUYFF

* * *

My dad dropped out of college before the second semester of his freshman year. Whenever someone asks him what he studied in college, he tells them he majored in "socializing." He sells fish for a living, gets up at four every morning so he can be in tune with the Asian markets, and then spends his days on the phone and on his feet, helping unload trucks, moving slats of wild salmon around in bedroom-size freezers, and making phone calls that ensure trucks full of tuna get from fishermen to wholesalers to your local northeastern grocers. He gets home around 2 P.M. and, without fail, reeks of fish. Not any particular fish—certainly not any kind of odor I've encountered outside of post-work hugs or rides in the car—but rather what I imagine every fish smell put together would smell like. Call it "fish essence."

I also have no doubt that, were my dad in charge, the United States would never have missed the 2018 World Cup.

Had I been born in another country, I'd probably be playing professional soccer right now. Or at least, I would've played professional soccer at some point. I was quick enough, I had the touch, and I had the vision to slow the game down. If I'd grown up in Amsterdam or Lyon or London, I would've joined up with the youth academy at a professional club, worked my way through the age groups, received the requisite developmental guidance, and ended up in the second division in Ireland or somewhere in Scandinavia. I probably wouldn't have gone to college; maybe, I'd have already retired and would be going to college right now.

Instead, I grew up in St. James, New York, a sleepy little middle-class enclave on Long Island tucked between a bunch of other, more affluent neighborhoods that residents referred to, unironically, as "hamlets." Robert Mercer, the shadowy hedge-fund master behind the election of President Donald Trump, lives 10 minutes away, deeper into the woods, up near the water. Trump held a campaign rally at a country club down the street from my parents' house. Ignore the various moral and ethical issues with this thought exercise for a second: If, for some reason, you wanted to ensure that a newborn child did not grow up wanting to play soccer, then putting them in a basket, attaching it to a parachute, and dropping the contraption into the heart of St. James would be one of your better non-Arctic or -Antarctic targets.

The American soccer ladder isn't quite broken, though it is missing a bunch of rungs, costs way too much money to use, and comes with plenty of purported guides who offer the wrong directions. I made it about as high as I could—I was a starter at the NCAA Division 1 level—but only because of the guy who smelled like low tide.

* * *

It's easy to identify a basketball player or a football player. Think about the last beautiful, non-pandemic day when you spent a large amount of time out in public, bumping into, walking by, smiling at, exchanging pleasantries with countless people you've never met before. OK, now think about how many of those people have the necessary body type to play in the NBA or NFL. Without even considering talent, sheer genetics provides a coldhearted selective filter for the player pool in both of those sports. LeBron James is six foot nine, 250 pounds, and built like a nuclear warhead. Tom Brady might be verging into dad bod territory, but he's still six foot four and 225 pounds. Anyone can dream of becoming the starting point guard for the New York Knicks, but only about 5 percent of the global population has the physical blueprint to make it happen.

Pretty much anyone can, in theory, become a professional soccer player. I'm five eight, 155 pounds, and look like a lesser Greek god when compared to the best soccer player in the world, the puny five-foot-six Lionel Messi. In fact, Australian researchers found that 28 percent of the global population has the necessary physique to become a professional soccer player.

And yet, soccer talent development in America for most of the 20th and 21st centuries has used the same filters as basketball and football. The bigger and faster kids get identified at the youngest ages and then get fast-tracked toward the best available training. Why? Because when you're 10, being bigger and faster is what wins soccer games. But youth trophies have little correlation with long-term development. France overhauled its youth system, and now French children play half as many competitive games as American children. They won the most recent World Cup. As David Endt, a former executive at Ajax, the Dutch club widely considered to have one of the best youth-development structures in world soccer, told the *New York Times Magazine*, "Here, we would rather polish one or two jewels than win games at the youth levels." Ajax recently reached the Champions League semifinals.

Soccer suffers from what is known as the *relative age effect*, where children born earlier in the year often perform better than those born later but are still funneled into the same arbitrary age group. After all, eight months of age difference matters way more when you're 10 than when you're 20. More than 30 percent of the athletes in European soccer's top leagues were born in the first three months of the year, and less than 20 percent have their birthdays in October or later. However, another study found that the players who win awards at the highest level—in other words, the kids who develop the best—are more likely to be born at the tail end of their age group.

My dad didn't know about any of these studies, or all of this data. He probably still has no clue. But he wouldn't be surprised to hear any of it because, somehow, he knew something was wrong. The first travel team I played for was the best travel team on Long Island, the Smithtown Thunder. I was one of the first kids who could both (1) run with the ball relatively close to my feet and (2) kick it in the air. So many of our games featured the same pattern: Someone would clear the ball up to me on the right wing; I'd dribble 15 or 20 yards forward and then lob the ball into the net from the sideline because 12-year-old keepers still can't touch the crossbar. Most of my teammates were particularly big or particularly strong or particularly both of those things for their age, and we had only a handful of smaller, more skillful players, like me. "The team had the perfect collection of talent to win games at that age group," my dad told me.

A paragon of unconventional sports wisdom my father is not: He's convinced Babe Ruth would be the best baseball player alive today, he doesn't understand why it was a mistake for the New York Giants to draft a running back with the no. 2 pick in the 2018 NFL draft, and his great basketball insight is that players don't "jam the ball" enough. He also doesn't have much personal experience to draw from. My mom was offered and accepted a full gymnastics scholarship from the University of Florida, but my dad's athletic career ended in ninth grade when he broke his ankle playing badminton against his gym teacher.

Despite that, he was able to turn himself into exactly what his son needed, and what the soccer world still doesn't have nearly enough of: a long-term thinker willing to go against the way things have always been done. He knew I wouldn't be able to keep lobbing the ball into the net. After all, those keepers were going to start growing at some point.

* * *

It was a Pieter Bruegel painting of the late-1990s American soccer scene: curly-haired me, in a bright-blue Carolina Panthers Starter jacket, sitting behind home plate in a dank, dark, and moldy indoor AstroTurf baseball field, crying my eyes out. My parents had taken me to meet a local private trainer with the air of an '80s Wall Street banker but an encyclopedic knowledge of Dutch soccer named Ron Alber—and they'd done it absolutely against my wishes.

A few weeks before, on the way home from practice with the Thunder, I had told my dad that I was bored. He had immediately gone out to the local soccer shop and asked one of the owners for the name of the most intense soccer-trainer he knew. When they spoke on the phone, Ron told my dad that if he ever decided that he disagreed with his methods, Ron would give him his money back. That was music to a fish salesman's ears. But even though I claimed I was bored at practice with the Thunder, I'd grown comfortable being the best soccer player on every team I played for. It was part of my nascent preteen identity. And what if it was no longer the case once I met Ron? I couldn't take that chance! So, I cried through the whole car ride there, and no doubt to the mortification of my mom and dad, I kept the tears flowing once we walked in the door.

But then I watched the kids play. They all manipulated the ball with Olympic-synchronized-swimming levels of precision—seamlessly shifting into a new, slightly different movement at the sudden command of the coach. Half of the training session was just that: you and the ball. Then the other half was passing drills—one-touch back-and-forths, short-short-long patterns—and a bunch of micro-games: 1-on-1 dribbling and defending, 4-on-2 possession in a box, three teams in a giant square. There were no keepers because there were no goals; no one took a shot at any point during the session. Somewhere along the way, my tears dried up; I was mesmerized, enchanted by the repetition in the patterns, by the way they broke the game down into its component parts and shifted the geometry away from the up-and-down, kick-and-score game I was used to. I knew I could do all of this, but no one had ever asked me to try.

Tear ducts closed (or exhausted) and with an Adidas track jacket in place of the Panthers parka, I showed up the following week. And then the next, and the next, and the next. I stayed with my club team for another year or so, but I kept going to the group training session and then added individual hour-long weekend sessions with Ron to my regimen. Eventually, I decided to leave the Thunder, along with my two best friends on the team and the other two best players, for the club team that Ron trained, the Huntington Boys Club (HBC) Elite.

From the outside, it must've seemed absurd. We'd won the Long Island championship with the Thunder, again, in our last season with the team. I think, deep down, prepubescent me knew that Elite were always better than us whenever we played them, even though we won more often than not. The way they moved the ball, both individually and collectively, was something we could never do. Sometimes my dad would talk about how we'd dominated a game and still lost; matchups against Elite were the only times he'd turn that statement around: They dominated the game even though we won. They'd win every aspect of the game—except for the final step: putting the ball into the net. It felt so satisfying to beat them, but it also felt like it wouldn't last. I guess even if you *can* beat 'em, join 'em.

What none of us realized at the time: We were all picking sides in a century-long battle over the right way to play the game. "The history of tactics, it seems, is the history of two interlinked tensions: aesthetics versus results on the one side and technique versus physique on the other," Jonathan Wilson writes, in *Inverting the Pyramid*, his own history of tactics. In Brazil, it's *futebol d'arte* and *futebol de resultados*. In England of the early 1900s, Herbert Chapman was one of the first managers to attempt to professionalize his charges. He installed a cohesive fitness regime and was constantly thinking of better ways to arrange his players on the field. His Huddersfield Town and Arsenal sides each won two league titles apiece. But even he seemed conflicted about the right way to achieve success. Chapman wasn't in the business of player development, but his language sounds remarkably similar to the folks at Ajax and the French federation: "The average standard of play would go up remarkably if the result were not the all-important end of matches. Fear of defeat and the loss of points eats into the confidence of players. . . . If we would have better football, we must find some way of minimizing the importance of winning and the value of points."

While the romanticism still exists somewhat, the modern version of this debate has shifted slightly. It's no longer about the merits of achieving some aesthetic ideal vs. winning as many trophies as possible. No, now one side of the argument claims that aiming for that ideal is also the best way to win as many trophies as possible. Manchester City manager Pep Guardiola, who prefers lots of possession and quick passing, has said, "We play leftist soccer. Everyone does everything." Meanwhile, Guardiola's philosophical obverse, José Mourinho, who likes his sides to sit back and wait for a mistake, has said, "Whoever has the ball has fear." As such, the debate rages on: Is it better to have the ball or not? Better to hit it long or pass short?

An ocean away, parents and kids on the Thunder couldn't comprehend what we were doing; they were Suffolk County's very own Mourinistas. We're the best team on Long Island! Not yet a teenager, I didn't have the vocabulary to answer those questions properly, and even if I did, I'm not sure the answers would've landed the right way, anyway. *Listen, your uncultured playing style is just not sustainable. The process, for kids like us, is more important than the results.* Our teammates weren't even really the issue. When I asked my dad if our leaving upset the parents on the Thunder, he laughed and said, "Yeah, that would be the tamest way of putting it."

With the three of us in tow, Elite became one of the best teams in New York, and then the Northeast. Joining up with them meant that I was always getting training from Ron, no matter where I was playing. The team eventually disbanded, right around 10th grade, because so much in American youth soccer isn't designed to last. Games and tournaments are still all that parents really care about, and the proportion of practice-to-games is still tilted way too far toward the latter. Moms and dads have to pay for their kids to be on most of these teams, so they expect their children to play in the games no matter how good they are; very few ever think that the training is what they're actually paying for.

From there, none of the teams I played on were as good, nor was the coaching. I bounced around from team to team, making sure I got to all the right college showcases. I kept improving because I kept playing, but I definitely didn't get the most out of what were probably the most important years on that path. Christian Pulisic, a 22-year-old who is already the greatest American soccer player of all time and was acquired by English club Chelsea for $73.1 million, credits his success to the Croatian passport that allowed him to legally join German club Borussia Dortmund before he turned 18. "Ask anyone and they'll tell you—those age 16–18 years are everything," he said. "From a developmental perspective, it's almost like this sweet spot: It's the age where a player's growth and skill sort of intersect, in just the right way—and where, with the right direction, a player can make their biggest leap in development by far."

I ended up getting recruited by a bunch of Division 1 programs, but none of them matched my ideal—almost no Ivy League programs, and none of the academic big shots from the Atlantic Coastal Conference, like Wake Forest or Virginia. I was on the verge of committing to Columbia, until the coach got fired during my recruitment. So, instead, I ended up at Holy Cross, a very good school with a very average soccer program. Our coach was Elvis Comrie, a smooth-talking British Jamaican man who'd won a National Player of the Year award when he played at the University of Connecticut in the '80s. He became the Holy Cross coach way back in the early '90s, which might as well have been the Bronze Age, given the rapid transformation American soccer had undergone over the ensuing two decades. His tactics never quite evolved, but he was an incredible recruiter, who turned your parents into putty and who made you feel like you were the next Diego Maradona. One of my teammates went on to have a successful career with the Bolivian national team; another one got an invite to the MLS Combine but didn't get drafted; most of us were too good to be playing where we ended up.

Of course, we eventually found out why Elvis was such a good recruiter: He'd made more than 300 illegal phone calls to prospective players, and the NCAA cited him for failing to "promote an atmosphere of rules compliance." No shit; we practiced four times a day during preseason of my freshman year (two was the limit), we were rarely given per diem funds for hosting recruits, and there was always a giant pile of unused apparel sitting in his office that we never got to wear. He resigned after my junior year and was eventually banned from coaching in college ever again. I was glad to see him go; we never got along. He called me "Kenny G" because of an unfortunate hairstyle choice I made as a freshman and because of my laid-back, "smooth" style of playing. I always got the sense that everyone on and around the team wanted me to play more, except for him.

Under a new coach my senior year, I immediately became a play-every-minute-of-every-game starter. We won our final game of the season—against Army—but missed the playoffs thanks to a near-impossible confluence of results that eliminated us via tiebreaker. We found out on the bus ride home from West Point, and I broke into tears, inconsolable for hours. I guess I could've picked myself up and made a run at playing pro in a lower league here or somewhere in Europe, but I didn't touch a soccer ball or even get my heart rate above "resting" for the first couple of months after the season ended. I was too burnt-out.

College soccer was a rewarding experience because of the lifelong friends I made—bonds that are literally impossible to describe to people who didn't go through what we did. But the soccer had almost nothing to do with that. The collegiate game suffers from the same problems the Thunder did, the same tensions that have been pulling at soccer from the start; not enough people care about developing players and, perhaps more importantly, not enough people care about building consistent systems for players to grow. Coaches have to win to keep their jobs, so they employ conservative tactics that are best played out by bigger and faster bodies. Innovation in the game was missing.

The one goal I scored in my career—I was a defensive midfielder for most of it, OK?—came at Boston College in overtime. It should be a kind of feather in my cap; Alejandro Bedoya, who started for the US at the 2014 World Cup, was on that BC team. But I didn't even feel like Bedoya was one of the five best players they had, and I'm not even sure he was in the top 50 of the best kids I played against in college. The technical geniuses, the kids who can manipulate a ball as if they're using their hands and who have PhD-level understandings of the dynamics of space, would too often fall through the cracks. It's getting better, with the advent of scholarship youth academies for all of the MLS clubs and a nationwide system of affiliated teams throughout the country, but we still haven't found a way to value and cultivate those innate technical skills—something researchers have referred to as "game intelligence"—ahead of those obvious traits that can be measured with a stopwatch and might produce some short-term results.

When I look back on my experience, what strikes me most about it is how random everything was. I sort of just got pulled along by these various currents that sanded down my edges for good or ill and spit me out at the end, exhausted from the ride. I think of other sports and how there's a much clearer conception of what a good player does—as long as he or she has the requisite physical profile. In baseball, you just need to be able to get on base or strike guys out. In basketball, you just need to be able to shoot. In soccer, how could we ever begin to boil that idea down to one sentence when no one can even agree on how we're supposed to play?

I was just one datapoint—churned through a global soccer machine with one governing fact: No one really knows what they're talking about, in any kind of objective fashion. And those who do, or come close to it? They still don't have much of a voice.

* * *

Baseball has had its data revolution; high-school teams now keep in-depth advanced stats. Kids across the world are perfecting their long-range shooting form because Stephen Curry and the Golden State Warriors proved that three is worth more than two. And as the NFL slowly realizes that the average pass gains nearly double the yardage of the average run, the best athletes are being discouraged from setting up shop in the backfield.

However, while the search for a better way—a right way—to play these games has created ripple effects up and down the various levels of professional and amateur sport, that hasn't been the case in soccer. For all the discussion about how to play the game, the conversation has always been more like a political debate or a form of art criticism—a means of affirming personal taste rather than an effort to find some previously undiscovered truth. Despite the philosophical agreements over tactics, the best predictor of performance at the highest level of professional soccer is how much a team pays its players. There's rarely been any data to back up the stylistic claims—until now.

We have finally entered soccer's age of disruption. A motley cast of bloggers, billionaires, basketball executives, motivational speakers, board-game nerds, anonymous religion professors, NBA GMs, Moneyball heroes, rich kids with nothing better to do, energy-drink magnates, particle physicists, and behavioral economists are all trying to chip away at the unknown and figure out what actually wins soccer games. Some of them have discovered ways to improve performance on the margins, while others have been spectacularly, destructively wrong as they've tried to get their arms around a dynamic sport that's always changing.

At the same time, while that search for optimization across sports has led to plenty of curses being broken and trophies being lifted, it's also created plenty of collateral damage. If you're an NBA fan, you have to suffer through a barrage of three-point attempts, night after night. The nimble big men who made their living 10 feet from the basket—gigantic ballerinas who could perform inside a phone booth—have been replaced by players who simply camp out beyond the three-point arc. "I hope that it's less specialists and more hoopers," five-time NBA All-Star and TNT commentator Chris Webber said recently about the future of the sport. "I hope teams and analytics allow players to play their style, rather than just standing in the corner." The aesthetic diversity of Webber's era has disappeared. If you're an MLB fan, you watch player after player strike out because they're trying to hit a home run at every at bat. The most exciting part of baseball—when the ball is bouncing around in play as fielders scramble to control it and runners scurry around the bases—is quickly being squeezed out of the product.

Certain parts of the labor force are feeling the squeeze, too. Baseball teams have gotten so good at identifying the right skillsets and developing them scientifically that veterans rarely receive the kind of post-peak contracts they used to. Why sign a big name when you can acquire a nobody, coach him up, and get 90 percent of the production for 20 percent of the price? Plus, as performance continues to be quantified on a more and more granular level, players become easier to view as commodities, rather than employees. Running backs used to be the stars of the show in the NFL; now the average career at the position lasts for about two years and the average salary is lower than it is for any position other than punter.

Soccer isn't close to being there yet—but we would be wise to heed the warning. Quantitative analysts have only recently begun to crunch numbers at a scale approaching other, more optimized sports. And thus far, all efforts to develop a unified theory of soccer value have proven to be fruitless. Plenty of new knowledge has been created, and there are lots of new levers that smart clubs and coaches can pull in order to gain an edge. But institutional inertia often prevents that from happening, as does the fluid, dynamic nature of the game: How do you put a value on anything when every action that occurs on the field is affected by the positioning of the 21 other players? And if you can, how do you convince a coach that you're right?

It's a daunting task, but lots of people are trying, searching for data that proves there is a right way to play. We're going to explore this new world of data in the world's most popular sport and try to begin to understand why it's been so hard to convert teams to any one set of consistent datapoints. We'll look at the ongoing searches for new knowledge across the soccer landscape. We'll profile the players, coaches, and owners who have managed to find an edge. And we'll also highlight the supposed disruptors who thought they found an advantage, only for it to suddenly blow up in their faces.

At the core of all this is a simple, incredible truth: Millions of people watch soccer every week, trillions of dollars are spent on it every year, and no one who claims to be an expert can truly explain to you what wins soccer games with any level of confidence. That is, except for maybe one person: that visionary fishmonger, still living out on Long Island.

CHAPTER ONE

THE CHALLENGE OF BIG DATA

At the start, the term "World Cup" was a bit of a misnomer. In the first 11 iterations of the event, six of the winners and two of the runners-up came from South America, the other five winners and nine of the runners-up hailed from Europe. In fact, of the first 42 semifinalists in the tournament's history, only one team came from outside South America or Europe: the good old US of A in 1930. But even that was an anomaly; this was just a 13-team tournament, and the Americans had to win only two games to qualify for the final four, where they got thumped, 6–1, by eventual runners-up Argentina. As the tournament expanded in size, Europe and South America just dominated more places. From 1934 through 1978, only three teams from outside those continents—Mexico, Cuba, and North Korea—even qualified for the knockout stages of the tournament.

However, the divide was most pronounced with Africa. Coming into the 1982 World Cup in Spain, only one team from the continent had even won a match at the world's most anticipated quadrennial competition—Tunisia 3–1 over Mexico four years prior. Tunisia also drew 0–0 with West Germany at the 1978 World Cup, though the West Germans seemed to have performed some kind of collective memory-purging ritual in the years that followed.

By 1982, Germany had acquired the aura of invincibility that would be codified by the famous quote from England striker Gary Lineker: "Football is a simple game. Twenty-two men chase a ball for 90 minutes and at the end, the Germans always win." They'd won two World Cups and reached the semifinals in five of the previous seven tournaments. At this point in the sport's history, the conceptual battle seemed to be between the beautiful, jazzy Brazilians—winners of three titles over that same span—and the organized, brute-force Germans. Though the Brazilians had won more often, their hold on the game always seemed tenuous, thanks to an approach that required 11 individual geniuses to hit the same notes at the same octave—at the same time. The Germans, meanwhile, just seemed to require 11 fit bodies to make the same set of systematized decisions. The Brazilian game was breathtaking; the German game was repeatable.

The worst part of it all? The Germans were getting high off their own supply. Before their opening match against Algeria in '82, one German player said, "We will dedicate our seventh goal to our wives, and the eighth to our dogs." Another, according to the Algerian fullback Chaâbane Merzekane, "said that he would play against us with a cigar in his mouth." German manager Jupp Derwall claimed that he would "jump on the first train back to Munich" if his team lost to the Algerians. Derwall didn't even show his players tape of their first-match opponents because he figured it would've just been a waste of time. Better to let them focus on what would come next. Yeah, about that: Algeria won the match, 2–1, in what is considered one of the biggest upsets in World Cup history. The German newspaper *Süddeutsche Zeitung* wrote, "This feels like the sinking of the *Titanic*."

The Algerians lost their next match to Austria, 2–0, but rebounded with a 3–2 win over Chile in their final match of the opening round. They became the first African team to win two games at the World Cup but had to wait another day to find out if they'd also be the first side from their continent to qualify for the knockout rounds—even though that seemed close to a formality. Anything other than a one- or two-goal win by Germany over Austria would see the Algerians through to the next stage, but either of those two specific results would mean qualification for both the Germans and the Austrians due to an unfortunate confluence of tiebreaker rules.

The West Germans took control of the match from the jump, with aggressive pressure and an overwhelming amount of possession, opening the scoring in the 10th minute. Suddenly, though, it became clear that the dynamic of the match had changed. The game quickly devolved into something that, in the words of columnist George Vecsey, "had all the precision of professional waltzers performing in a Vienna park." In the second half, the game offered up a grand total of three shots, none of which found the target. Neither side even considered defending the ball in the opposition half, which led to each team completing more than 90 percent of its passes—a significantly higher clip than the best clubs in the world complete today. Enraged by what he was seeing, the German announcer Eberhard Stanjek refused to continue commentating on the match midway through the second half. The following day, Spanish newspaper *El Comercio* published the result of the match under its "Crime" section, accompanied by the headline "Forty thousand people presumably scammed by twenty-six Austrians and Germans." During the game, Spanish fans mocked what they were seeing, chanting "*que se besen, que se besen*," or "let them kiss, let them kiss." The game ended, 1–0. Algeria was eliminated.

After the match, Benali Sekkal, president of the Algerian Football Association, said, "Their scandalous behavior was an insult to any sportsman and especially to the public, who had to watch this scandalous game." Benali filed a protest both against West Germany and Austria and against the Scottish referee, Bob Valentine. FIFA quickly dismissed both protests, but the blowback to the result was so intense that they changed the structure of the tournament four years later—teams in the same group would now play their final games at the same time. This match has since come to be known by many names, most notably as "The Disgrace of Gijón" or, my personal favorite, "The Non-Aggression Pact of Gijón." Fans booed the Austrians and the West Germans after their next matches; some even waved money at the players, suggesting that the game may have been fixed. The match united the soccer world in support of the Algerians and in disdain for all the world's official German-speaking nations.

However, the anger was slightly misguided. The fans, the commentators, the journalists, the Algerian coaches and players weren't really mad at the Germans or the Austrians. No, they should've been shaking their fists at the structure of the event—and the fundamental nature of the sport.

* * *

Forty years before the Non-Aggression Pact of Gijón, a group of scientists descended on a series of isolated, inhospitable volcanic plateaus somewhere in north-central New Mexico. A bunch of people had tried to live there—and everyone failed. The local Apaches and Navajos weren't very welcoming, and while a group of brave homesteaders settled on the land in the late 1800s, they found there wasn't enough water and that it was a lot warmer if you just moved a couple of miles south. In the early 1900s, a man from Detroit founded the Los Alamos Ranch School—an all-boys college preparatory-cum-survival-test. The school lasted for only 25 years and had only about six students per class, but it still managed to produce alumni such as writers William Burroughs and Gore Vidal. Despite its modest success, the Ranch School experiment ended when government officials decided they'd found the perfect place to begin theirs: altering the fundamental nature of reality.

Los Alamos National Laboratory was created, in secret, to speed up the creation of the atomic bomb. When I asked Luke Bornn what he did there, he told me, "Built bombs." I did a double take—I mean, you never know!—before he started laughing. "I actually worked on a really, really fun problem. You know I'm Canadian, so I didn't get to work on any of the top-secret problems or anything. But I got exposed to this really fascinating problem the day I arrived."

Helicopters were falling out of the sky, and nobody knew why until it was too late. If a helicopter blade was punctured once by, say, a bullet, then nothing happened. The pilot couldn't detect any tangible difference and the helicopter would fly just fine. A second bullet hole? Same thing—no problem at all, no one would feel anything different. A third bullet hole? The pilot still wouldn't notice a change, until the helicopter suddenly crashed down to Earth. Bornn was brought to Los Alamos to help figure out a solution.

"Can we detect those holes in the blades without actually outfitting the helicopter blades themselves with all these sensors?" he said. "Can we somehow detect the damage to the blade before the pilot can? And so, what we did is put accelerometers all over the body of the helicopter, which is not moving. And the basic premise is that the resonant characteristics of the helicopter changed slightly when the damage happened. And so you can actually detect the damage in the helicopter blade through the really subtle changes in the way that the helicopter vibrates."

The findings had a wide-ranging practical impact not just on the life span of helicopter pilots but on the health of various man-made structures. A similar idea has been employed to improve bridge maintenance. "You have a little bit of a crack, and it still looks like a bridge," Bornn said. "It cracks a little bit more, still looks like a bridge. Cars can still drive over it. Crack goes a little more, and all of a sudden, cars are dropped into a river." To keep the cars dry, engineers will now place accelerometers all over the body of a bridge, and then basically shake the bridge to see if its so-called resonant characteristics have changed enough to reveal an oncoming disaster. Next time you successfully drive across a body of water, you can thank Luke Bornn.

In a broad sense, what Bornn was doing at Los Alamos was using movement data to analyze the structural health of a larger system. Before that, he spent some time at the National Center for Atmospheric Research, a beautiful, geometric, maze-like complex built by the Chinese American architect I. M. Pei into the foothills of Boulder, Colorado. At NCAR, Bornn studied climate, specifically how various climate systems moved through space.

"I guess I have a bit of a non-conventional path," he said. "Most of the people that I've worked with in sports over the years, they have essentially wanted to work in sports their whole lives. Either they've been an athlete that converted to someone that wanted to work in the front office or a failed athlete—these are all people that wanted to work in sports. And I was fundamentally different than that. I was basically an academic."

After getting his PhD in statistics from the University of British Columbia, Bornn became a professor at Harvard University. And for a while, he really was an academic's academic. Forget the helicopter stuff. A lot of his early work went even deeper into perhaps the densest realm of scientific work imaginable: the modeling of modeling. If you've ever read a research paper before, you know there are some tricks for the layperson—read the intro, scan for some graphs, go through the results, and read the conclusion. Also: Ignore the "methodology" sections. But some of the papers Bornn was writing were essentially entirely methodology sections.

One of the problems, Bornn eventually realized, with studying move-ment is that there's not a ton of great data on it. There's movement everywhere you look—in the sky, on the street, maybe even right behind you. It's easy to observe movement patterns in nature, but it's hard to objectively record what you're seeing in fine-grained detail without wildly invasive technology or Los Alamos–level funding. One of the most comprehensive movement studies was published in the leading scientific journal *Nature* by a group of Hungarian researchers who put golf-ball-size GPS backpacks onto a flock of pigeons. Prior to this, pigeon-flight dynamics had to be inferred through mathematical models that predicted in-flock behavior, but for the first time, the *Nature* study showed exactly how the birds moved. Given the paucity of JanSport-wearing pigeons out there, these kinds of movement datasets were extremely rare, so Bornn was constantly looking for whatever detailed data he could find. As long as it related to movement, he didn't care what was doing the moving.

In 2005, a pair of Israeli scientists were on a journey similar to Bornn's. Gal Oz and Miky Tamir had both worked in missile recognition for the Israeli army, and then they decided to turn their same techniques toward a slightly more benign endeavor: team sports. They called their product SportVU, an automated tracking system—essentially, a collection of high-speed cameras—that could capture where every player on a field or court was at all times. They'd first set their sights on Israeli soccer—until the company was bought by an American firm that pushed the technology toward the potential riches of the basketball court. In 2010, a handful of NBA teams installed SportVU cameras in their arenas, and a few more teams signed up every year. Today, all 30 teams use them.

While the tracking data provided basketball teams with never-before-seen detail about how their players positioned themselves on the court, it transformed a sport into something Bornn was finally interested in: a rich dataset of movement patterns. In 2012, he stumbled onto the SportVU data. "To be clear, I hadn't done anything with sports at that point," he said, "but I got access to this data, and was interested in it not because it was basketball but because it was the richest space-time dataset I had ever seen—across any field. And I still believe that's true."

With the NBA data at his fingertips, the papers Bornn wrote changed from "Assessment and Management of Anemia in a Population of Children Living in the Indian Himalayas: A Student-Led Initiative" and "Efficient Stabilization of Crop Yield Prediction in the Canadian Prairies" to "Factorized Point Process Intensities: A Spatial Analysis of Professional Basketball" and "POINTWISE: Predicting Points and Valuing Decisions in Real Time with NBA Optical Tracking Data." The shift from "how's our wheat-crop output looking?" to "how many points is LeBron James worth?" gained Bornn a little more notoriety, but also helped narrow his academic focus.

"I ended up getting a lot of attention for those papers. I published 15 to 30 papers in sports analytics using this NBA tracking data and related data.

That spun into consulting and spun into jobs in quantitative gambling and so on. Basically, I realized that I was good at it and enjoyed it, and so I somewhat haphazardly stumbled out of academia and into sports."

Since then, Bornn has gone on to hold senior positions at NBA franchises and one of the biggest soccer clubs in the world. He's launched his own analytics company that now contracts with some of the most forward-thinking franchises in baseball.

On the SiriusXM radio show *Wharton Moneyball*, hosted by a group of sport-and-stat-obsessed University of Pennsylvania professors, they referred to Bornn simply as "the best person in analytics." He's combined academic research with cross-sport practical application in a way that no one else really has. And on a daily basis, he's now faced with maybe the biggest intellectual challenge of his life: decoding the Beautiful Game. "No question—it's the hardest sport of them all," he said. "Some of it is that it's harder to measure, and some of it is that it's just unmeasurable."

* * *

Bornn and the Algerian national team were and are grappling with the same fundamental problem: Soccer has no structure. Twenty-two players take the field, the ref blows the whistle, and whatever happens next is determined partially by two managers' pregame tactics, partially by the decisions each individual player makes in a given moment, partially by how well they execute on those decisions, partially by the weather, partially by the length of the grass, and partially by what everyone ate before the game. The other major sports don't have the same issues.

"If you look at the sport that's furthest ahead in terms of how people think about analytics adoption, it's baseball," Bornn said. "It fundamentally becomes easy because first of all, they play so many games. And secondly, you get these discrete pitcher-batter dynamics, so it becomes really easy to think about the game and break it into these discrete time events. Those dynamics mean measuring player value becomes really, really easy. In soccer, you're talking about 22 players and these complex dynamics and with no clear notion of possession and [also] super, super low-scoring [matches]. And then the other sports all fall somewhere in between. American football is much easier because you have clear resetting with each down. Basketball, you have like 200 possessions back and forth that give you a clear differentiator."

Take Super Bowl LII in 2018, for example. Philadelphia Eagles head coach Doug Pederson had a decision to make. The Eagles had the ball on their own 45-yard line, down 33–32 against the Patriots. The Eagles had never won a Super Bowl, and with quarterback Tom Brady and coach Bill Belichick, the Patriots always won the Super Bowl. In fact, they seemed to thrive in this exact situation Pederson was facing; Brady and Belichick had won five Super Bowls by an average of just under four points per game. No one has ever been better at what they call "situational football": being prepared for and executing in the game's highest leverage moments.

In case history wasn't a tough enough opponent, Pederson also had to conquer time. On 3rd and 1, Eagles quarterback Nick Foles had just completed a pass to wide receiver Torrey Smith, but Smith was wrestled down by Patriots linebacker Kyle Van Noy at the line of scrimmage. Fourth and one—and the clock was ticking.

With a 40-second play clock, Pederson had between 5 and 10 seconds to make the decision that could define his team's season: Do you punt and hope to get the ball back, or do you try to gain that yard for a first down?

Running a hyper-speed cost-benefit analysis in your head under the intense pressure of this situation would make even the most powerful mind short-circuit. Instead of focusing on the specifics, Pederson followed a slightly different decision-making tree. First, he asked himself: Do we want to win? *Duh, this is the freaking Super Bowl.* And then he asked himself: What gives us the best chance to win?

That question was also easy to answer. According to Brian Burke of ESPN's analytics department, the decision to go for the first down, regardless of the outcome, increased Philadelphia's chances to win by 7.3 percent. Situations like this had already been calculated by mathematicians and football nerds, and Pederson was aware of the odds. He called for a pass to Pro Bowl tight end Zach Ertz, husband of United States Women's National Team star Julie Ertz, whom Foles hit for a two-yard gain and a new set of downs. Three minutes later, another pass from Foles to Ertz gave the Eagles a lead they would never relinquish en route to the franchise's first Super Bowl win.

"I'm constantly being communicated with," Pederson said after the game. "I have a coach upstairs that's giving me this information in real time, game day.

'Hey coach, if we can get it to 4th and 2, 4th and 3, this is the success rate here in this situation.'"

At its core, the data revolution in professional sports is a revolution in probabilistic thinking: The Eagles and anyone else at the intersection of data science and sports are trying to figure out which events, however big or small, contribute to a team's chances of winning. Then they try to figure out how to create more of those events. The rest is left up to the gods.

In baseball, the all-encompassing value metric is called "wins above replacement (WAR)." By looking at a player's offensive and defensive production, it's determined how many wins he's added to his team's record, compared to a "replacement-level" player at his position. As the website FanGraphs describes it, "replacement level" means "the level of production you could get from a player that would cost you nothing but the league minimum salary to acquire." In basketball, the Golden State Warriors and the Houston Rockets have been at the forefront of a league-wide movement to phase out mid-range jump shots in favor of three-pointers and closer attempts near the rim. "Let's say a long two-point shot, you make that 50 percent of the time," Bornn said. "Two points on average, an expectation that's worth one point. If you step behind the three-point line, you go from 50 percent to 40 percent. So you're less likely to make that shot, but it's now worth three. So you have 40 percent times three, which is 1.2. You do that repeatedly, that has a significant benefit. That's not fancy modeling, and it's had a massive impact on the game of basketball."

Some coaches and GMs are so intent on optimizing their approach that the wins and losses are almost less important than sticking to a mathematically sound gameplan. When the Rockets lost to the Warriors in Game 7 of the 2018 Western Conference Finals after missing an unfathomable 37 of 44 three-pointers despite averaging a 36 percent make rate over the full season, then-general manager Daryl Morey seemed unbothered by the result, focusing instead on the probability of his team's shots. "We should have won," he said. Their 27 straight three-point misses were a postseason NBA record, a succession of events with a 1-in-72,000 chance of happening. Houston played the odds right, even though the odds were against them that night.

However, trying to optimize win probability in soccer is like trying to put together a puzzle made of Jell-O—whenever you attempt to pick something up, it changes shape in your hands. Without downs or innings or constant television time-outs, there's little room for any kind of winning in-game decision-making—outside of free kicks and throw-ins, which we'll eventually get to. In soccer, the clock never stops, and the only things outlawed are excessive physical contact, the use of hands, and standing behind the defense when a ball is passed to you; that makes the play constantly fluid and much harder to measure. Two teams, after all, could theoretically spend an entire game staring at the ball as it sits at the center circle, daring the other side to take the initiative.

* * *

Bornn's first crack at the problem came with AS Roma, where he was hired to be the head of analytics in June 2016. Roma are Italy's lovable losers. The club badge is quite literally an image of Romulus and Remus suckling from the teats of the Mother Wolf. But despite the club's unsubtle positioning of itself as a founding pillar of Italian soccer, they've won the domestic league (Serie A) only three times, the last win coming in 2001.

Roma share the Stadio Olimpico, a wide-mouthed, inefficient, 70,000-person stadium built in 1927 on the banks of the river Tiber, with intra-city rivals Lazio. A faction of devout fascists are also devout Lazio fans, frequently threatening Roma's minority players. In 1998, during a match between the two sides, known as the *Derby della Capitale*, Lazio fans unfurled a banner reading, "Auschwitz is your country; the ovens are your homes." When the two sides play, violent clashes between both sides of supporters and police are the norm. In 2004, a massive riot forced the Derby to be suspended three minutes into the second half after false rumors spread throughout the stadium that a boy had been killed by a police car. In 2015, ultras (the term used to describe a team's most, um, ardent supporters) from both clubs boycotted the match because glass partitions were installed inside the stadium to separate fans. In 2017, after a 3–1 victory, Lazio's ultras hung mannequins wearing the jerseys of Roma players Mohamed Salah, Radja Nainggolan, and Daniele De Rossi from a footbridge outside the stadium, accompanied by a banner that read, "From a well-wisher: Keep the lights on at night when you sleep."

Bornn was hired four years after the club was purchased by billionaire American investor James Pallotta, who was also a co-owner of the Boston Celtics. While Bornn was at the club, they identified a succession of stars who would eventually be sold for massive profits to some of the richest teams in the world: winger Mohamed Salah and keeper Alisson Becker to Liverpool, center back Antonio Rüdiger and fullback Emerson Palmieri to Chelsea. And in 2018, shortly after Bornn left the club, Roma made a surprise run to the semifinals of the UEFA Champions League, a competition that features the top teams from every league across Europe.

While it's hard to think of an environment that would be less open to a stats professor from Harvard influencing decision-making than soccer in Rome, from the outside it certainly looked like analytics had somehow conquered the chaos of the capital. The team was fantastic, powered by a bunch of stars that no one else had identified. But that wasn't the case—at all. "I had remarkably little impact," Bornn said. "I think I had more impact than most, but still close to zero in some sense. It wasn't quite zero, but it feels like there were much bigger points of influence than data, certainly."

While Bornn was in Rome, the club was managed by Luciano Spalletti, an impeccably tan, attack-minded manager with a gigantic, shiny cranium and a perfectly manicured goatee. "He's a super, super nice guy," Bornn said. "Made me more espressos than I care to count. Doesn't speak English, was a good guy, but really had no interest in data. So, I figured, 'OK, I can't influence him directly, in terms of making data-driven decisions, but look where he gets his information from.' And it turned out that most of his information about opponents was coming from the video coaches and analysts. And so I spent a lot of time helping video analysts make better video. Prior to my arrival, their approach for opponent scouting was to watch the last two or three matches of the upcoming opponent. From those matches, they'd put together a highlight reel of the team's tendencies. But now with the data, I was able to say, 'Here's what this team has done over the last 20 or 40 matches,' so that you're actually getting a real signal of something that's repeatable. Even though I wasn't getting in a room with Spalletti on a regular basis, I was able to make it so that the information he was getting was a lot better."

Rather than attempting to continue to Trojan-horse his way into the heart of Roma's decision-making apparatus, Bornn left the club in 2017 to become the vice president of strategy and analytics for the Sacramento Kings. While in Sacramento, he worked with the chain-smoking seven-foot-one Serbian, Vlade Divac, who was the franchise's general manager. Divac admitted that he "did not know" how the NBA's salary cap rules worked when he was hired by Sacramento. There's a picture of Bornn and Divac sitting together at the NBA's Summer League exhibition tournament in Las Vegas in 2017. Divac is pointing toward the court, looking like he's made some kind of grand proclamation about a person just out of frame, while Bornn appears as if he's blinking out a form of Morse code, silently pleading for a friend on the other side of the arena to come and rescue him.

Eventually someone did: Billy Beane. In the summer of 2020, Bornn and the Moneyball star partnered with the private-equity firm RedBird Capital Partners to do two things. One was to create the RedBall Special Acquisition Corporation. SPACs are essentially blank-check investment vehicles, which go public and raise money without telling investors exactly where their money will eventually go—and oftentimes, without the SPAC itself knowing where the money will go. Like most things in finance, it's a confidence game. RedBall was the first-ever SPAC dedicated specifically to sports, and it had the benefit of being fronted by the only sports executive ever to be portrayed by Brad Pitt in an Oscar-nominated film. The SPAC was used to take the ticket-buying platform SeetGeek public. In addition to RedBall, Bornn, Beane, and RedBird created a holding company, which then bought a majority share of French second-division club Toulouse, where Bornn now serves as a co-owner and board member. He currently splits his time between making sure that Toulouse are making the right high-level strategic decisions and managing Zelus, an analytics company he founded with Doug Fearing, the former director of research and development with the Los Angeles Dodgers. The holding company is also an initial investor in Zelus. "We're essentially partnered with a handful of teams in each sport and really doing the sort of extreme far end of the analytics side," Bornn said. "All we do is the really high end, complex modeling tasks: player valuation and all that kind of stuff with modern data sources, tracking data, pose data, all that fun stuff."

Zelus hasn't partnered with any soccer clubs because, well, its founder runs his own club, and so the company is instead currently functioning as the in-house analytics department for Toulouse. Plus, all of the "fun stuff"? Soccer still isn't ready for that. It's not even close.

* * *

To understand the state of data collection in the world of soccer, we first need to reflect on the Prozone massage chair.

In the mid-1990s, a fledgling company called Prozone, short for Professional Zone, had developed a chair that emitted electrical impulses they hoped would one day stimulate the muscles of professional soccer players. And in 1996 it eventually convinced Derby County, then a Premier League team playing their home games at a stadium called the Baseball Ground, to install 22 of the chairs inside a portable cabin equipped with a video monitor. Every morning, the Derby players would hop in the chairs while the team's young assistant manager, Steve McClaren, would show them tape about a previous or upcoming game. McClaren, who eventually would go on to manage the England national team for one brief and disastrous year, was obsessed with breaking down tape and would stay late into the night in his office, burning the midnight oil and splicing together key moments from Derby's previous matches.

The founder of Prozone, Ramm Mylvaganam, figured there had to be a better way for the no. 2 at a Premier League team to be spending his time. Couldn't someone else chop up the tape for McClaren and allow him to focus on solving some higher-level problems? But McClaren told Mylvaganam that he didn't trust anyone else to know which moments actually mattered and which ones belonged on the tape. So, if coaches weren't going to allow their underlings to do it, Mylvaganam wondered if there might be a way to automate the recording of what happened in a soccer game, a way to get a full-field view of the fluid movements of all 22 players across 90 minutes. An engineer by training, Mylvaganam knew of a French university that had developed technology that could track the movements of players and render it into a 2-D visualization of 22 dynamic dots. He bought a stake in the company and soon had eight cameras installed in Derby's new, not-quite-as-confusingly-named stadium, Pride Park.

Derby County, then, had tracking data—more than a decade before it came to the NBA and before anyone had begun to comprehensively collect the kind of play-by-play data that some baseball watchers were recording all the way back in the 19th century. Prozone's technology accurately rendered the movements of all the players in a given situation and provided the kind of bird's-eye view of the entire field that broadcast cameras couldn't catch. It not only visualized soccer teams as the kind of complex, dynamic systems that they are; the tracking data also made it possible to see how far and how fast players were running over the course of a match. "Everything starts with football," said Paul Power, an analyst who worked at Prozone in the early days. "You're talking 20 years ago for tracking, 15 years ago for GPS. It's only been about four years now that the NFL have even had this type of data. Basketball? Eight years maybe."

If you've watched a soccer game at any point over the last decade-plus, you've likely (1) seen a player remove his shirt and (2) seen said player wearing a kind of brassiere under his shirt. These are miniature GPS tracking systems that monitor things like a player's physical movements and heart rate. Players started wearing the GPS vests in training back in the mid-2000s, and in 2015 FIFA approved their use during gameplay. Soccer has been at the forefront of measuring detailed physical outputs of players, which has given teams a better sense of when a striker or a midfielder is being overextended and needs a break. While the NBA just recently got into the "load management" game, soccer teams have been rotating their stars out of their starting lineups for more than a decade now.

Prozone's first-stage tracking data couldn't be used in training, and it didn't tell you anything about a player's heart rate. But it captured all of the other relevant physical data: how many kilometers a player ran over the course of a match, how many times he sprinted, how often he wasn't moving. And with its bird's-eye visualizations, Prozone's data held the potential for something beyond sprinting statistics: a new systematic understanding of how soccer works, how the players move in relation to each other. The data was almost perfect—except for one tiny, round, indispensable element.

"The whole idea was to use it to re-create a set piece or a goal instead of a replay," said Power. "But the main issue was, it didn't have the ball. Steve McLaren was like, 'Obviously this is great, and we know how far everyone's running, but we don't know the context of the ball.'"

It was an easy fix, according to Power. Someone just had to watch footage of the game along with the tracking data and annotate when a number of simple events occurred: passes, shots, tackles. By combining the record of the events with the moving dots, you could then re-create where the ball was and estimate how it was moving. This created the exact kind of rich movement dataset that Bornn would eventually be chasing after, but it turns out that not many Premier League teams wanted it. It was expensive to install the cameras in your stadium, and you'd also be limited to tracking data only from games that took place in stadiums that had the cameras. However, you needed only a tape of a game and some manpower in order to collect the event-based data, which meant it was cheaper for teams to acquire and it could be collected for the entire league. And so, the Premier League's demand economy shifted the focus of the sport back away from the movement of the 11-man organisms and toward whatever was happening on the ball. Seeing proof of concept, professional clubs wanted to know who was taking shots and who was making tackles, so this is what Prozone and its eventual competitors started to collect.

"Initially, it took about five hours to collect event data for a match," Power said. "I've done it myself, and it's painstaking. You have to be sure of the player ID and you have to remember that back then there was no HD. So you got this really fuzzy picture. VHS tapes were being taken from the stadium and driven up to the center because you couldn't live stream the game either, because it wasn't available then. Eventually it got to DVD, which is obviously great. And then eventually you could transfer it via the Internet. It's really mad. It's covered the whole technology spectrum."

Prozone competitor Opta Sports, launched in 1996, became the official data provider for the Premier League in 1997—a position they still, sort of, hold today. Opta mainly focused on collecting on-ball data, while Prozone collected a hybrid of movement and on-ball information. In 2015, the company Stats Inc. bought Prozone. Ownership of Opta changed hands multiple times over its first decade of existence, before it was purchased by the British media company Perform in 2013. In 2018, Perform split into two: DAZN (pronounced "Da Zone"), which was a sports streaming service, and Perform Content, an amalgam of Perform's B2B operations that included Opta. A year after that, Perform and Stats Inc. merged into . . . Stats Perform, an umbrella under which Opta now technically still exists. That's all very confusing, and Power himself was pulled along via the various corporate currents: first as a Prozone employee, then as a Stats Inc. whiz, and then finally as a director at Stats Perform.

For every Premier League game today, Stats Perform records roughly 4,000 events, which are just things that happen with the ball: shots, passes, dribbles, attempted tackles, clearances, saves, and so on. That adds up to 30,000 events per week, and 1.14 million datapoints per season—and those numbers wildly undersell the scale of the operation. Every weekend, an army of coders across the world watch not just every Premier League match but every match in more than 1,000 other leagues across the world. Stats Perform now has offices everywhere from Chennai to Castelfranco, and it takes about two hours to log each game. One person watches the away team, another focuses on the home team, and a third person serves as a kind of auditor, making sure that no mistakes were made. After about 30 minutes of post-match editing in which the coders go through their results and check for anything that doesn't make sense—say, a pass followed by a throw-in, rather than a throw-in followed by a pass—the game is done. The relatively new demand for real-time event data was driven by teams who want the information as soon as possible but also by sportsbooks who are taking bets on how many tackles or shots a given player will have over the course of a match. Despite that, most of this information still isn't publicly available.

Most of the coders are college-age men who do it to make money on the side, but there are a select few who can make a career out of it and get entrusted with the weekend's highest-profile matches. No longer are they logging relatively easy-to-define events, like shots, passes, tackles, fouls, etc. Now, they also mark various qualifiers: Was it a left-footed shot from the center of the box? Did he pass the ball with his head to an offside player? Did the tackle occur as the last line of defense before the goalkeeper? With access to Stats Perform's database, you can pretty easily find, say, which teams attempt the most failed tackles in the left side of the attacking third while trailing in the final 30 minutes of a match refereed by Anthony Taylor. In addition to the event data, Stats Perform collects another 15,000 qualifiers per match. Combined with events, qualifiers create an even deeper collection of detailed and unique datapoints. All in all, Stats Perform's coders are collecting 150,000 unique datapoints per week and 5.7 million per season. And that's only in the Premier League. In terms of what's happening with the ball, Stats Perform has come pretty close to catching it all. The scale of the data is totally overwhelming. It's also completely insufficient.

If soccer has a modern forefather, it's Johan Cruyff, the gangly, free-speaking, free-smoking, and free-living Dutch superstar of the 1970s. Cruyff was the leader of the famed Netherlands, Ajax, and FC Barcelona sides who pushed forward the concept of Total Football, a style that required all 10 outfield players to constantly interchange and be as comfortable on the right wing as in central defense. Cruyff then went on to manage at Ajax and Barcelona, where he maintained the same philosophy from his playing days. "In my teams, the goalie is the first attacker, and the striker the first defender," he said.

Cruyff was something like a Yogi Berra for European football intellectuals. He once said, "There is only one ball, so you need to have it." Really makes you think, huh? And he also had his say in the romance-vs.-winning debate: "Quality without results is pointless. Results without quality is boring." There's a poignant quote from him for just about everything. An avowed atheist, Cruyff commented on the religiosity of the players in Spain, saying, "I'm not religious. In Spain, all 22 players make the sign of the cross before they enter the pitch. If it works, all matches must therefore end in a draw." Cruyff passed away in 2016, at the age of 68, of lung cancer. He still had his say about soccer's data revolution, even if he didn't know it at the time. "When you play a match, it is statistically proven that players actually have the ball 3 minutes on average," Cruyff said. "So, the most important thing is: what do you do during those 87 minutes when you do not have the ball. That is what determines whether you're a good player or not."

Luke Bornn agrees. "If you think about baseball: If you know what's happening with the ball and if you know what's happening with the guys on bases, you've captured 98 percent of the game," he said. "The same can almost be said about basketball. But in soccer, the fact that a team will actively give up the ball as part of their offensive strategy tells you that what's happening away from the ball is critically important."

Of course, Derby County were recording what was happening away from the ball, and Prozone offered the services to any other Premier League clubs that wanted to have the cameras installed in their stadium. But there were—and still are—all kinds of issues with using tracking data in soccer, beyond how expensive it was. The first: What the hell do you do with it? The number of people working in soccer with the computational skills and modeling instincts of Bornn or Power is still comparatively tiny today; back in the mid-1990s, there was almost no one who would've known what to do with detailed movement data. On top of that, the data wasn't as detailed as it needed to be; it tracked how fast all the players on the field were moving and provided a fluid animation of how all 22 players were moving, but teams didn't have access to the raw data beneath it: the x- and y-coordinates of where all the players were at any given moment. And then there was the problem of availability: Derby (or any other Premier League team with a Prozone deal) would get tracking data for all of their home matches and then any away matches in stadiums where the Prozone cameras were installed—and that's it. Thirty-eight matches is already a small sample to try to glean actionable insight from, and you were basically cutting that in half. Plus, this also meant that you had tracking data for an opponent for just one or two matches. And so tracking data was essentially useless from a scouting perspective—both in prepping for opponents and in searching for new players to sign.

That's still an issue today. According to Power, about 15 leagues across the world now have deals with a provider for tracking data. In 2013–14, the Premier League signed its first leaguewide tracking deal, with New York–based ChyronHego, to have its frame-by-frame tracking system installed in all of its stadiums. Teams now get the raw data, too: x- and y-coordinates of all players and the ball, at a rate of 25 frames per second. This meant that clubs no longer had to pay for the cameras to be installed or for access to the data, and it also meant that teams now had access to tracking data from all the matches in the league—eventually. "It took a couple of years for that data to be shared across all teams," Power said. But access to tracking data for all the teams in your league still isn't enough. Although the data might be shared within a competition, teams typically still can't access tracking information from other leagues, which again severely limits the data's usefulness for identifying players to acquire. One Premier League club went so far as to ask Power if it was even worth looking at the new Second Spectrum data. "I was like, yeah? You're not using it? They said, 'There's no point because we can't use the GPS tracking in any other league.' And it's a really relevant point."

Instead, much of the data's insights get re-packaged as previously unknowable trivia—marketing tidbits disguised as useful information. Amazon Web Services provides the tracking data for the German Bundesliga, and if you watch a match from that league, you'll be bombarded with context-free information about how fast players are running, as if Amazon themselves were the first ones to even think of recording this kind of information. "There is very little new," Power said. "A lot of what you see teams use was invented 20 years ago. You see a lot of companies say, 'Oh, look at this, we can highlight the speed of the players.' Like, yeah, so what? We already did this."

* * *

Stats Perform has an army of harshly graded and meticulous soccer-watchers who are recording tens of millions of discrete events across a season. Other data companies employ a similarly exhaustive process that produces more information than any one human brain could ever process and organize. If Cruyff and Bornn are right, 97 percent of the game is nowhere to be found in those numbers—and only a select group of clubs have very limited access to the other numbers that might begin to show what's happening beyond the 3 percent. Soccer, then, suffers from two problems, pulling at it from opposite sides: There's not enough information, and there's too much data. That is, unless you ask Bruce Arena.

The Portland Timbers and Los Angeles Galaxy serve as two of the major success stories from the fledgling history of America's first-division soccer league: Major League Soccer. The Galaxy, of course, signed David Beckham, and they've also employed Landon Donovan, perhaps the most accomplished American soccer player of all time; Robbie Keane, perhaps the greatest Irish soccer player of all time; Steven Gerrard, perhaps the greatest English midfielder of all time; and Zlatan Ibrahimović, definitely the greatest Zlatan of all time. They're about as stereotypically LA as can be. The Timbers, meanwhile, were one of the league's earliest expansion successes. Rather than chasing big names like the Galaxy, they ported over a rabid, grassroots fanbase from a Timbers club that existed in various forms and various leagues dating back to 1975.

When they met on July 23, 2016, it was technically a battle between the league's past two champions. Keane and Donovan led LA to their record fifth MLS Cup in 2014, and then Portland snatched it away the following year, winning the championship in just their fifth season in the league. Before the season, this might have seemed like one of the games of the year, but by the time the summer came around, both teams were a ways off first place. The Galaxy eventually made the playoffs but lost in the second round; the Timbers didn't even reach the postseason. So, unless you were at the game or share a blood lineage with one of the 27 players who featured, you would have no reason to know that the Galaxy won this specific match, 2–1.

After their win, Galaxy coach Bruce Arena, a tell-it-like-it-is Brooklynite who guided the United States Men's National Team to their best-ever finish in the modern era of the World Cup in 2002 and in 2021 led the New England Revolution to the highest-ever MLS season points total, was asked if he was concerned by the fact that although his team won, they conceded 18 shots and attempted only 9 of their own. "We won the game. That's what you do in soccer games. We were on the road in a venue where the team does pretty well at home. What are we complaining about? Then some moron will write that they had more shots than us thinking that's important," he said. "Actually, analytics in soccer, if no one here has figured it out, doesn't mean a whole lot. Analytics and statistics are used for people who don't know how to analyze the game. I'll be very honest with you, this isn't baseball or football or basketball. We have a very important analytic, and that's the score. That distorts all the other statistics."

Arena seemed to be playing the pantomime villain who's existed in all the other major sports: the proud lifer luddite, the veteran coach who knows that numbers can't measure heart and a computer can't see better than his own two eyes. Not long after claiming that the most important analytic is the score, Arena would oversee the final stages of USMNT's embarrassing failure to qualify for the 2018 World Cup. The familiar narrative took a step further: He who proudly stands athwart progress will eventually be destroyed by it.

But in a way, Arena was right. The score, ultimately, is the only thing that matters. And those goals really do distort everything that happens in the game. Just maybe not in the way he thinks they do.

Goals mess with your head. The average NBA team scores north of 100 points per game. In the NFL, it's around 25. In MLB, it's only about 4.5, but they make up for the lack of scoring by playing 162 regular-season games—ten times more than the NFL and double the number of games in a typical NBA season. The average match in one of European soccer's five major leagues—England's Premier League, Germany's Bundesliga, France's Ligue 1, Italy's Serie A, and Spain's La Liga—contains about 3 goals, combined. In basketball and football, there's enough scoring that it's relatively easy to connect the other events that happen with the ultimate scoring play. Not so in baseball, but there are so many freaking games that patterns start to emerge and the things that are likely to lead to runs being scored can be identified. But soccer has so few goals on average and so few games, just 38 in the Premier League. The micro and macro samples are both too small to confidently separate the signal from the noise.

The best coaches probably watch soccer matches somewhat similarly to the Stats Perform annotating crew. They're seeing and noting everything that happens with the ball, and they're also much more attuned to the stuff that's happening without it than the average set of eyes. Then, a couple of times a game, the ball goes in the net, and their brains reach for something amid that morass of 15,000 unique datapoints to explain the why of the goal they just scored or conceded. And then they keep doing it over and over and over again until they develop their theories on how goals are scored.

"Eventually, your brain just starts to say, 'OK, here are the things that matter. Teams that do lots of short passes? They tend to score more,'" Bornn said. "I watch it, though, and my brain says, 'Teams that actually make really aggressive downfield passes are the ones that tend to score more.' Our brains are not that good at extracting signals, and there's a lot of biases that come from that. Even if you assume that coaches are optimizing to maximize goal differential, it's really clear to me that there's no reason that any two coaches would have the same system to do that, because they've watched different games. They have their own internal biases, and one of them might think, 'OK, our goal is to hold the ball as much as possible until we move the ball around until we see a passing lane,' and then another one just says, 'We're going to boot it downfield because that gets us in a better scoring position.'"

Might the history of soccer tactics—*futebol d'arte* vs. *futebol de resultados*—just be a bunch of observational biases screaming at each other?

More so than in any other sport, coaches in soccer—managers—get all the credit and all the blame. They're philosophers and celebrities. When José Mourinho was hired by English club Chelsea (the first time) in 2004, he proclaimed at his introductory press conference: "I am not from the bottle. I am a special one." A former Manchester United player, Wilf McGuinness, said of his coach: "Matt Busby was a god. We used to look up at him when we were growing up. We thought: 'There he is. That's the boss.' That's what we called him. 'Boss.' He was a wonderful man." Former Arsenal manager Arsène Wenger was so respected that in order for the club to get a bank loan to build a new stadium the bank required that the club retain Wenger for five more years as a precondition. As for Pep Guardiola, Douglas Costa, who played for him at the German super-club Bayern Munich, said, "He's a genius. I can learn more from him in an hour than from others in one year. He not only lifts you to the next level on the pitch, but also in your mind. He has revealed totally new options to me. I did not know that was possible when I got to Munich."

Today, after every match, you can find detailed tactical analysis of how Mourinho's and Guardiola's teams played: What position did the striker take up out of possession? How did the midfielders stagger themselves up and down the center of the field? Which fullback pushed high up, and which one slid into the center? What are the center backs doing when the ball is near the other goal? New words and fractional numbers seem to be invented every week to account for whatever complicated new player role has been invented. Managers are often treated as if they're both supercomputers and masters of the universe: not only able to predict how all 11 players should be positioned at all times but able to control them, too.

Eduardo Galeano would've hated this. In 1995, the late Uruguayan poet wrote *El fútbol a sol y sombra* (published in English in 1998 as *Soccer in Sun and Shadow*), both a love letter to the Beautiful Game and a warning as to where it was headed. When it came to managers, Galeano was no fan: "His mission: to prevent improvisation, restrict freedom and maximize the productivity of the players, who were now obliged to become disciplined athletes." He continued: "Today they talk in numbers. The history of soccer in the twentieth century, a journey from daring to fear, is a trip from the 2-3-5 to the 5-4-1 by way of the 4-3-3 and the 4-4-2. Any ignoramus could translate that much with a little help, but the rest is impossible. The manager dreams up formulas as mysterious as the Immaculate Conception, and he uses them to develop tactical schemes more indecipherable than the Holy Trinity."

Bornn and Galeano are unlikely allies in this fight. Those numbers Galeano mentions are common notation for the formations of each team: defenders, then midfielders, then attackers. As the sport has become more profitable, the number of defenders has increased—a large-scale example of a kind of conservatism that Bornn bemoans, too. Like the Uruguayan poet, the Canadian quant is skeptical of the veneration of, and the complexity ascribed to, the modern manager.

"The vast majority of papers out there say coaches don't matter, basically," he said. "I'm oversimplifying, but that's basically it."

A study from the *Economist*, which used a team's individual player ratings from the video game *FIFA* to predict point totals and ascribed the over- or underperformance to the team's manager, found that the managerial effect didn't carry over when a coach switched clubs. A 2013 paper, titled "The Performance of Football Club Managers: Skill or Luck?" and published in the journal

Economics & Finance Research, put an even finer point on it. The researchers predicted a team's expected results through a combination of spending, payroll, and injuries, and then they, once again, ascribed under- or overperformance to the manager. The researchers found that when teams employed an interim manager between firing the previous guy and hiring his full-time replacement, they exceeded expectations by a whopping 0.42 points per game, better than all but eight of the 60 coaches included in the study. And a 2017 paper, "Towards Smart-Data: Improving Predictive Accuracy in Long-Term Football Team Performance" in the journal *Knowledge-Based Systems,* estimated that an improvement to team personnel or injuries to key players could be worth around eight points a season, while a change in coach typically gained or cost a club about one whole point.

"There may be a small signal that coaches seem to have some sort of small impact, but we're not able to individually identify which ones are great and which ones are bad," Bornn said. So, if your coach doesn't matter and the game is too complex to accurately model from the front office, then how do you run a soccer team?

* * *

As we move forward, surveying soccer's age of disruption, we'll return to Bornn from time to time. Given the number of not only sports but general fields of inquiry he's worked across, Bornn has a clearer view of the shortcomings of soccer's old and new schools than anyone I've ever spoken to. He's run the data operations for one of the biggest clubs in the world, and now he's part-owner of another club in France. Unlike some of the other characters we'll meet, he doesn't have a vested interest in pushing soccer's hottest new statistic or claiming that the data revolution is coming, get in or get out of the way. No, all that matters to him is what works, what wins games.

In his first season with Toulouse, most of Bornn's work was spent getting the club's finances in order—a task that was complicated by a global pandemic that kept fans out of the stands and a billion-dollar broadcast deal that collapsed.

"Running it like a proper business is not normal in soccer clubs," Bornn said. "A lot of soccer clubs are run like family businesses or vanity pieces, so the vast majority of clubs just hemorrhage money. We came in and tried to get the club to run properly; the unfortunate thing is that's something that fans never see. But would I rather have an owner that makes a lot of poor decisions but funds the club at a $5-million deficit every year? Or would I rather have a club that's breaking even, but makes lots of smart decisions? I would way rather have the latter because it puts the club on a much more sustainable footing. But the truth is that fans just aren't exposed to that information. Most fans have no idea whether their club is profitable or breaking even or losing money. It's always remarkable when you see something like, 'Oh, yeah, this club sold a player. Oh, great. How are we going to use that money?' And oftentimes what you use that money for is paying off the massive deficits that you're burning day in, day out."

One of Toulouse's first clear analytically inclined strategies was simply to get younger. Research suggests that performance for players in the top-five European leagues tends to peak somewhere between the ages of 24 and 28—with minor differences by position. Center backs and goalkeepers tend to peak a couple of years later, whereas wide attackers tend to peak a year or two earlier. One simple way to improve performance, then, is to try to pack your team with players toward the beginning of their peak years, and that's exactly what Bornn and his team did. For the 2020–21 season in France's second division, Toulouse's average age—weighted by minutes played—was 24.2, second youngest in the league. But even that idea comes with a caveat, according to Bornn. A year before he arrived in Italy, Roma bought languid Bosnian striker Edin Džeko from Manchester City. Džeko had scored tons of goals, but he was 29, and the problem with acquiring a 29-year-old is that you're likely paying for past performance and bringing him in right as he's about to decline. "What's funny is that at the time, I remember thinking, 'Oh, we should probably think about his age,'" Bornn said. "And he's continued to be a beast even well into his 30s. He defied age." Džeko played six seasons for Roma and averaged at least 0.5 goals+assists per 90 minutes—an above-average rate—in all of them. Džeko never relied on his athleticism to score goals, which could've suggested that he would age more gracefully than other players at his position. Or it could've meant that even the most minor of physical declines to his already-limited physical skills would've suddenly rendered him useless. It turned out to be the former, and Roma would've missed out on one of the best players in Italy had they stuck to a hard-and-fast peak-age recruitment policy.

The other simple strategic implementation at Toulouse? Be aggressive. Humans are naturally risk averse, but the people whose livelihoods live and die by the wins and losses of a group of 20-somethings whom they can only partially control rank as some of the most risk averse among us. Countless studies have found that most coaches don't act the way Doug Pederson did with the Philadelphia Eagles. Instead, they constantly choose the options that will look less bad if they fail.

"When I see coaches choosing particular strategies and choosing particular players, certainly now as a team owner, I'm pushing always towards being more aggressive," Bornn said. "That's in player selection, that's in tactical choice, all those kinds of things." The outcome backs up his claims, too. In the 2020–21 season, Toulouse conceded 42 goals, just slightly better than the league average, but they also scored a league-high 71, seven more than the next-best offensive team.

All in all, it added up to a plus-29 goal differential, which was second-best in Ligue 2, and the third-most points. In France, the top two teams in the second division are promoted to Ligue 1 after each season, meaning Toulouse missed out on automatic promotion (by just two points). Instead, they were given a home-and-away series against the third-to-last-place team from the first division. Whoever scored the most goals over two games would get to be in Ligue 1, with the loser spending the next year in Ligue 2.

Bornn's partner famously once said, "My shit doesn't work in the playoffs"—a reference to how all of the edges he built up with the Oakland A's would lead to lots of wins over a 162-game season but could all be destroyed by the randomness of the small-sample postseason. Beane often couldn't even bring himself to watch playoff games; he'd lift weights in the bowels of the Oakland Coliseum instead of putting himself through the emotional torture of rooting for what was, to his mind, essentially a series of coin flips. For all the reasons Bornn has already described, soccer is basically a season-long version of this problem, and when you distill it down to just two matches, only a true masochist could find joy in the experience.

Bornn, himself, is unnervingly self-assured—even when he's talking about how unsure he is about something. Within the current structure of his work-life, he's basically the soccer version of Jonah Hill's Paul DePodesta, except instead of a nebbish neurotic, he's a confident, plainspoken Canadian who owns a bunch of electric guitars. "I used to play in bands and I actually taught at a music studio," he said. "I used to be a half-proficient player. Nowadays, I could probably play you 'Stairway to Heaven.' And that's about it." When I, a person who stopped taking saxophone lessons in seventh grade, expressed my astonishment at his ability to play an entire eight-minute song, he said, "I should have been clear: I can play you the *intro* to 'Stairway to Heaven.'"

Frankly, it's easier for me to envision Bornn noodling away on some chords while his team decided its future than to imagine him pacing around a stadium box or his living room, living and dying with every shot for 180 minutes. He put his processes in place; whatever will be, will be. But even Bornn couldn't help himself from getting bitter when I brought up what happened. Before I could even finish asking my question, he said, "When we lost on a tiebreaker?"

In the 2020–21 league-promotion playoff, Toulouse lost the first match to Nantes, 2–1, but won the second, 1–0. On aggregate, the teams were tied, but Toulouse didn't score in the right games. The tiebreaker was "away goals," and the first game was at Toulouse, the second at Nantes, so despite losing Game Two at home, Nantes retained their place in the first division. The margins are thin enough to make you want to vomit.

"First off, you just realize how random those sorts of things are," Bornn said. "So we missed automatic promotion by just a few points. And then a tiebreaker is why we didn't get promoted. There are all these little decisions that were made along the way, some made by other people, some my own mistakes. So you think, 'Geez, if I had done that right earlier in the season, or if I had the wherewithal to spot this error after the second game instead of after the fifth game, we maybe would have won another game. We would have been promoted.' That's how close it is and there's so much randomness. But I think oftentimes, the nature of sports is that it just feels like there's so many little things you can always do better. And so there's this constant struggle to figure out where you should focus your time and attention. And it was actually a good experience, because, by not being promoted, it forced everyone to realize little decisions matter. When you miss promotion by just a couple points, it really makes you hammer home that flipping one of those losses to a win or maybe even one of the draws to a win would have done it."

* * *

For all the issues Bornn has with deconstructing soccer and properly applying data, it still is better to try to use the data than to completely ignore it. When he ran the Oakland A's, Billy Beane infamously discounted defense because he couldn't measure it. That's since been disproven, and defensive ability and strategy now play a huge role in MLB on a day-to-day basis, but even though they were missing out on half the game, the A's still wildly exceeded their expectations because they were the only ones trying to systematically measure anything different. Bornn and Beane have taken this attitude to France now, too. "I think this way with everything: if we can't measure it, I'm not going to pay for it," Bornn said.

Running a soccer team in the current era is kind of like walking toward a destination through the dark. Would you rather have a flashlight or not? The people in complete darkness have to operate through feel, trying to use their senses to get a notion of the way the Earth around them is contoured and if there might be a tree or a stop sign or a fire hydrant in the way. They can try to remember what it was like last time and attempt to pass that knowledge on to others, but by necessity this means operating conservatively, lest they go running off a cliff. Now, there might also be people using flashlights who get overconfident, too, assured of their ability to see better than everyone else, only to get tripped up by the crack in the ground that they couldn't see because their light was pointed elsewhere.

However, the majority of soccer clubs are still moving through the world without the flashlight turned on. Some of them own the equipment and just refuse to use it. Some others think that their flashlight can show them everything they need to see. And only a select few are navigating the darkness in the same way the average person would: accepting whatever information they can find, while acknowledging that they're nowhere close to seeing the entire picture.

"My experience is that sports teams are insanely inefficiently run," Bornn said. "I think we're so far ahead in our analytical understanding of the game, relative to the state of execution within clubs. For a club, I wouldn't be like, 'Oh, we really need to better evaluate center backs.' It's like, 'No, you need to figure out how to actually incorporate all this information into your decision-making.'"

I asked Bornn what he regretted most about his first season with Toulouse—what were the things that could've turned that one loss into an extra win? His answer wasn't something like figuring out soccer's version of shooting more threes or trying to hit more homers or attempting to convert more fourth downs. "Making sure your best players play, as simple as that," he said. "When we took over the club, we turned over half the roster. So, at the time, we were still left with, you know, a mixed bag in terms of skills. It's as simple as: The highest-performing assets should be on the pitch." But how hard is it to objectively determine who your best players are with any kind of confidence? "I think it's really challenging," Bornn said. "But it's literally how I make my living."

Back when he was still working for the Kings, I asked Bornn for a metaphor to describe the current state of our collective objective knowledge about how soccer works: What wins games, what matters, what doesn't? "It's like the equivalent of if in basketball we only had data on dunks," he said. "We would spend all our money on seven-foot guys and guys who can get to the rim because that's what we would have data on. And it would just show that dunking was for winning games." We might miss out on Stephen Curry that way, but after all, LeBron James and Michael Jordan were pretty damn good at dunking the ball.

CHAPTER TWO

DUNKS ONLY

Forget the mysteries hidden beneath the complex spatial dynamics of soccer for a second. Did you know Jesus had a brother?

I went to a Catholic high school and was very much *not* taught that Jesus had any siblings. There's that whole "perpetual virginity of Mary" thing. There are references to "your brothers and sisters" in the various New Testament gospels, but I was taught not to take the Bible literally. It was *symbolic*, and those words were used to emphasize Christ's spiritual closeness with *everyone*. His followers were all brothers and sisters.

"It is true that figurative family language is everywhere in early Christian literature, but I don't find it particularly compelling," said Mikael Haxby, a religion scholar with a PhD from the Harvard Divinity School. "No one else is called literally 'the brother of Jesus' or 'the brother of the lord,' it's a specific thing about James."

At the Divinity School, Haxby's dissertation was titled "The *First Apocalypse of James*: Martyrdom and Sexual Difference." The *First Apocalypse* is a so-called Gnostic text—outside of traditional Christianity, non-canonical—that was discovered by an Egyptian peasant named Muhammad Ali al-Samman sometime in the first half of the 20th century. Gnostic texts date back to the third or fourth century. The *First Apocalypse* is an imagined dialogue between James and his brother: Jesus Christ. They know they're both going to be martyred, but James is scared. As Jesus tells him, "You are ignorant concerning yourself." But by the end of the conversation, with help from his brother, James overcomes his fear, saying, "I have come to believe all these things, and they are properly within what is in my soul."

Although accounts differ on how James's martyrdom occurred, the Gnostic text is considered one of the earliest descriptions of Christian martyrdom, sometime after the death of Christ in the year 32 or thereabouts. Strangely, the story doesn't appear in the Bible.

"James has a peculiarly fraught position in early Christianity," Haxby said. "He is not mentioned at all in the Gospels despite what we know from the letters of Paul about his importance, which seems highly suspect. As early as the Gospels, he was being written out of the story."

Haxby's dissertation—and the text he wrote about—sought to re-center James as *the* leading figure in early Christianity and Christian martyrdom in particular. But Haxby also challenged another form of orthodoxy by looking at the portrayal of feminine and masculine martyrs. In the *First Apocalypse*, Jesus mentions seven women martyrs, and he implores his brother to imitate *them*. As Haxby's dissertation concludes: "I believe the text has a greater opportunity to articulate visions of the perfected martyr which can intermingle male and female or masculine and feminine characteristics."

We still don't know the actual truth of this story; we can't know the truth. Who knows what texts were destroyed along the way, who knows who was allowed to write down and interpret the events of early Christianity? Given that, folding in the *First Apocalypse* and other non-canonical texts seemed obvious to Haxby. Every further piece of information could clarify the stories we'd been telling ourselves. And those stories, it turns out, are usually wrong.

* * *

Michael Caley liked playing the role of baseball nerd on the Internet.

Caley grew up in western Massachusetts and considers himself a veteran of the online baseball wars of the early 2000s. Michael Lewis's *Moneyball* had just been published. The jocks and the scouts and the guys who loved to attempt to attain peak athletic performance with plum-size wads of chewing tobacco lodged in their lips weren't having it. At the same time, blogging had temporarily democratized publishing in a good way, and the kind of person willing to start a blog—an untraditional thinker with *a lot* to say—was often the same kind of person willing to accept the idea that the people who run baseball teams don't really have any clue what they're doing.

The ultimate battle—the Gettysburg of the discourse, if you will—was waged between Mike Schur and Joe Morgan. The latter was one of the best baseball players of all time, a Hall of Fame second baseman for the Cincinnati Reds, and the color-commentator for ESPN's *Sunday Night Baseball*. Morgan was your stereotypical jock-turned-commentator—near-impossible to parody. He refused to read *Moneyball* and mistakenly thought that Billy Beane himself was the author. "That moneyball theory is overrated," Morgan wrote in an online chat for ESPN.com. "No one has ever won with it. PLAYERS win games. Not theories." A couple of years later, he told *Deadspin*'s Tommy Craggs, "Anytime you're trying to make statistics tell you who's going to win the game, that's a bunch of geeks trying to play video games."

Schur, who has since gone on to create a number of hit sitcoms, including *Parks and Recreation* and *The Good Place*, first created the blog *Fire Joe Morgan* with a bunch of his TV-writer friends who wrote under pen names. Aiming their sights at "conventional wisdom and poor journalism in baseball," the *FJM* crew would find the worst columns available on the Internet, and then break them down with vicious, line-by-line commentary. Early on, Schur offered up his thoughts on one of Morgan's rambling on-air commentaries concerning the New York Yankees: "I am honestly beginning to wonder whether Joe Morgan has ever played in, seen, or heard about a Major League Baseball game."

Caley never wrote for *FJM*, but he was on their side, commenting on various message boards, defending advocates of statistical analysis against luddite baseball traditionalists. "I was a huge baseball fan, huge Red Sox fan," he said. "I was one of those people who wasted a good chunk of my 20s arguing about baseball stats online."

Soccer wasn't his thing, but the drama and pageantry of the World Cup caught his eye every four years. By the end of the aughts, what with the Boston Red Sox ending an 86-year World Series drought by building a team through the use of statistical analysis, the fight for the soul of baseball had died down quite a bit. After wrapping up a massive research and writing project, Caley had some time on his hands. His interest in using data to better understand sports hadn't disappeared, and with the 2010 World Cup approaching, he decided to set his sights on soccer.

The first problem: Compared to baseball, which for all its internecine arguments has a long history of statistical record-keeping, there were basically no stats. "I remember trying to get a number of shots, shots-on-target, not just attempted but conceded," he said. "If you want to see how good a team's defense is, you want to see how many shots they've allowed and how many shots on target? Didn't exist. You had to go through individual games and collect the data from each game from the other team's shots and shots-on-target."

The second problem: figuring out what you want to figure out. Even without the knowledge that Stats Perform is recording millions of datapoints per match, a soccer game can appear impossibly complex to the naked eye. There are 22 players, all moving independently of each other, all playing offense and defense—at the same time. The ball can seem to move just arbitrarily across the field at times, and with such a high-speed precision at others that the moments seem pre-planned.

But this is where Caley's background in baseball—and his novice soccer eye—helped him. A lifelong soccer fan would've brought all kinds of preconceived notions about what matters and what needs to be appreciated to their maiden statistical analysis of the sport. Caley, though, had no such problems. He knew that goals won games, so he set out to figure out what creates goals. "The baseball model is you're trying to find the component principles," he said. "You're trying to find what makes up a run, what makes up a win. And try to analyze it, literally break it down into its components and see what makes it up. That was what I was looking for."

During the *FJM* heyday, the analyst Tom Tango popularized the idea of "linear weights," which is an awful name (derived from the mathematical process that creates the stat) but a very intuitive idea. The concept was that every plate-appearance affected a team's likelihood of scoring a run. This is how it works, crudely: You look at every walk, single, double, triple, and home run for a set of seasons. Then you figure out the average number of runs that were scored every time each one of those things happened. If there were—pick a number, any number—50,000 singles hit across the five seasons studied and there were 35,000 runs scored directly from those hits, then linear weights would tell you that singles were worth 0.7 runs. (I cheated; this is the actual value of a single, according to the site FanGraphs.) This was a better way of assessing player performance than just on-base percentage because it didn't treat all hits and walks as created equal. And it was also better than the much-maligned runs batted in (RBI) stat because it judged the batter on what only he could control—his at-bat—and not whether his teammates were able to get on base before him.

The beauty of linear weights is that it both scratched at any seasoned baseball watcher's intuition *and* created new knowledge about the sport. It was obvious that a triple was a more valuable play than a single, but the most popular statistic of the time—batting average—didn't show it. At the same time, linear weights both revealed a closer-to-true value for all players and also put a needle through the balloon of "clutchness." The Joe Morgans of the world truly believed that certain players had a special ability to get a hit when there were men on base, as opposed to the simpler alternative: A hit was determined by the batter's matchup with the pitcher and the opposing defense. The other stuff was out of his hands.

Despite the boring, esoteric name, linear weights elegantly valued all players and all actions through the sport's common currency: runs. With a bunch of time suddenly on his hands, Caley set out to do the same thing for soccer.

* * *

Mikael Haxby and Michael Caley are the same person.

When Haxby finished his dissertation and started blogging about soccer, he created "Michael Caley." If he was going to continue his career in religious academia—and you don't write a 100-page dissertation about sexual difference in non-canonical apocalyptic literature concerning Jesus's controversial brother if you don't want to pursue a career in religious academia—he needed to separate himself from the guy blogging about Burnley and Barcelona.

Caley started off by writing for *Cartilage Free Captain*, a fansite for the English club Tottenham Hotspur that was and still is part of the SB Nation network of fan-run sites. The name of the publication refers to Ledley King, a graceful central defender who spent his entire career—from age 16 through 31—with the club. Arguably the best center back in England when healthy, King was Spurs's standard-bearer. Swelling from a chronic knee injury eventually prevented him from playing soccer more than once in a seven-day span. Toward the end of his career, he wasn't even able to practice. "There's no cure," Tottenham manager Harry Redknapp said of his captain's injury in 2008. "There's no cartilage, nothing to operate on."

Over time, Tottenham earned a reputation as serial chokers: capable of producing sublime performances filled with teamwide pass-and-move coordination against the best sides in England, only to throw it all away the next week against the last-place team. There's even a word for this phenomenon: "Spursy." A tendency to inevitably fail to live up to expectations. To consistently bottle it.

It all seems very "armchair psychologist." However, there is an actual economic explanation for Spursy-ness. Tottenham have typically prioritized an aggressive, attacking style of play. The problem is, attackers are the most expensive players on the field, and for most of the Premier League era, Spurs were—at best—the sixth-or-so richest team in the Premier League. And so, if Tottenham acquired a truly great player, he would quickly leave for a bigger club that could pay him more money. And the players who *didn't* leave all had some kind of flaw—injuries, lack of consistency—that prevented the richer clubs from targeting them. Tottenham were destined to have a roster of young players on the verge of leaving, would-be stars if only they could stay healthy, and volatile veterans. In other words, it was the exact kind of squad profile that would produce plenty of breathtaking moments but not enough consistency to win anything across a 38-game season.

In a sense, Spurs were the perfect team for someone looking to reveal novel insights about the way the Beautiful Game works. Tottenham would frequently find ways to lose games that seemed impossible for them not to win. Could anything explain that? If so, was there anything a coach could do about it? Or did those players really just not have enough heart or grit or whatever other Morgan-ism tickles your fancy? On top of that, the club's constant top-level personnel turnover offered up a number of new pathways of inquiry into how exactly individual players might affect a team's overall performance.

To begin his analysis, Caley decided to break down goals into component parts, starting with the shot. While baseball provided him with a framework to think about how value is produced, the connections between the two sports were much more theoretical than practical. One had outs and segmented matchups between a hitter, whose goal was to get on base, and a pitcher, whose goal was to prevent him from doing so, while the other was a chaotic, continuous chain of decisions and actions made by players that sometimes led to a scoring chance but more often than not led to nothing. Theorists have referred to soccer as an "invasion game." All invasion games involve a ball; the team in possession of the ball tries to score by advancing the ball into some predetermined goal; the defending team tries to both regain possession of the ball and stop their opponent from scoring. Unlike baseball, all invasion games involve transition phases between attack and defense—where the ball is not clearly possessed by either side, and it's impossible to define which team is attacking and which team is defending. No matter the invasion game, the team in possession typically tries to create space, while the team out of possession tries to limit or destroy it.

Though basketball and American football remain the two most popular invasion games in the United States, neither one has a predetermined goalkeeper who is given the luxury of fancy equipment designed both to differentiate him from other players and to help him tend his goal. Instead, Caley owes his early work to a different sport that he didn't particularly care for.

"As I started reading around, I saw that there were already people doing this work," he said. "A lot of them were hockey fans and so they came into it with a lot of the assumptions you get from hockey about shots. It's an easy flip from the importance of shots in hockey to the importance of shots in soccer. Because I don't have a hockey background, I learned the hockey analytics from learning soccer analytics."

Hockey's first big analytical breakthrough came sometime in the late aughts. There was a blogger who went by the pen name "Vic Ferrari" and wrote about the Edmonton Oilers for his site, *Irreverent Oiler Fans*. Mr. Ferrari created a stat called Corsi—named for former Oilers coach Jim Corsi for no other reason than that Ferrari "liked his mustache." (It *is* a great mustache.) Corsi was just the difference between a team's shot attempts and their shots allowed. So, what's the big deal? Although imperfect, Corsi proved to be a quite powerful predictor of future performance. A team with a positive goal differential but a negative Corsi was likely to soon start perfuming worse, and a team that was getting outscored despite outshooting their opponents was likely to soon start winning games. Related to Corsi was "PDO," which doesn't actually stand for anything and is just the online username for the person who proposed it. PDO was a team's combined shooting and save percentage. Across the entire NHL, the league's PDO always equaled 100 since every shot on target either went in the goal or was saved. It's essentially a measure of luck: If a team's PDO was significantly above 100, they were likely to regress to league average shooting and save rates, and vice versa.

The beauty of Corsi—the stat, not the mustachioed man—wasn't just that it provided a somewhat stable way to assess team quality and predict future performance. The simple ratio also revealed a basic truth about the sport: The best teams and players tended to be the ones who took the most shots, rather than the players who were especially skilled at converting those shots into goals. In fact, the finding, and the research it has since inspired, were so powerful that Ferrari eventually revealed his identity. It turned out he was a financial analyst living in Chicago named Tim Barnes. In 2013, Barnes was hired by the Washington Capitals as an "analytics consultant." As Barnes was eventually promoted to "director of analytics," *Irreverent Oiler Fans* went dormant. In 2018, the Capitals lifted their first-ever Stanley Cup. The nerds had won again.

Inspired by Barnes's findings, a number of soccer bloggers, including Caley, applied a version of Corsi to soccer. There were so many great mustaches to choose from across the sport. (Personally, I'd have gone with "Bergomi," for Italian defender Giuseppe Bergomi, who both sported a unibrow and looked like he had a miniature rodent living on top of his mouth.) But they instead went with a simpler designation: "total shots ratio," or TSR. The more prosaic name produced roughly similar results. A spate of analyses by the blogger James Grayson in 2012 and 2013 found that TSR was a strong predictor of performance, much more so than simply looking at a team's previous point total or goal differential. His analysis of 12 Premier League seasons found all the league winners and most top-four finishers to be toward the top right of the plot, while all the teams that were relegated populated the bottom left.

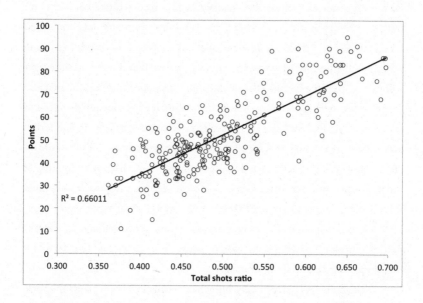

Grayson also found that after about five games in a season, TSR became a stable predictor . . . of itself. That meant that certain teams had an inherent ability that made them more likely to win points. This was a kernel of new knowledge about the way the game worked: The best soccer teams took a lot of shots and didn't concede many. For the people who were writing about soccer stats on blogs, TSR became the currency of quality.

For all its predictive power, though, TSR didn't prove satisfying. Not all shots are created equal, after all. An empty-net tap-in gets counted the same way as a hero-ball attempt from midfield, even though the former is way more likely to turn into a goal than the latter. The people doing the analysis knew this; there's an underlying current of trepidation to many of these blog posts—*we found this thing, but . . .*—and they were hamstrung by a lack of readily available fine-grain data. The shots numbers-people like Grayson were using had no context attached to them; each shot was just a shot; you couldn't see where it came from; these were brief flickers of light in a pitch-black soccer stadium.

One way to work around the limits of the data was to try to find statistical markers from which you could infer some of the things you could not see. Under the pen name "shuddertothink," Benjamin Pugsley wrote an impressive collection of early statistical analyses for another SB Nation blog, *Bitter and*

Blue, a Manchester City fansite. In early 2013, Pugsley looked at "shots on target," rather than just pure "shots," the thinking being that if a shot ended up on target it was probably a higher-quality shot than one that didn't. There was also a theoretical aspect to it. In hockey, a shot that didn't find the target still proved valuable because the puck could ricochet off the back boards and scramble the defense while the attacking team retained possession. In soccer, a shot that didn't find the target was usually just a turnover. Grayson had found little difference in using TSR for all shots compared to using it for just shots on target. However, Pugsley twisted the lens slightly, and rather than looking at predictive season-long correlations, he looked at more than 1,000 individual Premier League matches in which there was a winner. Over a four-season sample, he found that teams that produced more shots on target won 72 percent of their non-draw matchups, compared to just a 63 percent win rate for teams that simply outshot their opponents.

Those findings seem obvious, but when coupled with Grayson's findings, Pugsley's analysis raised more questions than it answered. Over a full season, the best teams in the world tended to be the teams that outshot their opponents by the widest margins. But the way these teams won matches was by putting these shots on the goal frame. Was it simply that attempting more shots overall made you more likely to produce more shots on target? Or was it that the top teams were producing shots that were more likely to be turned into shots on target? Something was still missing.

Caley found it, but it took him a while. He came across a trove of Opta data on the website Squawka, a clunky stats database that, at the time, was filled with ads and was slow to load. It offered location-based event data for the Premier League. You could click on a game page, wait for a couple of minutes, open up another tab, wait for another couple of minutes, click on *another* tab, wait *another* couple of minutes, and then see where and when all of the passes or shots occurred for a given match. But then the information for that specific game—and all other specific Premier League games—just sat there, cordoned off in its own little bucket. Squawka didn't organize any statistics beyond some basic stuff, but beyond its frustrating, cumbersome exterior, there was a vast library of information just floating out there about how the most popular sport in the world was played. Except, all the books had been thrown from the shelves, and the pages were ripped out, and everything was written in a language you couldn't understand.

They don't teach you to code at Harvard Divinity School. At least, not yet they don't. Failed by his most recent degree, Caley had to first teach himself how to gather the game-by-game information hidden inside Squawka and then he had to teach himself how to interpret it, too.

"Once I started collecting data, I always would teach myself just enough programming, just enough statistics to get over to the next problem," he said. "Suddenly you have a lot more data than just the number of shots the team has conceded. I'd just start playing around with that. I think the evidence becomes clear very quickly. Teams are trying to create different kinds of shots, and different decisions to create shots lead to different goal likelihoods."

At *Cartilage Free Captain*, Caley messed around with a number of projection systems that began to layer in more information as he came across it. He wanted to find a way to predict future performance more accurately than just by shots. The shots were always the core, key component, but he kept adding in and removing various contextual factors as he tried to figure out what truly mattered. He toyed with including the state of the game when a shot was taken and also how good a team appeared to be at turning its shots on target into goals. Both would seem to be vital pieces of information—the state of the game changes the way teams play, and why wouldn't you want your model to know how frequently a team converts its chances?—but neither one proved to have much predictive power.

Instead, Caley initially settled on three categories to include in his predictions:

- Location: This is simple. Where was the shot taken from? How far from the goal line and how far from the center of the goal mouth?
- Shot and assist type: Based on the way Stats Perform's coders were tagging events, Caley came up with a simple taxonomy for every shot that occurred in a match. There were five: (1) a header from a cross, (2) a header *not* from a cross, (3) a non-header from a

cross, (4) a shot after a dribble, and (5) a regular shot
(or, in other words, anything that doesn't fit in the other
four buckets).

- Speed of the attack: How quickly did the ball move up
field before the shot was attempted?

What Caley's model did was first classify the type of shot, then contextu-
alize it with both the speed that led up to it and the location where it occurred.
Using that information, the model would then spit out the likelihood that any
given shot would turn into a goal. If you added up those likelihoods across a
single 90-minute match, you ended up with a very specific prediction, down
to the second decimal place, for the number of goals the average team would
be expected to score and concede from that specific collection of shots. When
tested against shots or goals or shots on target, this metric was significantly more
predictive of future goals and future wins. Thus, one version of expected goals,
soccer's most powerful modern statistic, was born.

* * *

Gordon Strachan was *not* happy. He'd just been to the doctor's office, where
he found out that he would no longer be able to indulge in some of his favorite
foods. As he stormed into the conference room at Hampden Park in Glasgow,
he was ready to take his anger out on whoever got in the way.

If you were going to create a Joe Morgan for soccer in a lab, he'd look a hell
of a lot like Gordon Strachan. He has one of those faces that seems permanently
set to "scowl." And whenever he smiles, it doesn't look like he's happy. No, it
looks like he's mocking you for that thing you said that you thought was very
clever but, based on Gordon's facial expression, was very dumb. A reporter once
asked him, "Gordon, can I have a quick word please?" He said, "Velocity," then
walked away. A few other classics of the genre:

- After a loss to Middlesbrough, he was asked, "What
areas do you think Middlesbrough were better at than
you today?" His response: "What areas? Mainly that
big green one out there."

- After another loss, this time ending a long run of matches without a defeat, a reporter asked him, "Can you take it?" His response: "No, I'm just going to crumble like a wreck. I'll go home, become an alcoholic and maybe jump off a bridge."

Before becoming a manager, Strachan was a star midfielder for the Scottish national team and played for a number of top clubs in Scotland and England, including Aberdeen, Manchester United, and Leeds United. He became a player-coach at the tail end of his career and then directly transitioned into management. As a five-foot-six—and that's being generous—central midfielder, Strachan had to figure out a way to make his presence felt since the other guys who played his same position couldn't see him unless they looked down. He did it with a combination of spatial intelligence and rigorous planning. Strachan played until he was 40, which he says comes down to his ability to read space better than his opponent and a specific diet that mainly consisted of porridge, bananas, and seaweed tablets, combined with frequent trips to the acupuncturist and even more frequent afternoon naps.

Being told he had to change was not something Strachan liked, and he also didn't like being told he was wrong, especially by an outsider. The first had just happened at the doctor's office, and Paul Power was waiting in the conference room to do the latter.

Power is one of the godfathers of the modern analytics movement in soccer. Everyone knows him; most people have worked for or with him. He's a sweet, sarcastic polymath with a thick brogue. In the mid-2010s, he was living in the North East of England, working as a sports development manager for the Sunderland City Council. Wondering what the hell a sports development manager is? As Power explained it, "I was in charge of creating participation pathways, building swimming pools, those random things." Before that, he worked for the local club, Sunderland AFC, doing a similar community-outreach-type job. Unlike the stereotype of the socially awkward stats nerd blogging from his mother's basement, Power made a living by working with people, communicating with strangers every day. Of course, he also *did* start blogging at some point. He wrote about coaching and tactics and quickly found that other people were interested in his thoughts about coaching and tactics. He didn't think of it as a replacement for what he was doing every day; it was more of a hobby that he could easily justify because it was kind of related to his day job.

Then, two things happened that changed everything. First, he came across a mention of *Moneyball* on another blog, *Zonal Marking*, written by Michael Cox, now a staff writer at *The Athletic*. "I was like, 'What the hell is this?' Bought it myself, read it, and I was like, 'Damn. This is what analysis should be doing.'" Now, "man reads *Moneyball* once and becomes one of the smartest people in soccer" would be way too convenient a story. The book opened Power's eyes to how evidence-based thinking could challenge and ultimately conquer conventional wisdom in sport. And even though it'd been done before in another sport, soccer's traditions were even more deeply entrenched than baseball's. Disrupting the world's most popular game sounds great in theory, but when you start to think about how to do it in practice, you feel really small, really quickly. Power needed a push, and unfortunately, he got one when the global recession hit in the late aughts.

Unlike, say, Tim Barnes, who went straight from blogger to working for the Capitals, Power went back to school and got his master's in sports performance from the University of Sunderland. His interests initially took him toward video analysis and psychology, but then he read about the birds and the fish. The paper was called "Sports Teams as Superorganisms: Implications of Sociobiological Models of Behaviour for Research and Practice in Team Sports Performance Analysis," published in the journal *Sports Medicine* by a group of Portuguese researchers from the University of Lisbon and the University of Algarve. "And it was talking about complex dynamic systems theory, which is a derivative from chaos theory," Power said. "Basically, you look at flocks of birds, shoals of fish, and how you have thousands of different agents, how they interact. And I was like, 'Wow, this is actually what football is.'"

More broadly, this affirmed in Power a desire to quantify and then interpret what was happening on a soccer field. While he was getting his master's, he interned as a video analyst at Sunderland AFC. One of the oldest clubs in England, Sunderland have won six first-division titles and finished in second five times—but not since 1936. The 21st-century story of Sunderland was of a club with significant resources and an impressive youth academy and absolutely no plan whatsoever. Frankly, if you happen to buy a soccer club at some point, a good team-building principle would be "Just do the exact opposite of what Sunderland did." They waffled back and forth between the Premier League and the Championship (England's second division) in the early part of the century before finishing no higher than 10th in the Premier League for nine straight seasons. They cycled in manager after manager and former big-name player after former big-name player without any real regard for quantifying what wins soccer games. After being relegated from the Premier League in 2017, they were immediately relegated to the third division the following year. The club is such a disaster that Netflix made a multi-season docu-series about their struggles.

While Power was with Sunderland, he had access to some early data from Opta and from his eventual employer, Prozone. It was basic stuff—number of shots, number of passes, and so on—but it was still something. Given the number of managers that have been in and out of the doors at Sunderland, it's not easy for Power to remember who he actually worked with. But he recalls trying to show some stuff to Martin O'Neill and Paolo Di Canio. O'Neill has managed 10 different teams over 30 years and maintains a bizarre interest in unsolved murder cases. Di Canio, meanwhile, has described himself as "a fascist, not a racist." In his autobiography, the former Lazio player wrote that Benito Mussolini, of whom he has a tattoo on his back, was "deeply misunderstood." Regarding his attempts to share data with the amateur criminologist and the avowed fascist, Power said, "They wouldn't even look at it. It just meant nothing to them."

Except, Power doesn't blame either of them. "They were open to getting better, but when you get told you have so many shots it doesn't really mean any-thing," he said. "It lacked all the context; it was the usual complaints." After seeing what Prozone was providing at Sunderland, Power got them to send him his own dataset by telling Prozone that their data was, well, shit. He contacted Prozone and told them that their data lacked all kinds of useful context, so they sent it over to Power with a challenge: "Show us what you can do." Using Microsoft Excel, he built a model that found a way to value the space that players were creating with their runs, and then wrote his master's thesis about it. Prozone liked the work, offered him an internship, and then quickly hired him full-time. Since then, Power has spent most of his days building models and consulting with clubs and coaches. Which is what brought him face-to-face with a grumpy Gordon Strachan.

Strachan coached Scotland from 2013 through 2017, and the Scottish FA decided that it would be a good idea to bring in Power to consult on some best practices for the national team. It was a move made by people *above* the coaching staff. At around nine thirty in the morning, the first to arrive were a pair of Strachan's assistants. One was Stuart McCall, a former Premier League player for Everton and Scottish giants Glasgow Rangers in the '80s and the '90s. The other was Mark McGhee, a former Premier League player for Newcastle United and the other Scottish giant, Glasgow Celtic, in the '70s and '80s. Both went on to manage a number of mid-tier clubs in England and Scotland. While McGhee was managing Aberdeen in Scotland, he defended himself after a loss, saying, "Go and look me up on Wikipedia. I've got a track record. I know how to manage a football team but I need the players out there to do it."

McCall and McGhee entered the room, said hello, took their seats, and then just stared at Power as they all waited for the boss man to arrive. After a couple of unbearable minutes, Strachan finally showed up. He looked at the one guy in the room who had never played for or managed a professional soccer team before and skipped his hello: "Right, what's this shit you're gonna show me?"

Rather than trying to tell them that his shit was, in fact, the good shit, Power used a brilliant little sleight of hand. He sounds nothing like an academic, and part of that is because most of his life was spent outside of academia and not knee-deep in the finer nuances of Voronoi diagrams and chaos theory. But no matter how he sounded, he was still an outsider who had to figure out how to convince these three men—who had more than a century's worth of combined playing and managerial experience on him—that he knew something about this game that they didn't. And so rather than talking directly to them, he didn't even try.

"I showed them a video of this really famous interview of Roy Hodgson when he was England manager," Power said. "The journalist said, 'Roy, you only had two shots on target.' And you hear Roy Hodgson going, 'Two shots on target, two fucking shots on target? Oh no. Two shots on target—don't effing give me that.' And then he went, 'What about when [striker] Daniel Sturridge was through on the keeper and the defender blocked it off the line? What about when he lifted it over? What about when we did this and the defenders got in the way?'"

Power played the video for them, and then looked right at Strachan.

"What do you think of that?" he asked.

"All right. He's right," Strachan said.

"That's expected goals," Power said.

"What do you mean? You're telling me why one shot is harder than another, aren't you?" Strachan said.

"Yeah," Power said.

"So you're just telling me the chance of scoring?" Strachan said.

"It's the chance of scoring. That's all it is," Power said.

The three coaches looked at each other and nodded: "Oh, OK, I like that."

Power likes to tell this story not only because it makes him look good but also because it shows how important it is for data to be presented in the right way to the right people. "The best example of this is expected goals," he said. "The name 'expected goals' has destroyed and set back football analytics, ironically, even though it's the bastion of football analytics and it's everywhere now. When that first came out, it did a huge amount of damage because of the way it was sold."

* * *

Michael Caley can't quite claim credit for Power's hated "expected goals." Once again, the blame might belong with hockey. A blogger named Alan Ryder used the phrase in a paper he wrote for his site, *Hockey Analytics*. In 1993, researchers at the University of Sheffield used the phrase "lower than expected goals against" in a paper, "The Effect of an Artificial Pitch Surface on Home Team Performance in Football (Soccer)," which appeared in the *Journal of the Royal Statistical Society*. But that was more an accidental grouping of the two words in sequence than a coining of a phrase. In 2009, on his site, Soccermetrics, Howard Hamilton wrote about the sport's need for an "expected-goal value" in a post titled "Moneyball and soccer." According to Caley, Sarah Rudd, formerly of Arsenal, and Sam Green, an early employee at Opta, were both working on expected-goals models in the late aughts and early 2010s. Some others surely were, too.

"Once you're trying to get the components of goals, a lot of people have come to that independently," Caley said. "I certainly didn't discover anything because other people had already done it. But I think it's an idea that makes sense once you start working with the data you have."

Now, Caley *does* claim that he was the first person to come up with the abbreviation "xG." And beyond Power's criticism about the name, the power of xG is that it both scratches at the intuition of anyone who has ever watched a soccer game before and at the same time upends conventional wisdom. Caley and the like were the first to codify the idea with both a term and a mathematical model, but everyone who watches a soccer game is doing so with some kind of expected-goals model in their head. He didn't know it at the time, but when my dad suggested that I leave the best youth team on Long Island to go play for another team that we were constantly beating, he was essentially making a bet on xG: They were creating better chances than us, but we converted more of ours. He knew, somewhere in his gut, that over the long run those conversion rates would not last.

This is something that soccer managers have been talking about forever, just in their own terms. In spring 2018, Arsenal manager Arsène Wenger spoke to the team's media group after a sad 2–1 loss to lowly Newcastle United toward the end of his tenure with the club. "There's a difference between the performance and the result because I felt we played very well in the first half especially and should have put the game to bed," he said. According to data from Stats Perform, Arsenal created 1.2 xG in the match and conceded just 0.8 to their opponents. The numbers help to quantify something coaches always say; the result is the score, and the performance is the xG.

At the heart of all of this is an uncomfortable, often-unacknowledged reality for people whose livelihoods are determined by the final score of matches: On a game-to-game basis, soccer is incredibly random. If it were not, the distinction between result and performance would essentially be meaningless, and past goals would be the best predictor of future goals. While xG itself is a relatively new concept in a sport that's existed for at least 150 years, the academic study of soccer's randomness is not. "I find it difficult to imagine that anyone, who had ever watched a football match, could reach the conclusion that the game was either all skill or all chance," statistician I. D. Hill wrote in the *Journal of the Royal Statistical Society* in 1974.

In 2009, an astrophysicist named Gerald Skinner took a break from improving our ability to see into outer space to try to help us see what wins soccer games. He cowrote a paper with a researcher from the University of Warwick named Guy Freeman, titled "Are Soccer Matches Badly Designed Experiments?" Perhaps to fend off any detractors, NASA is listed as one of Skinner's accreditations on the paper, which was published in the *Journal of Applied Statistics*. As the authors write, their goal was to figure out the probability "that the outcome of the experiment (match) truly represents the relative abilities of the two teams." Using a lot of fancy math, they essentially make the argument that if the results of soccer games were a sound determinant of team quality, then you would never see a situation where "A beats B beats C beats A." In the World Cup, from 1938 through 2006, there were 355 examples of three teams all playing each other. Removing the examples that included draws left Skinner and Freeman with 147 triples, and 17 of them (12 percent) led to the A-over-B-over-C-over-A scenario. However, if the results of matches were *completely* random, you'd still only expect that 25 percent would lead to what they call the "intransitive triplet." Skinner and Freeman's research found that anything less than a three- or four-goal victory "lacks the 90 percent confidence which within quantitative disciplines is frequently considered a minimum acceptable level of confidence in the outcome of an experiment." They were so disturbed by how badly designed soccer matches are that they suggested either making the goal bigger or letting games run on for however long is necessary until one team reaches the three-to-four-goal threshold for confidence. Perhaps the Algerians can take some solace from Skinner and Freeman concluding their paper by saying, "there is less than one chance in three that it was the best team that won the cup."

Expected goals, then, both amplifies the sport's unpredictability and gives teams a tool to navigate through it. In February 2017, Sunderland went on the road and beat Crystal Palace, 4–0, with all goals coming in the first 45 minutes. Sky Sports called Palace "sorry," while the *Guardian* said they were "broken," and the BBC went with "abject." At halftime, a fan ran onto the field to confront Palace midfielder Damien Delaney to, one assumes, kindly ask that he and his teammates improve their performance in the second half. The result dropped Palace into a tie for last with Sunderland, putting both teams two points back of 17th place, or the lowest spot in the standings that does not get relegated from the Premier League. Based on the reaction and the result, it seemed like Sunderland were headed toward safety and Palace were destined for the second division. Except, expected goals told a different story. Per Stats Perform, Palace created 2.24 xG and conceded just 0.58.

Given the chances both teams created, this was something like a once-in-a-century result for both clubs. Now, I doubt Delaney could've placated the Palace supporter by saying, "Listen, mate. We've got them on the xG.

Positive regression is coming our way. Just be patient." But he would've been right had he done so. Palace went on to finish in 14th place, comfortably clear of the relegation zone, while Sunderland won only one more game for the rest of the season and finished dead last.

"Expected goals captured a significant piece of traditional soccer wisdom," Caley said. "It's pretty easy to talk to someone who does soccer professionally or someone who has had soccer around them their whole lives and explain the concept. 'Well we're trying to figure out how good a chance the good chance was.' I think that's all very clear. At the same time, there are other pieces of similarly traditional soccer wisdom that are less compelling under this framework."

CHAPTER THREE

MYTHICAL FINISHING

In January 2018, it seemed like Cristiano Ronaldo was cooked. His 33rd birthday was just a couple of months away, and while he'd extended his peak well beyond that of the typical player, time comes for everyone. Some go through a gradual, graceful decline; others fall off a cliff. Three months into the season, one of the greatest players of all time seemed to be tumbling back to Earth. After averaging nearly 32 goals per season over the previous 11 years, he'd scored just four halfway through the 2017–18 season—and one of them came from the penalty spot. The city of Madrid, the country of Portugal, the cyber-army of anonymous teenagers with "CR7" in their Twitter handles—they were all getting acquainted with the Kübler-Ross model. Multiple publications called it a crisis, while Ronaldo himself was forced to then "downplay the crisis." The typically center-line Reuters went as far as to say that Ronaldo's "best days may well be behind him."

With 83 attempts to his name, Ronaldo was still shooting; he just couldn't kick the ball into the net. Except, here's the thing: The most prolific European goal-scorer of all time? He's never been all that good at kicking the ball into the net. And thanks to Michael Caley's work and other similar xG analyses, we now know that most of Ronaldo's contemporaries aren't all that good at it, either.

Even though announcers are constantly lauding certain attackers as "clinical finishers," most players who are good enough for the highest level converted their chances—turned expected goals into actual goals—at roughly the same rate. (By position, forwards tend to score more goals than xG suggests, midfielders remain roughly even, and defenders tend to underperform.) The primary skill, the thing that all the top goal-scorers have in common, is the ability to register lots of shots from high-quality positions.

For the five Premier League seasons from 2016 through 2021, all players classified by Stats Perform as "forwards" took 19,759 shots worth 2,761.99 expected goals and turned them into 2,779 goals. This means that 99 percent of the goal-scoring by the players paid to score goals in the richest soccer league in the world can be explained by a collection of contextual factors that completely ignore what happened once the ball left the player's foot or head. In other words, for professionals in the Premier League, the ability to find the space to get the shot is drastically more important than the ability to convert the shot into a goal. The players who take lots of shots—and take them from high-probability locations—are the ones who score the most goals.

However, that's not to say that certain players aren't better at turning their shots into goals than others, but rather that it's difficult to confidently identify finishing skill, and to the extent that it exists, it's a marginal skill rather than a primary one. A 2017 study by the analyst Marek Kwiatkowski looked at seven years' worth of shots from Europe's five biggest leagues and found that there were only 46 players—among the 98 teams, all of which employ upward of 20 players—who could be identified as an "above-average" finisher with at least a 75 percent confidence interval. Beyond that, there were only *ten* players whom the study identified as above-average finishers with at least a 90 percent confidence interval. Top of the list was Lionel Messi, the greatest soccer player of all time. But even he shows the limitations to the value of finishing skill. In the 11 seasons for which Stats Perform has data, Messi scored 386 goals from 300.81 expected goals in Spain's La Liga. That's about 85 extra goals—an absurd 28 percent above average for more than a decade, giving him an additional nine goals per season—but even for the greatest kicker of a ball the game has ever seen, more than 70 percent of his goals can be explained by a model that doesn't care who he is or where the ball goes once it leaves his foot.

And although Ronaldo seemed to be endangering fans, teammates, and opposing players with his shooting in the first half of the 2017–18 season, the model didn't care. No, it expected him to—and, in a sense, assumed that he *did*—score 11.36 times, rather than 4. So, one of two things was happening: Either (1) Ronaldo had maintained the physical skills that allowed him to get all those great shots in the first place but had developed some Chuck Knoblauch-ian kind of yips-like psychological ailment that prevented him from redirecting the ball between the goal posts, or (2) he was suffering a multi-month stretch of rotten luck.

If you look at the game through the lens of xG, nearly every shot requires some form of luck. Although each miss feels like an embarrassing failure, penalty kicks are converted only 76 percent of the time. No shot, not even an empty-net tap-in is going to earn an xG value of 1.00—what if the guy trips, or the ball hits a bump, or a fan runs onto the field and tackles him before he kicks it?—so every goal that gets scored is a temporary victory against the odds. The average team takes around 12 shots per match, and the average shot is converted around 10 percent of the time. The best teams will attempt 15 or so shots in a given match, and the best players will average 4 or 5. These teams and these players aren't just flipping a double-sided coin; no, it's one of those rigged quarters and it's got a 90 percent probability of landing tails. Given that, it's no surprise that teams and especially players would be prone to wild fluctuations in goal conversion over a small sample of matches.

"The things that you always had debates about from the moment expected goals came onto the scene is a player or a team on a hot or a cold finishing run," Caley said. "There's always these stories about why *this* team is different, why this player is different. These stories have always been a part of soccer lore because there have always been various hot streaks and cold streaks in the game. So, you're challenging those."

The post hoc stories usually have something to do with "confidence"; if a player stopped scoring goals, it's because he's "lost his confidence," and if he can't stop scoring goals, it's because he's "full of confidence." And the nice thing about tautological confidence-based analysis is that it's impossible to disprove—even if that's what Caley's work has done. Players go through slumps because the majority of shots are more likely to miss than end up in the net, and sometimes you just stack a sequence of misses on top of each other—even when you've won the Ballon d'Or five times.

Over the remainder of the 2017–18 season, Ronaldo went on a tear, finishing the season with 26 goals in league play, one more than the previous season despite playing 200-plus fewer minutes. He also scored 15 goals in the Champions League, while no one else in the competition scored more than 10. And on May 26, Real Madrid won their third Champions League title in a row.

Cristiano Ronaldo was never in danger of losing his spot in the lineup because he's Cristiano Ronaldo, but you could see how another, lesser-known player at a smaller club might be. And you could see how he might be replaced by a worse player who just isn't getting on the end of the same number of chances and therefore isn't in danger of *missing* as many chances, so it doesn't seem like he's playing as poorly as the guy he replaced. Yet, over the long run, the team's performance suffers even though they can't blame the guy who couldn't kick the ball straight anymore.

* * *

In 2005, a former NASA roboticist named Randall Munroe launched a web comic called *xkcd*. The tagline describes it as about "romance, sarcasm, math, and language." With his stick figures, Munroe pokes fun at various illogical collective wisdoms, three times a week. In the 904th edition, Munroe released a comic called *Sports*. One person says, "A weighted random number generator just produced a new batch of numbers." The other person responds, "Let's use them to build narratives!" And below them sits the phrase: "All Sports Commentary."

More so than any other major sport, Munroe was describing soccer. The result of each individual match and every individual shot has only a tenuous connection to the actual quality of the team or player producing it. But within the typical European-league structure, a 38-game season with no playoffs, each result *is* incredibly valuable. While xG now gets mentioned on broadcasts across the world from time to time, it still isn't anywhere close to being widely adopted. And the media surely benefits from the current relationship it has with fans; every weekend there are a couple of results that get presented as referendums on a team's season, and fans get mad that their team sucks or that the coverage of their team says that their team sucks. Using xG as a baseline for more level-headed analysis would remove a lot of that emotion.

ALL SPORTS COMMENTARY

For teams, though, it *should* be an invaluable tool. It's undeniably a better way to assess player performance and team performance than what was being done before. More importantly, it's a way to pull yourself out of the wild ups-and-downs of results-based thinking. By judging yourself based on the quality of the chances you're creating and conceding rather than a couple of successive scorelines, you can identify when you're getting lucky or unlucky, and then you can make changes or stand pat even though the recent wins and losses suggest you should do the opposite. If a young Billy Beane were running a soccer team, you could easily picture how he would've found value in the market: Sign players that underperform their xG totals for a season and sell on whichever guys you employ that overperform theirs. And well, that is exactly what the guy who works with Billy Beane did.

In January of 2019, Glasgow Celtic, the biggest club in Scotland, paid $2.30 million for a player you've never heard of, from a team in Bratislava. Born in the Ivory Coast, Vakoun Issouf Bayo was a lively, explosive center forward from a country that produces lots of that specific kind of player. Celtic manager Brendan Rodgers said of his team's newest signing, "He likes to get in the box and attack the ball. He's an out-and-out striker, whereas some of our other strikers like to roam and link the game up. He's one that plays the game simple outside the box, but when it's in wide areas he's in the box looking to score." However, a little more than a month later, Rodgers left Celtic to go manage Leicester City in the English Premier League. Bayo played a whopping two minutes over the remainder of the 2018–19 season and then made eight appearances and just a single start the next year. He didn't score a single goal. To Celtic fans, journalists, and management, he was, for all intents and purposes, a complete bust. Except, Luke Bornn realized that Brendan Rodgers was right. Bayo kept getting into the box and kept getting shots. They just weren't going in.

"He played about three full matches and generated 1.67 xG, which per match is actually a really high number," Bornn said. "Didn't score a single goal, though. And so the narrative on him with the fans and I'm sure even with the leadership itself, it goes: 'This guy can't score goals. He's useless at scoring goals.' Whereas we had data on him before he joined Celtic. He was at Dunajská Streda, and he scored 10 goals on 9 xG. So we knew that this was just a short-term blip. They were excited to get rid of him because he didn't score three goals; he's a striker. We were like, 'We don't care.'"

Toulouse acquired Bayo on loan from Celtic for the 2020–21 season. (Teams will often pay a small fee and/or some portion of a player's contract to acquire him for a single season.) He scored 10 goals, second-most on the team, which was nearly enough to push them up to Ligue 1. "We can see that underperformance of xG is not something that is repeatable over time," Bornn said. "We just know that it's random. There are very few players that consistently over- or underperform xG. So, yeah. Brought him in, knocked in 10 goals, and we got a great deal."

Beyond Bornn's specific experience, Caley believes that the transfer market shows how far away teams remain from optimizing their use of xG. The proof is in the price of players. In the summer of 2019, Antoine Griezmann became the sixth-most expensive player of all time, as he moved from Atlético Madrid to Barcelona, and Eden Hazard became the ninth-most expensive player when he went from Chelsea to Real Madrid. And yet, in the season prior to their moves, neither one was even in the top 25 among all players in combined xG plus expected assists. (An added benefit of xG is it applies to passing, too; while assist numbers are reliant on another person kicking a ball into a goal, xA determines the number of assists a player can expect to accrue from his passes.) "I think until we see forward prices line up with xG plus a little bit of finishing sauce, we know there is a ton of value not being picked up," Caley said.

Today, Caley has given up on the academic world. He works as an organizer for the leftist wing of the Brooklyn Democratic Party and still produces a multi-weekly podcast about soccer analytics called *The Double Pivot* with Mike L. Goodman, a former colleague of mine and the first American to serve as a full-time analytics-based soccer writer. The latter fact might also seem like an indicator of the game's lagging adoption of xG; shouldn't Caley be working for a team by now? But that's more by choice. Caley produced analyses of English clubs Everton and Nottingham Forest for a group of investors that were considering buying one of the two clubs. Neither sale happened, and the whole thing soured Caley on the idea of doing proprietary work.

"I got paid more than I got paid for a freelance article. It was ultimately really enervating," he said. "I put together these reports and at the end of it maybe 10 people saw them. I know people who have gotten jobs inside, and it's really exciting to them. One, you get the funding to do lots of more cutting-edge research, and two, you have the fun of 'I identified that winger! Look at him go!' That did very little for me professionally or emotionally. I kind of was like, *eh.*"

Although Caley has given up on the academic excavation of the martyrdom of Jesus's nontraditional brother and the radical interpretation of gender roles in apocalyptic gospels, he feels like he just moved the same work over to something else.

"In a very broad way, there is something appealing about trying to figure out problems in which you are lacking a lot of the data that you need," he said. "Understanding soccer through on-ball data, you have this one little piece of the puzzle and you know there's all the stuff that you don't have, but there's still things you can say about it. The history of antiquity, the history of ancient religions, you know all the time that all you've got from these people are a couple of texts and you can extrapolate from some archaeological data. It isn't theirs. Who wrote the text? We don't know, but you can put these little bits and pieces together to try to come up with a coherent story."

CHAPTER FOUR

THE MONEY WAY

This whole thing started with a Scottish linen salesman living in Birmingham. Blame him, revere him—it really depends on how you feel about cartels.

In the mid- to late 1800s there were a bunch of people swinging bats on one side of the Atlantic and a bunch of people kicking balls on the other. As both baseball and soccer evolved beyond their infancies and into something big enough to be commodified, the two sports dealt with similar problems. Baseball's popularity grew in the United States because it presented a livelier, faster-paced option to the multi-day marathons of cricket. The ball was in play more often, the athletes were constantly doing athletic things, and the players weren't constantly stopping for tea and finger sandwiches. In England, they're still playing test cricket to this day, but for all the obvious reasons described in the previous sentence, the sport maintained a limited commercial appeal. Instead, soccer became the national sport.

It's important to note here that this version of soccer was only vaguely related to the version of soccer that you're now able to watch on your TV screen every weekend. There was a goal, sure. And a ball, yes. And even the same number of players, true. But the reason the game captured the national imagination in the first place is that it was brutal and chaotic. The idea of "passing the ball" wasn't popularized until sometime after the game began to be played at an organized level. You'd kick the ball upfield or try to run through a mass of defenders, you'd fall, and then you and your teammates would try again. It was a litmus test for your morality and your masculinity. This was Victorian England; people were literally freaking out that their boys were masturbating too often. "The masturbation panic was so ubiquitous there was a strong emphasis against solitude, against privacy, against individualism," Katherine Mullin wrote in *James Joyce, Sexuality and Social Purity.* "All sorts of team sports, football in particular, were brought in as an antipode to solipsism."

Two of the biggest clubs in the world today, Liverpool and Manchester City, were initially founded as church teams in an effort to save local boys from "dirty thoughts." Not all teams had religious beginnings, but most were affiliated with one of the elite English public schools, and then when that initial wave of boys became men, they kept on playing and maintained those same allegiances even after graduating. Within this setup, soccer quickly became a game of the monied class, much like cricket and baseball initially were.

However, it proved impossible to keep either soccer or baseball away from the lower classes; you needed just a ball and/or a bat to play. Each sport had a national governing body of sorts—the Football Association in England and the National Association of Base Ball Players in the States—but just about anyone could start their own team. Over time, the classes started to mingle on the pitch and on the diamond, and the average outcome looked something like this: rich guys getting their asses kicked. With people up and down the social ladder interested in the same game—and with a diversifying player pool that produced increasingly entertaining feats of athletic excellence—it quickly became obvious that there was lots of money to be made.

Sensing a sea change, on both sides of the ocean, various self-proclaimed protectors of the games began to cry "amateurism." In the States, gamblers and priests joined the gentlemen in their opposition to the potential professionalization of baseball. The gamblers worried that players wouldn't be so easily influenced if sport became their job, while the church claimed that weekend baseball would distract from adherence to proper religious practice. And of course, the gentlemen were the only ones who could afford to play the sport for free forever. Their hope was that maintaining the game's amateur status would eventually crowd out the working-class dudes who kept working them on the diamond.

The reality is, though, that players were already getting paid. As Stefan Szymanski and Andrew Zimbalist point out in their book, *National Pastime*, it was common practice to give skilled players "soft jobs" on a city's payroll to encourage them to join a local baseball team. Unconcerned with amateurism and frustrated with the sometimes sloppy play and the influence of gambling on the pseudo-amateur sport, the president of the Chicago White Stockings, William Hulbert, decided to form America's first professional baseball league in 1876. As Szymanski and Zimbalist note, the "National League appears to be the first example of a closed professional team sports league anywhere in the world." Membership in the NL was limited to eight teams initially and potential future members were to come only from cities with at least 75,000 people. Decisions were made by the league's eight team presidents, and although players now had professional contracts, they were given no managerial power. They became the labor to Hulbert and Co.'s capital. With this structure in place, the focus shifted from the sport itself to the league—crushing the competition and growing the overall revenue in order to fill the pockets of the owners. A lot has changed since then, but Hulbert himself created the structure that every other major American sports league would eventually follow: owner control in a closed, cartelized system with exclusive membership.

Right around the same time, the Brits were fighting their own battle over amateurism. In the early 1880s, a bunch of the northern industrial towns formed their own teams; these sides were organized not by school but by factory affiliation. The northern clubs began to win national competitions, and much like in baseball, these teams figured out a way to pay their players without actually paying them: The factories would just hire the best soccer players and pay them as factory workers.

This was professionalism by another name, and it all came to a head in 1884 when the factory team Preston North End defeated the fancy London club Upton Park in the FA Cup, the country's national soccer tournament, which still exists today. Upton Park claimed the match should be ruled null and void due to the presence of paid players, and in response, Preston withdrew from the competition—only to then form a union with 30 other, mostly northern teams who all threatened to break away from the FA if professionalism wasn't quickly normalized.

The FA, sensing its pending irrelevance, soon overturned its prohibitions on player pay, but there was nowhere for the potential pros to go. There was no national league, and no National League. Teams played in all kinds of ad hoc cup competitions, but this made playing schedules incredibly unpredictable—and it really annoyed William McGregor.

Born in Scotland, McGregor moved to Birmingham around 1870. He opened a draper's shop and sort of stumbled into an administrative role at one of the local clubs, Aston Villa. In March of 1888, he sent a letter to five other major northern clubs, asking for what he called a "fixity of fixtures" throughout the season. "If [a club] was thrown out in the first round, they had blank days," he said. "If they kept in longer than they expected to remain, then fixtures already arranged had to go by the board. Spectators, too, became disgusted by the intermittent fare provided for them." His proposal was for a group of teams to play each other: a pair of games between each, home and away. A month later, the Football League was formally established. This structure, too, has changed, but McGregor's idea—two games between every team, one home and one away—was adopted and is still being used by every major European soccer league today.

Unlike the National League, the Football League continued to exist within the sport's national governing body, the FA, and its teams continued to compete alongside amateur clubs in the FA Cup. McGregor and his fellow founders also never envisioned a closed-off league; early on they advocated for a version of the promotion and relegation system we still see today. In theory, it was—and still is—possible for anyone to start a soccer team, join a local league, win that league, and then win another league, and another, and another, and another before ultimately reaching the top.

Why the drastically different initial approaches to professionalizing sports? The Football League was founded within a settled, confident, comfortable culture: imperial England, conquerors of the world, where, as Szymanski and Zimbalist write, "any innovation was required to fit into the social order." Hulbert's National League came about in post–Civil War America, where the economy was getting its first high off the idea of winner-take-all competition. "Ruthlessness in the economic sphere became a virtue," they write. Hulbert's idea, thought up almost out of thin air, with no real antecedent, was as ruthless as it gets.

Although they were initially shaped by various somewhat random, temporary cultural factors, McGregor's and Hulbert's ideas are still being felt today. Is it any surprise that the world's first breakaway, financially optimized, cartelized sports competition became Major League Baseball, the most mathematically optimized league in the world today? The one where former players have been almost completely replaced by Ivy League general managers and legions of scouts have been rendered irrelevant by algorithms? The search for an edge has been a part of professional baseball's DNA since the moment it started. On the other side of the Atlantic, competition was really only one part of the Football League's founding impulse. Initially, directors of the clubs weren't even allowed to take salaries and annual investor profits were capped at 5 percent. The global appeal of the parochial game was eventually gobbled up by the capital machine, but it took a while. There's still not quite a Billy Beane of soccer—other than, you know, the actual Billy Beane—and there are still so many "known unknowns and unknown unknowns," as Luke Bornn put it. Structurally, soccer is harder to understand than any of the major American sports, but the game also got a late start. In England, they've been doing the "ruthless competition" thing really for only about 30 years.

* * *

Ruthless competition is what Stefan Szymanski has always been after. Not for himself, no. He just really wanted to know how others did it.

After getting his PhD in economics, Szymanski accepted a job at the London Business School, where he and his colleagues studied, as he self-mockingly referred to it, "The Sense of a Business Strategy." They wanted to figure out how businesses became profitable relative to their competitors. Seems simple enough, but in the mid-1990s things had started to change. Deregulation led to at least some form of monopolization in most major industries. "And as economists we took the paradigm: well, it's easy to understand the monopoly," Szymanski said. "If you don't have competition, it's easy to understand how you make money: People don't have an alternative, your buyers don't have an alternative. So, how can you miss?"

They could've studied how certain businesses became monopolies, but this presented a different problem. Most monopolies rose to monopoly-dom by differentiating themselves to such a degree that they essentially sidestepped the competition, rose above, circled back around, and crushed everyone below them. That wasn't too interesting, either. So, as Szymanski's options continued to dwindle, he found himself doing something he almost never did: He started thinking about sports, and soccer in particular. "You can't really differentiate in soccer in the way of saying, 'OK we're now going to play with 12 people on the field, and we're going to play with a square ball.' It's no longer soccer, right? You're actually constrained by the rules of the game to play the same game over and over again," he said.

Like Bornn's, Szymanski's hard right turn into sports was driven by the availability of data. This was all purely theoretical—*wouldn't that be fun, but oh well*—until he and his colleagues realized that the annual financial statements for English soccer clubs were readily available to anyone who knew where to look. Perhaps more importantly, they were easy to understand, too. "Financial statements of soccer clubs in England are very revealing, precisely for the reason financial statements are not generally very revealing in other contexts," he said. "If I look at the financial statements of Apple, for example, the problem I have is knowing which bit of the business is generating the money and which isn't. In the soccer clubs, they only do one thing: play soccer."

And so, Szymanski set off on what I consider to be the landmark study of professional soccer in Europe—the piece of literature that revealed the core truth about how this mysterious game works and why some clubs move through the darkness better than others.

"I think it was my boss at the time, John Kay, who said, 'You should look and see if higher spending leads to more success,'" Szymanski said. "And I think my response as a casual fan was, 'No, you're not going to find much there, it's pretty random.'" Remember, this is long before efficiency became the goal for many sports teams, both on and off the field. "And then—lo and behold—we looked at it, and he was damn right. We could see his correlation just stood out by a mile. Basically, the fundamental principle has not in my mind changed since then."

In 1991, Szymanski copublished his first paper on soccer with Filippo Dell'Osso in the *Business Strategy Review*, "Who Are the Champions? (An Analysis of Football and Architecture)." It's the work that first pushed him toward finding and then fine-tuning that fundamental principle: Player wages are the main predictor of team success. Not tactics, not any specific kind of coach, no, just money. An updated version of this initial research found that from 1974 through 1999, the correlation between wages and position in the table in English soccer was 94 percent. (For comparison, Michael Caley's work on xG found the correlation between xG and future points to be about 52 percent—and that's the *strongest* statistical correlation anyone has found for any kind of on-field performance.) Similar studies have found comparable results outside of the UK, too, as teams with wage bills outside of the top three in a given European league win the title just 15 percent of the time. And so while their philosophies of play may differ wildly, there's one thing that all of the most successful managers have in common: They worked for teams that paid their players a lot of money.

However, there's an important distinction to make here. The market for soccer players functions very differently than the market for baseball or basketball players. In baseball, you get traded or you run out your contract or you get released. That's how you move teams. In soccer, players can run down their contracts, though they rarely do. Instead, players tend to move thus: Liverpool decide they want to acquire a central defender from Sevilla in Spain. In order to do so, Liverpool have to come to a financial agreement with both Sevilla and the player. Sevilla has to accept a transfer fee from Liverpool—essentially a sum of money that allows Liverpool to buy out the player's current contract—and then Liverpool have to agree to a new contract with the player. Despite the seemingly complicated multi-level negotiation process, the summer transfer window—there are two periods throughout the year (between seasons and in January) when teams are allowed to make transfers—is a complete free-for-all because theoretically any player can change teams for the right amount of money. Although there was a global pandemic in 2020 that caused mass economic contraction, that summer Premier League clubs spent more than a billion dollars just on the fees that allowed them to then sign new players to contracts. What's more: Szymanski's later research has found almost no correlation between transfer spending and success.

That initial paper set Szymanski off on his path toward becoming The Soccer Economist, the guy everyone turns to when they want to try to understand how all the money sloshing around the Beautiful Game affects what's happening on the field. He's written countless books on the topic, most famously *Soccernomics*, coauthored with the journalist Simon Kuper. Now a professor at the University of Michigan, he joked, "In some ways I've been rewriting that paper my whole life."

* * *

Soon after Szymanski wrote that first paper, though, everything changed. The 22 teams at the top of the Football League ladder, the same one William McGregor thought up back when he was selling fabric to people who didn't know what electricity was, broke away to form their own league. They called it the "Premier League." And while the league still maintained its connection to the other leagues through promotion and relegation, the teams in the Premier League were now free to negotiate their own television deal. Previously, revenues from broadcast rights were shared equally among teams in all four of the professional divisions. Now, the clubs in the first division would get to keep it all for themselves.

The initial package was purchased by Rupert Murdoch's BSkyB for, as David Goldblatt writes in *The Ball Is Round*, his global history of the sport, the "then astronomical figure of over £304 million over three years." The Premier League was the first European league to focus so openly on commercialization. The various club owners at the time became enamored by how the NFL packaged and sold its product: making every game feel like the most important game of your life, surrounding matchups with hours of pre- and postgame chatter. "In terms of commercial attraction, it was amazing," said then Tottenham owner Irving Scholar. "You could see the future." The league's broadcaster felt the same way, too. One of Sky's initial innovations was to schedule games on the first weeknight of the week. They called it Monday Night Football.

Since the Premier League was a breakaway league founded by 22 teams, the initial financial structure of the competition remained relatively democratic so as to appease all the members equally. The payout for the last-place team compared to that for the first-place team was a ratio of about 1-to-1.6, while in other countries like Spain where there were historically just a couple of dominant clubs, the payouts were closer to 1-to-3. This close-to-equitable structure was the launching pad that sent the Premier League into orbit. Despite the reduced top-line prize money, the best teams still wanted to win trophies because the payout was still massive thanks to the new TV deal and because winning helped you acquire better players and more fans and more money that would bring in more new players and more fans and more money and on and on. Meanwhile, the teams at the bottom of the table fought for their lives on a weekly basis, as the difference between relegation and survival was huge. In the final season before the Premier League was created, the difference in combined revenue of the 22 top-tier teams and the 24 second-tier teams was £58 million. Ten years later, it was 10 times that. By 2016, the gap was multiple billions of dollars. "The founders of the early 1990s had created a framework to keep the smaller clubs comparatively rich and make relegation a financial castrophe," Joshua Robinson and Jonathan Clegg write in *The Club*. "Every game mattered now."

Thanks to Sky's slick packaging and a financial structure that layered drama onto almost every match on the calendar, the Premier League has become the most popular league in the world. Per game, the league's TV revenue is more than double that of any other league in the world. Liverpool and Manchester City were founded by church groups to prevent young boys from masturbating; now Liverpool are owned by an American billionaire who got rich by creating an algorithm and trading soybean commodities, while Manchester City are a plaything of Sheikh Mansour, a member of the Abu Dhabi royal family who went to community college in Santa Barbara.

Despite some increasingly uncompetitive changes to the ways teams qualify for the Champions League—and the spectacular failure of the breakaway Super League in April 2021—the promotion-and-relegation structure has remained. So, too, have the fans. In some ways, these were both supposed to be bulwarks against the commodification of the sport. Promotion-and-relegation maintained a "we're all in this together" feeling that William Hulbert's National League explicitly tried to destroy from the get-go. And the fans were the reason the teams existed and the reason why owner dividends were limited and club directors were initially unpaid. These clubs were supposed to be held in some kind of public trust, to serve the interests of the supporters in the local community rather than the bottom line of whoever was cutting the checks.

However, in a strange twist, the open structure of the league and the dedication of the fans were two of the main things that allowed the league to be commodified. Relegation added that new layer of drama and the local fans created the atmosphere in the stadium that was then bought, sold, and broadcast across the world.

While the World Cup used to be the only time fans would get to see the best players from around the world compete against each other, they now get to watch them every weekend in the Premier League and in the other major leagues across Europe. The rising revenues have concentrated all of the global talent in Western Europe. The best players all play together and they're coached by the best coaches, day in and day out. There was a time when, say, Pelé's Brazil was probably the best soccer team in the world, because no club could ever have all of the best players from the best soccer-playing countries playing in the same team. But now clubs will have the best players from Brazil, England, Portugal, and Egypt all in the same starting lineup—and they're getting daily training from the best German coach.

With global commercialization comes ruthless competition—you might assume. When club owners were only half-interested in turning their teams into indomitable winning machines, and weren't able to profit massively from their revenues, and weren't deathly frightened by the financial fallout from relegation, is it really that surprising that the richest teams won and the least-rich teams lost? With very few organizations searching for competitive edges via a top-down institutional mandate, the market did its thing. The teams with the most money attracted the best players and the best coaches, seemingly, because there were no other forces working to prevent that from happening.

Except, now that working-class administrators are gone—butchers have been replaced by billionaires and oligarchs have taken the place of optometrists—nothing has changed. Well, everything has changed, and the Premier League is awash in billions of dollars and it attracts the best coaches and the best players from across the planet now. Every game is on television in the United States. People like me can make a living writing about the league for an audience of Yanks. But the driving factor behind winning—the one variable with the tightest correlation to a team's season-ending point total—hasn't budged. For the seasons starting in 2007 and ending in 2016, Szymanski rewrote his and Dell'Osso's 1991 paper and reran their study. The result: Over that time span, wages still explained 90 percent of the variation in team performance.

* * *

Szymanski has done more work to increase the general public's understanding of the Beautiful Game than maybe anyone else in the world. He has simplified a game that often seems purposefully opaque, both on and off the field. And I think he's wrong about what it all means.

To him, the ruggedness of the wage-to-performance correlation is proof that these teams are all innovated out. That soccer clubs have all figured out the best ways to play and the best players to sign and the right things to measure, as much as they can. If anything, he thinks the structure of the Premier League should have inspired soccer teams to be *ahead* of their American-sport counterparts on their journeys through the darkness. "As an economist, I would say if you were looking for innovation, you would look to the competitive markets," he said. "Competition generates innovation, not monopoly. And the major leagues in the United States are organized on monopolistic, cartelized grounds, so they're less likely to be innovative, not more likely to be innovative."

Szymanski's initial work is one of the driving principles behind this book you're reading. As of now, wages—not possession percentages, not shots, not expected goals, not the number of tackles, not any kind of philosophy—are what create winning in the world's most heavily romanticized sport. To me, that's proof of the exact opposite of what he's saying: that no one is really innovating. It's proof that everyone's basically doing the same thing that they've always been doing, and when they change, they all change at the same pace. The only truly groundbreaking innovation, as things currently stand, is to get bought by an oligarch or a petrol state with a trillion-dollar sovereign wealth fund so you can eventually pay more money for better players and (maybe) better coaching. It's not "let's figure out a new way to play or a new way of scouting or a new way to score goals."

Take Manchester United as an example. They're the New York Yankees of soccer—just more popular. If you've ever met a Yankees fan, you know: 27 rings, bro. The Bronx Bombers have won the World Series 27 times; no other franchise has more than 11 titles. This is the most successful team in American sports history, and it's one of the richest, too.

The Yankees, of course, were the team that Billy Beane set out to defeat when he was with the scrappy Oakland A's. "If we do what the Yankees do, we lose every time, because they're doing it with three times more money than we are," Beane said in *Moneyball*. However, as Beane's A's started to have success despite their limited payroll, the Yankees (and baseball's other big-money clubs like the Los Angeles Dodgers, Chicago Cubs, and Boston Red Sox) eventually caught on. They started developing much of their resource advantage to the exact things that had brought Beane success: finding, developing, and creating new information that would allow them to identify undervalued players. Except, their outsize payrolls also allowed them to develop even better information while still outbidding their competition for the top talent. Now the Yankees were doing what Beane did, and with three times more money.

The richest teams in baseball had enough of a built-in advantage that they really only had to avoid being wildly inefficient with their spending in order to succeed. But instead, they've become some of the most efficient teams in the sport. Combine that with a sizable financial advantage, and you dominate—before the playoffs, at least.

Much like the Yankees, Manchester United lead all English clubs with 20 first-division titles. And much like the Yankees, they're richer than everyone else. In 1998, the accounting firm Deloitte created something called the "Football Money League," which tracks, analyzes, and ranks the richest clubs in the world by annual revenue generated. It started with just 10 teams and has since expanded to 30. Manchester United have "won" the Money League twice; they've never finished lower than fourth; and they've been the richest English club every year. More titles, and more money: The Szymanski system triumphs once again—sort of, and not really anymore.

"Back in 1990, we thought Liverpool was the shining example of a successful club," Szymanski said. "And Manchester United was the classic example of the underperformer back then because they hadn't won anything in decades."

From 1981 to 1990, Liverpool won six of nine first-division titles. Next closest were cross-city rival Everton and North London's Arsenal, both with two. Manchester United, meanwhile, had been stuck on seven titles since 1967, a year after England won its one and only World Cup. And then Sir Alex arrived.

With the club hovering near the relegation zone halfway through the 1986–87 season, United took a chance on a ruby-cheeked Scotsman with a brogue so thick it often seemed like he had teeth only on the bottom of his mouth. When Alex Ferguson took over as manager at United in 1986, his greatest challenge, as he put it, was to "knock Liverpool off their fucking perch." Come his retirement in spring 2013, Manchester United were wrapping up their 20th league title, while Liverpool were still stuck on 18. Ferguson took down Liverpool, and the rest of England in the process.

His managerial tenure was one of the most successful not just in sports but in any field where people worked for other people. So successful that, in 2012, the *Harvard Business Review* conducted a case study of Ferguson's work with United. In a 2013 *HBR* follow-up, Ryan Giggs, one of the Premier League's greatest-ever players, told the author: "He's never really looking at this moment, he's always looking into the future. Knowing what needs strengthening and what needs refreshing—he's got that knack."

It was discovered that, over his last decade in management, Ferguson's team spent less money on player transfers than any of their main rivals. And when they did spend, they spent a larger proportion of their money on players under the age of 25, compared to their competitors. The transfer market is inefficient and players peak earlier than you think—Ferguson had an innate understanding of the things we'd eventually learn. As Giggs perhaps hints at, he was ruthless when it came to squad management, often preferring to sell players when they were still at their peaks, lest they suddenly decline and see their transfer value plummet.

"Although I was always trying to disprove it, I believe that the cycle of a successful team lasts maybe four years, and then some change is needed," Ferguson told the *HBR*. "So we tried to visualize the team three or four years ahead and make decisions accordingly. . . . The goal was to evolve gradually, moving older players out and younger players in."

At times, Manchester United's titles felt inevitable—metaphysical, even. It was as if the structures of the sport bent to Ferguson's whims, as if soccer couldn't exist if Manchester United didn't win. Critics had a different name for it: "Fergie Time," the idea that referees would add extra time to the end of matches if United weren't winning. Conspiracy is an easier explanation for 13 titles in 21 years than, say, complex man-management and constantly evolving squad-building, but the critics weren't totally wrong, either. A study from Opta actually found that between the 2010 and 2012 seasons there were 79 seconds more than average in matches that United were losing.

Except, that was only part of it. United won so many games late in matches because, well, United won so many games, period. But they also prepared specifically for these moments. According to the 2013 *HBR* study, over Ferguson's final 10 seasons, United had a better record than any other Premier League team when the game was tied at halftime and when the game was tied with 15 minutes remaining. Ferguson's teams would practice how they would play with 10 or fewer minutes left on the clock—even or down a goal.

"I am a gambler—a risk taker—and you can see that in how we played in the late stages of matches," Ferguson said. "If we were down at halftime, the message was simple: Don't panic. Just concentrate on getting the task done. If we were still down—say, 1–2—with 15 minutes to go, I was ready to take more risks. I was perfectly happy to lose 1–3 if it meant we'd given ourselves a good chance to draw or to win. So in those last 15 minutes, we'd go for it. We'd put in an extra attacking player and worry less about defense. We knew that if we ended up winning 3–2, it would be a fantastic feeling. And if we lost 1–3, we'd been losing anyway."

Ferguson had revived a sleeping giant. The club was saved from bankruptcy in the early 1900s by a wealthy brewer by the name of J. H. Davies. Davies poured money into the club and oversaw the construction of Old Trafford, the same stadium United play in to this day. Critics back then called the club "moneybags United." According to Szymanski, tragedy then helped turn them into a brand name. Under the legendary manager Matt Busby, an especially young United team won back-to-back league titles in 1956 and 1957. The "Busby Babes" were expected to dominate the next decade. But after defeating Yugoslavian club Red Star Belgrade in the semifinals of the European Cup in 1958, the team plane crashed while attempting to take off in a blizzard. Eight of the players, and 15 other passengers, died. Busby himself barely survived.

"The tragedy shocked fans and nonfans alike, not just in England but throughout the world," Szymanski wrote. "Without question, it changed the attitude of many towards the club and certainly made it a household name. From this time on, Manchester United became one of the best-supported clubs in the country."

The team, improbably and impossibly, rebounded to win the European Cup—under Busby—exactly 10 years later. After Busby finally stepped away in 1971, Liverpool dominated the next two decades. However, despite 20 years of mediocre performance, Manchester United's fanbase didn't waver. From 1972 through 1990, United didn't win the league once and finished higher than third only a single time—but the club still led the league in attendance in 16 of the 19 seasons. And in the other three, they finished second.

Ferguson was clearly a special leader and a visionary thinker—and he had the resources to properly execute his ideas. From the founding of the Premier League through his retirement in 2013, Ferguson's teams won 13 of a possible 21 league titles. And yet, for the majority of his tenure at Manchester United, he was working for the richest club in the country and managing the highest-paid collection of players in the league. When those are your circumstances, you're supposed to win more often than not. But boy has that "supposed to" been doing a lot of work over the past decade at Old Trafford. Since Ferguson retired, Manchester United hasn't won another title, unless you want to count the ones the accountants at Deloitte are handing out. Their average Money League ranking among English clubs since Sir Alex stepped down: 1.0. Their average finishing position in the league: 4.38. The wages-and-results chain has been broken by at least one team over the past decade. United just pulled the link in the wrong direction.

* * *

In 2005, Manchester United got its own billionaire owners. American real estate magnate Malcolm Glazer and his family agreed to pay $1.8 billion for a 98 percent share of the club. The Glazers acquired United through a leveraged buyout, meaning they borrowed money and then transferred the debt from the purchase directly onto the club. You can probably imagine how this image—Americans coming in and injecting their beloved club with debt—went over in Manchester. When Malcolm sent his sons Joel and Avram over to first attend a match in person, they arrived to a lovely chorus of United fans, chanting in unison: "Die, Glazers, Die." Advertisers were spooked, too. The team's shirt sponsor, multi-billion-dollar telecom corporation Vodafone, broke off its four-year, £36 million deal just two years in because they were suddenly scared of being associated with the biggest brand in soccer.

It really seemed like the takeover would end in disaster, especially as United were enduring their longest title drought in the Premier League era: three years. In 2003–04, Arsenal's famed Invincibles won the title without ever losing a match, and then in the following two seasons, José Mourinho's Chelsea, financed by the unlimited funds of billionaire Russian oligarch and then-owner of the world's largest yacht Roman Abramovich, took home the trophy. On top of that, Liverpool had just won the Champions League in 2005. Could a debt-ridden United really keep up?

What a silly question, in hindsight. Behind the emergence of a noodle-legged and formerly profligate Portuguese winger who suddenly turned all of his stepovers into goals, United won three straight league titles from 2006 through 2009, plus another Champions League. And then, despite selling Cristiano Ronaldo to Real Madrid in the summer of 2009 for a then-world-record fee of

£80 million, Ferguson's team won two of the next four Premier League titles before his retirement in 2013.

The real reason that United haven't won—or even come close to winning—the Premier League since Ferguson left isn't that they've hired the wrong coaches or signed the wrong players. No, it's that they replaced Sir Alex with a banker.

When the Glazers were attempting their takeover of the club, most banks shied away for the same reason Vodafone did. But JP Morgan decided to help push the deal through. The Glazers' point person on the purchase was a young banker named Ed Woodward. Woodward had no real connection to soccer; he was more of a swimmer, according to his friends; he attended a bougie private school in Essex and got a degree in physics from the University of Bristol before joining PricewaterhouseCoopers right out of school and then eventually jumping to JP Morgan. The Glazers and Woodward struck up a relationship—funny how helping someone execute a takeover of arguably the world's most popular sports team can do that—and the owners poached Woodward from JP Morgan after completing the takeover.

In 2007, Woodward was appointed head of United's commercial operations. United's menu of sponsors has grown to an absurd degree, totaling something in the realm of 80-plus global and regional deals. Not only does the team now have an official "Lubricant Partner and Fuel Retail Partner" and an official "Global Mattress and Pillow Partner"; United also has an "Official Indoor Entertainment Centre Partner for the People's Republic of China" and an "Official Soft Drinks Partner for Nigeria." The parceling out of United's image in micro-deals across the globe has been a massive success; even with the team's proportionally pathetic performance on the field, they still lead the league in commercial revenue every season.

After nailing his first remit, Woodward was then promoted to chief executive in 2013, right as Sir Alex retired. This was a weird time in soccer. Ferguson, along with Arsène Wenger, was one of the sport's last true "managers." The essence of the idea was formed by Matt Busby. This man wasn't just the coach; he was the face of the club, and he had his hand in everything from scouting to youth development. Ferguson *was* United, but most other clubs had already begun to structure their teams to at least vaguely resemble the American-sports structure, where a general manager sat on top of or at least next to the coach.

The term varied from club to club, but the commonly accepted descriptor of the newish role was "director of football." Like their American GM counterparts, the DoF was supposed to focus on acquiring players, implementing a certain playing-style philosophy across the club, and making long-term decisions about player contracts and the makeup of the team. This, in theory, would then allow the manager to focus on one thing: maximizing the performance of the players at his disposal. In theory, it would also allow the team to function at a high level even if a manager departed.

In 2013, Woodward essentially took over the GM duties from Sir Alex, and to call it a "failure" would be generous. Finishing lower than fourth place on average with the league's highest revenues and typically its highest wages is a violation of Stefan Szymanski's golden rule. To toss away that financial advantage, you almost have to actively be harming your team, relative to what an average decision-maker would do. Woodward could have hired someone to oversee the team's football operations while he stuck to the deal-making he was actually good at, but he clearly enjoyed interacting with soccer stars. In 2015, he talked of other teams getting "shivers down their spine" after seeing a player he signed, Germany and Bayern Munich legend Bastian Schweinsteiger, in a United uniform.

Of course, Schweinsteiger was already 30 when Woodward signed him—past his prime in soccer years—and he started only 13 Premier League games for the club before joining the Chicago Fire of MLS a year and a half later. Under Woodward's wayward guidance United spent a ton of money. Before the summer of 2021, the three most expensive signings in Premier League history—midfielder Paul Pogba, defender Harry Maguire, and striker Romelu Lukaku—were all Woodward-era signings. David Moyes, the man Ferguson selected to replace himself and who was fired before the end of his first season with the club, said of Woodward: "I don't know if this man is a genius or a clown." The coach who succeeded Moyes, Champions League winner Louis van Gaal, called Woodward "an evil genius." In 2018, United fans hired a plane to fly a banner above the Burnley stadium before a match. It read: "Ed Woodward: A Specialist in Failure."

In 2021, due to blowback from supporters over United's efforts to join the failed Super League, the club announced that Woodward would be stepping down from his role as chief executive. Bizarrely, Woodward claimed to be "proud of the regeneration of the club's culture and our return to the Manchester

United way of playing." A reminder: United won five Premier League titles and a Champions League in the seven years before Woodward's ascension to the top of the club's hierarchy; none of those things have happened since.

So, why were United so bad under Woodward? Just how could a club squander such a financial advantage? Back in 2018, a concerned investor asked Woodward about the team's poor play. After finishing in a surprising second place the year prior, they'd dropped down to a mid-table place more than a third of the way through the season. Woodward responded by saying the quiet part out loud: "Playing performance doesn't really have a meaningful impact on what we do on the commercial side."

* * *

One of the unintended consequences of the Moneyball revolution in baseball is that it totally revamped the demographics of the front office. Billy Beane's origin story is that he was a first-round pick out of high school—your classic "looks great but hasn't produced much" prospect. Despite a smooth swing and lithe, lanky body, Beane played only 148 games in the majors over a six-year career. His desire to find a new way to build a baseball team was driven by Oakland's financial constraints but also by his own experience: Billy Beane wanted to beat all of the idiots who thought it was a good idea to draft Billy Beane.

The people who followed in Beane's footsteps, though, weren't fellow former elite prospects. They did not, as Beane put it in *Moneyball*, look good in jeans. No, the people Beane inspired were more akin to his deputy in Oakland: Paul De Podesta, the nebbish Yale grad portrayed by Jonah Hill in the film. According to an ESPN study conducted in 2020, the number of Ivy League grads in general-manager roles in MLB increased from 3 percent in 2001 to 43 percent in 2020. Concurrently, the number of former pros in GM roles has decreased from 37 percent to 20 percent. This isn't to say that the development is necessarily good or bad, but rather that one in-club has been replaced by another.

Chris Anderson sort of fit into both clubs—and maybe that was the problem. After a career as a semiprofessional goalkeeper in Germany, he became a professor of political science at Cornell University. Anderson read *Moneyball* and then wondered if some similar principles could be applied to soccer. He started blogging about the numerical side of the sport, cowrote a book about it

(*The Numbers Game*) with the economist David Sally, and eventually became the managing director at Coventry County, who were in England's third division (confusingly named "League One") at the time. He set out to revolutionize English soccer through data and sound decision-making—only to step away from the job after just 11 months.

European soccer, and English soccer in particular, is still very much controlled by the first in-club. "English football's full of guys, coaches, agents, hangers-on who are still in the game and who have survived," he said. "And the reason they survive is because they can convince the next owner. And so what kind of skills do they have? They have the skill of getting themselves another job."

One of Anderson's employees at Derby was a former Premier League player with 500-something professional appearances to his name. "He didn't own a computer," Anderson said. "Part of my personal-development plan for him was to get a computer, learn how to open a Word document and an Excel sheet."

Most clubs with a director of football are still being run by former players. And most English soccer players stop getting an education in their mid-teens in order to focus on getting their first professional contract. Almost no pros in England attend college, and most of them don't even get the equivalent of an American high-school diploma. Soccer is their job and their education, and they inherit the way things are done from the previous generation. So, when most professional players are experiencing the world in the same way and learning to think within the same environment, there just aren't many cultural factors driving the soccer-playing population, which then becomes the soccer-coaching and soccer-team-building population, to do things differently from the way they've always been done.

Of course, the opposite end of the spectrum is clearly just as bad, if not worse. Ed Woodward had a college diploma, it was his job to understand numbers, and we can probably assume that he owned a computer; he just seemingly had no interest in figuring out what actually wins soccer games. Almost every Premier League team now does have at least one person with the word "analytics" in their title, but most of the people I've spoken to who work for clubs or once occupied one of these roles say that the majority have very little impact on the team's decision-making. Teams hire them because it would look bad if they didn't.

"How ridiculous is that?" Bornn said. "You're spending hundreds of thousands of dollars between data and analysis. And then to just totally ignore all that when you're making decisions. Doesn't that just seem absurd? Look, let's frame this a different way. Let's say the team went out and hired a nutritionist who created lots of diet plans: Here's what we're going to eat pregame, postgame, recovery, etc. And then when it actually came time to order the food, you just bought McDonald's. *But what about the nutritionist's plan?* Yeah, we usually eat McDonald's and pizza. Let's do that."

And thus: The wages-and-results chain rarely gets broken.

"It's changing now, because the age profile of coaches is a lot younger, but 10 years ago, most of these guys were footballers who probably didn't go to school from the age of 14," Paul Power said. "So they haven't had math and science education. With a laptop, it's just not what they're used to. I think there's an element of fear of numbers and fear of the unknown."

Structural factors play a role, too.

"I think relegation is probably the extreme case of people being really risk averse, and making the potentially problematic decisions," Bornn said. "Being relegated out of the Premier League is such an extreme financial penalty that teams do crazy things sometimes."

Relegation poses the ultimate, most expensive version of the NFL's fourth-down problem, where the right decision is the one that looks the worst if it goes wrong. Given the massive financial disparity between being the 17th-best team in the Premier League and the 18th-best, clubs that see themselves in danger of being relegated tend to opt for the same option that everyone else has gone for in the past: They hire Sam Allardyce. In each of his four Premier League jobs—Sunderland, Crystal Palace, Everton, and West Bromwich Albion—Allardyce was hired midseason to help keep a struggling team from falling out of the Premier League. Though it worked the first three times, not even the presence of Big Sam was enough to save West Brom.

Why do they keep doing it? Take the 2020–21 version of Brighton & Hove Albion. According to the best expected-goals models, the Seagulls were one of the five or six best teams in the Premier League. Yet, some freakish bad luck saw them finish the year in 16th, just two spots clear of relegation. Due to its low-scoring nature, a sound process is less likely to be rewarded in soccer than it is in any other sport. A forward-thinking owner could buy a team, revamp the front office, hire an analytics superstar to make the decisions, and fill the management staff with all kinds of people with different backgrounds and perspectives and ways of thinking.

They could mine the xG market for undervalued players and identify the right kind of risk-forward manager. It could all come together, the team could create great chances, prevent them on the other end . . . and still get relegated because a bunch of opposition keepers played well, some penalty calls went against them, and their strikers didn't kick the ball as accurately as they normally do.

Amid a sports culture that's skeptical of laptops, let alone any kind of outside thinking, this theoretical team would be the laughingstock of the league. *Numbers can't measure heart!* It would be seen as proof that the traditional way was the right way. *There's a reason we don't do things like that, you know.* And so, rather than risk facing the fallout, rather than trying to implement a new institutional structure that might work and still fail, it's way easier for teams to opt for the traditional model and convince themselves that they'll just be slightly better at it than their opponents. After all, there's really only one thing worse than being relegated: being relegated without hiring Sam Allardyce.

* * *

Stefan Szymanski doesn't just disagree with my ideas of how slow soccer clubs are to innovate. No, he also called for some personal introspection: Why are you, an American, looking at soccer as a puzzle that needs to be solved? Might these games exist for reasons beyond optimizing efficiency on the pitch?

"I think it's a very interesting subject for an American to write about because I think there is a fundamental difference between the American concept of team sports and team sports as conceived in the rest of the world," he said. "What strikes me as a foreigner about American sports is how all American sports are built around the concept of 'the play.' And the play is a plan. We will have a plan of how we will do it and we will have a general in charge who will decide what the plan is for the players. So the coach is the general and the players on the field are the foot soldiers who are there to carry out orders of the general."

I don't quite agree with the metaphor, but he's circling around the point I agree with. Though coaches in soccer have been deified forever, it's still really hard to imagine a front-office executive in the soccer world becoming as beloved and famous as someone like Billy Beane. Even the NBA's version of Beane, Philadelphia 76ers general manager Daryl Morey, has achieved a level of notoriety unimaginable to soccer execs. My old boss Bill Simmons affectionately refers to him as "Dork Elvis." He has hundreds of thousands of Twitter followers. There are now kids who go to college dreaming not of becoming the next LeBron James or Steve Kerr; no, they want to be the next Dork Elvis. It even extends to fans, too. In my old job as a sports editor, readers always seemed way more interested in stories about how teams were built than in stories about how they played. Traffic was the highest during the off-season: when there were no games and the GMs were the protagonists of the story. Frankly, it's a lot easier for certain NBA fans to relate to a white guy in a suit than to someone like Kevin Durant. Hell, the premise of this book is playing into that desire, too.

"If the team wins, it's the general's genius," Szymanski said. "That is obviously true in football. It strikes me that basketball is a sport which in principle could be played in a number of different ways, and you could leave the players to make the decisions for themselves on the court and yet still, even in basketball it's a very highly coached, play-based game. And one thing you've seen in America lately is when the sport is not particularly well suited to the play, the rules have been changed to make it more suitable to the play. Old *jogo bonito* is not like that at all. Look at the coach screaming and waving his arms on the side of the pitch. He's a pathetic figure. We laugh at the coach. The idea that the coach is creating the plays that make the game happen? It's laughable. Everything happens in soccer on the field. And part of it is no one's ever tried to redesign soccer to make it more amenable to the concept of the play." While set pieces—moments when the game stops and the players can execute a combination of pre-planned movements—present this possibility, we'll later see how most teams have been hesitant to make them a bigger part of their practice.

However, there's no better example of the philosophical differences between soccer and America's major sports than the championship ceremonies on both sides of the Atlantic Ocean. Who's the first one to lift the Lombardi Trophy when a team wins the Super Bowl? It's whatever billionaire owns the majority stake in the franchise. But when a soccer team wins a title, the owner is nowhere to be seen and even the coach is somewhere off to the side. The team captain is the first one to lift the prize.

Boston Red Sox owner John Henry has accepted the World Series trophy four different times. He also owns Liverpool but was nowhere to be seen when the club won the Premier League in 2020. "Could you imagine handing the European Cup to John Henry on the field? You'd have riots on the streets of Liverpool," Szymanski said. "He'd never be able to show his face again."

All of these sports were sort of randomly designed, developing haphazardly from some initial crude version of the game that barely had any rules and was usually way more violent than whatever we see today. Most of the tweaks made along the way were arbitrary—these are manufactured games; there's no essential truth at the heart of American football that every rule change is bringing us closer to realizing—but every tweak *was* made within the sociocultural environment of the time. Much like how William Hulbert's decision to create a closed league fit within the turbo-charged free-market competition of late-1800s American and William McGregor's open Football League jibed with the complacency of the late-stage British Empire, the way these sports have been fine-tuned still contain some echoes of the values of the societies they exist within. "The interesting point is we designed soccer specifically to exclude the coaches [and managers] from a really participatory role," Szymanski said.

What if soccer, quite simply, was just never meant to be solved?

CHAPTER FIVE

A PASSING FAD

Over the past 30 years, there's been a great re-unleveling. The Premier League quickly became the richest league in the world, and although Germany, Spain, Italy, and France lag behind, they're still way ahead of everyone else. The central nervous system of the soccer world now sits somewhere in Western Europe. At the four most recent World Cups, only one of the 12 top-three finishers came from another continent.

In the 1980s, no one would've believed this outcome. Soccer was exploding, across the world. At the end of the previous decade, the great Pelé had predicted that an African team would win a World Cup before the turn of the century. A few years later, Algeria was beating Germany, and a few years after that, Morocco was reaching the quarterfinals. Three decades ago, you could spin a globe, stop it with your finger, and land on some city where someone was probably playing soccer successfully. Diego Maradona was dribbling through England's entire team, scoring goals with his hands, winning World Cups with Argentina, and winning league titles for un-fancied Napoli from the south of Italy. The Champions League was as wide open as ever: Teams from England, Germany, Italy, Romania, Portugal, and the Netherlands claimed trophies. The likes of France and the Netherlands won their first-ever international tournaments, at the European Championship, and they both beat teams that had never won before—Spain and the Soviet Union, respectively—in the finals. Mexico hosted the 1986 World Cup and took the Germans to penalties in the quarterfinals. Honduras, New Zealand, Cameroon, and Kuwait all appeared in their first World Cups, too. But according to Richard Pollard, the most sophisticated analysis in the soccer world was happening in Fiji.

A trained mathematician and statistician, Pollard grew up in England and got his education at McGill University in Montreal, Canada. He married an American woman who eventually and understandably got sick of all the rain in London. So, they packed their bags for Melanesia, where the average monthly temperature never drops below 72 degrees Fahrenheit and never gets above 81. It's the image that pops into your head when you hear the word "paradise." While in Fiji, Pollard started writing for the national newspaper the *Fiji Sun*. The editor at the time loved stirring up controversy, so he would give Pollard at least a full page in the *Sun*, and sometimes more, to rip professional soccer in Fiji to shreds. He gave Pollard the room and didn't particularly care what he was writing—as long as it was critical. While pretty much no other newspaper in the world at the time would've been receptive to this style of analysis, Pollard knew math, and he used numbers to tell all the coaches in Fiji that they were doing everything wrong. "Fiji was probably better informed about performance analysis than anywhere else in the world," Pollard said.

For part of Pollard's time in Fiji during the 1980's, the national team coach was a bighearted German named Rudi Gutendorf. They called him "Restless Rudi." His first job was managing Blue Stars Zürich in the Swiss league in 1955. His last job was with the Samoa national team in 2003—not *American* Samoa. No, the *smaller* Samoa. In between, he managed 53 other professional teams. The German government and Football Association funded him as a sort of football diplomat, spreading both the sport and a vague sense of Germany as a benevolent force to the developing world. Gutendorf managed the Chilean national team while the socialist Salvador Allende was president, but then he had to quit the job and quickly flee the country after the military dictator Augusto Pinochet staged a coup. He was named manager of the Rwandan national team in the late 1990s and had to find a way to balance a squad of Hutus and Tutsis in the aftermath of a brutal genocide just years before. He lost his job as manager of Iran because the ayatollah thought only a practicing Muslim should be coaching the team.

No one coached more national teams than Gutendorf's 18, and no one coached more teams, period, than his 55. He's in the *Guinness Book of World Records* for it.

"He was very well informed," Pollard said. "He knew what he was doing, but I didn't like his style of play at all."

Though no one has literally seen it all, Gutendorf came pretty close. And despite coaching through coups and post-genocides, something about this Pollard guy just annoyed the hell out of him. Gutendorf came to countries to help modernize their national teams; the soccer people were usually thankful for his presence. Typically, it was the authoritarians he had to worry about. But now there was this British journalist, with bushy hair and an even bushier beard, using statistics in a Fijian newspaper to call into question everything he'd ever taught his players. He got so annoyed that one day, after reading Pollard's latest column, he called the *Sun* from the team's locker room to complain about the coverage.

"In those days, people had opinions which were not based on fact," Pollard said. "They were all subjective opinions about the best way to play soccer. It was always short passing out of defense. Occasionally there were teams like Real Madrid and Brazil, who were basically very skillful at short passing, and the idea was that if you tried to emulate them, you'd be more likely to be successful than if you tried to emulate somebody that just booted the ball up the field. It became a very popular concept, even in England, that short passing was the right way to go."

To Pollard's mind, Gutendorf's team was passing too much, screwing around with the ball in the areas of the field where the only real danger was the danger you brought onto yourself. You couldn't score from your own defensive third, but your opponents could, so why take the risk of turning the ball over in that area? Get it away from your goal and move it toward theirs as quickly as you can. Unlike other right-way-to-play philosophies, however, Pollard's theories were not based on a career of subjective assumptions. He didn't come to his understanding of how goals are scored in the way, as Luke Bornn described, most coaches do: by grasping for a unifying explanation for what was a collection of mostly random events.

No, Pollard had done the math, and his math showed him a couple of things. First, that the team that reaches the final third with the ball more often tends to be the team that wins the game. He called this collective action "reaches." And second: "On average, one goal comes from every 10 shots." These two ideas worked in concert to create a framework for how the game was meant to be played: You tried to move the ball into the opposition third as quickly and as often as you could so you could then shoot the ball as quickly and as often as you could.

The Fijian national team was terrible. Still is terrible, mind you. Sure, they beat the crap out of the likes of Vanuatu and the Solomon Islands, but they've won only six of their 33 matches against Tahiti. A couple years before Gutendorf took over, they lost a game to New Zealand's rugby rejects, 13–0. Richard vs. Rudi was about as low-stakes as it gets, but right around the same time, on the opposite side of the globe, a similar battle was being waged in the birthplace of the Beautiful Game. Math and tradition were at war, and to many, it felt like a fight for the soul of the sport.

* * *

For the English, war and soccer have been inextricably linked—almost always to detrimental effect. The writer Simon Kuper has referred to the English national team's primary strategy of "defending in their own penalty area and hoofing balls clear" as part of an urge to reenact the battle of Dunkirk. In his sociological history of English soccer, *Those Feet*, David Winner writes, "Footballers in other countries don't talk in this instinctively military manner. But then they haven't traditionally taken the same pleasure from fighting as the British." During World War I, British and German soldiers famously put down their weapons, threw up some makeshift goalposts, and played a game of soccer against each other on Christmas Day. There are also stories of officers encouraging their troops to advance on the enemy by throwing a soccer ball in the direction they wanted them to go. "War was a game," Winner writes, "and football was a metaphor for war." While the connection between the two was not quite as explicit during World War II, the strategy of the English national team would eventually come to mirror the strategies of the Royal Air Force.

Thorold Charles Reep was born in Cornwall, England, on September 22, 1904. He loved math, and he loved soccer—among very few other things. As a child, he was a regular at Home Park, the home ground of his local club, Plymouth Argyle. Reep earned a scholarship to Plymouth High School at the age of 10 but dropped out nine years later to take a job as an accounts clerk. In 1928, he became a certified accountant and won a competition for a place in the Royal Air Force's nascent Accounting Division.

One of the reasons Reep joined the RAF was the soccer-related opportunities it provided. His first post with the air force was just outside of London. He played as a right midfielder for his station's soccer team and served as one of the club's organizers. One evening in 1933, Charles Jones, the captain of nearby Arsenal, visited the camp to give a lecture. Under their legendary manager Herbert Chapman, the Gunners dominated the English first division in the early 1930s, winning three of the decade's first four titles. As Jones outlined to Reep and his station-mates, Chapman's teams were so successful because they would coax their opponents out of their own half by defending deep in their own defensive third—only to then rapidly shift the ball up field to their wingers as soon as they won possession. Sure, we'd just call that "counterattacking" today, but at the time, no one was thinking about the game in terms of creating space and maximizing efficiency.

After an initial three-hour lecture, Jones would later return and give another similar talk of similar length. Over those six combined hours, Reep became rapt. Anti-intellectualism had long been a defining feature of English soccer. "It was a game imbued with martial values played with heavy leather balls in thick, ankle-high boots in seas of mud," Winner writes. "Creative players, where they existed, tended to come from Scotland." Thinking too deeply about the game was a sign of weakness; *just get out there and run around a bit, lads.* Reep had never seen anyone break soccer down into something resembling a science, or at least a complex system of component parts. Jones's presentations convinced Reep that the sport he loved was something like an equation, and that he would be the one to solve it.

Despite initial misgivings from Prime Minister Winston Churchill, the Royal Air Force engaged in what were known as "area" bombings during World War II. Rather than focusing on a specific German military target, they began to "aim" their raids at the centers of various industrial towns in an effort to, as John Dower writes in *War Without Mercy*, "destroy civilian morale." No longer were bombing expeditions done with precision; the goal was widespread destruction. "You are accordingly authorized to employ your forces without restriction," read a directive issued by the RAF on February 5, 1942. Drop enough bombs in the same general location, and you'll eventually hit the target.

As World War II roared on, Reep bounced between various stations throughout England and even spent some time in Germany toward the end of the global conflict. He eventually returned home, only to find a sport still yearning to be figured out. And on March 19, 1950, he finally did something about it. Well, maybe. He definitely did *something* about it at *some* point in March. Reep claimed that he watched Swindon Town play a match on March 19 at their home stadium, the County Ground, but the club never actually played a game on that date. As Jonathan Wilson points out in *Inverting the Pyramid*, it's likely that Reep attended the match on March 18, a 1–0 victory for Swindon over Bristol Rovers.

Whenever this match he attended actually took place, the first half drove Reep mad. He was fed up with the inefficiencies he thought he saw from both teams. So, rather than breaking down the door of the home locker room and trying to talk some sense into the manager, Reep decided to record everything that happened in the second half from the stands. The County Ground did not have floodlights, so Reep put on a miner's helmet, turned on the headlamp, and scribbled various symbols, words, and squiggly lines in his notebook. He was the proto-Opta coder; the first person on record to see the collection of movements and actions across the 90 minutes of a soccer match as a sea of datapoints waiting to be quantified.

Reep and his headlamp would go on to analyze thousands of matches. He developed an intricate form of shorthand that enabled him to record every action across a 90-minute match. According to his analysis, only two out of every nine goals came from possession sequences that involved more than three passes. To Reep, this meant that a team's tactics should be designed with the sole purpose of getting the ball up to the opposition penalty box as quickly as possible in order to maximize possessions of three or fewer passes. It was area bombing made miniature. As his dataset grew, Reep soon became a fundamentalist—a long-ball true believer amid a sea of short-passing heretics. "Passing has become such a fetish that when watching 'modern' play one sometimes has the impression that goal-scoring has become the secondary objective," Reep wrote, "with 'stroking the ball about' in cross-field moves, taking first place."

He became obsessed with the three-pass rule: "Not more than three passes," Reep told the BBC in 1993. "If a team tries to play football and keeps it down to not more than three passes, it will have a much higher chance of winning matches. Passing for the sake of passing can be disastrous."

So, too, could confusing correlation with causation, which is exactly what Reep did. Since he had observed that 77.8 percent of goals scored came from three passes or fewer, Reep concluded that it was desirable to avoid passing the ball more than three times. Through his exhaustive and one-of-a-kind data collection, Reep found that 91.5 percent of all possessions consist of three or fewer passes. Here's a simple chart:

Number of Passes	Percentage of All Possessions	Percentage of Goals Scored	Differential
Three or fewer	91.5	77.8	minus-13.7
Four or more	8.5	22.2	plus-13.7

The man in the miner's helmet had discovered something; he'd just misunderstood what it was. Sure, more goals were scored from abbreviated passing moves, but you were more likely to score from possessions that contained four or more passes. Without realizing it, Reep was insisting that teams double-down on the kinds of inefficiencies that had led him to undertake his analysis in the first place.

"It is, frankly, horrifying that a philosophy founded on such a basic misinterpretation of figures could be allowed to become a cornerstone of English coaching," Wilson wrote in *Inverting the Pyramid*. And yet, that's exactly what happened.

* * *

In the 1960s, Reep wrote a series of articles for the magazine *World Sport* called "Soccer Under the Microscope." A sample headline: "Are We Getting Too Clever?" And a sub-headline: "CHARLES REEP, whose complicated match records can trace every move—good or bad—for more than 500 games, continues his 'Soccer under the microscope' series by looking at England's performances during the last two seasons." But the ideas and theories weren't what Richard Pollard found intriguing about Reep's work. No, he was drawn to this part of display copy: "complicated match records can trace every move—good or bad—for more than 500 games."

"I was very interested in the idea that somebody could analyze a soccer game by first recording the data," Pollard said. "And then—he had this shorthand system—sitting down and analyzing it." It's really impossible to overstate just how different Reep's process of analysis was at the time. "In the 1960s, I don't think we even recorded shots," Pollard said. "There's goals and attendance and that was it."

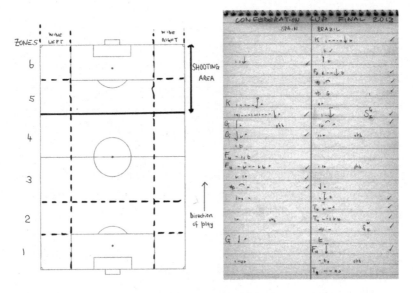

When Pollard first came across Reep's work, he'd recently turned 18 and was about to head off to McGill. He and his buddy John Goodbody, who would go on to work as a sports reporter for the *Times* of London for 20-plus years, wanted to know who this strange man was. Why was he trying to quantify this game? And could it actually work? Goodbody sent Reep a letter to tell him that he and Pollard were intrigued by the writing he was doing for *World Sport*. Reep responded, almost immediately, inviting the two of them to come visit his house in Suffolk, some 60 miles north of London. Pollard had just recently passed his driver's test, so he and Goodbody made the trip to meet the man who wore the miner's hat.

"He spent about four or five hours with us, telling us what he was doing," Pollard said. "He gave us a huge afternoon tea, which his wife prepared. We had a very nice time. He was extremely nice to us. We went up two further times to visit him, then I'd departed for McGill. And so I started corresponding with him. And over the years, I must have hundreds of letters that I've still saved in my garage. We remained great friends until he died in 2002, although I very seldom saw him, it was mostly over the telephone and with correspondence."

According to Pollard, the first formal work Reep did with a professional club came in the 1950s with Stan Cullis's Wolverhampton Wanderers. He provided analysis to Cullis for a couple of years—for free—as Wolves consistently finished at or near the top of the English league table. Reep's first *paid* job came with Sheffield Wednesday at the end of the '50s, but there was little to no fanfare about an accountant encroaching upon England's national game—in part, because no one knew it was happening. "Reep liked to stay in the background," Pollard said. "He didn't like the football world knowing that he was there. He wanted to work absolutely as anonymously as possible."

In the 1960s, it wouldn't have been too easy for Reep to stand out anyway. In 1966 came the country's greatest sporting triumph, as they won their first and only World Cup with a 4–2 win over West Germany at Wembley Stadium in London. Then, two years later, Manchester United, led by the dazzling, debaucherous, shaggy-haired, could've-been-the-fifth-Beatle winger George Best, became the first-ever English club to win the European Cup. A British club had never even made the final, let alone won the whole thing. But a victory for Scottish club Celtic the year prior meant that Great Britain had finally regained its power atop the game it invented. And the next 15 years might've been even better—at least for the club teams. From 1977 through 1982, English clubs won an absurd six-straight European Cups: three for Liverpool, two for Nottingham Forest, and one for Aston Villa. Liverpool won again in 1984, to make it seven from eight.

Despite the unmatched success of all its club teams, the English national team wasn't able to build on its World Cup win. In hindsight, that victory now looks a bit like an aberration: the result of superior fitness and the fact that they hosted the tournament before the advent of affordable, readily available global air travel. Playing at home proved to be a massive advantage. The Three Lions didn't qualify for either the 1974 or the 1978 World Cup. And while they were there while Germany and Austria were making a disgrace of themselves in Gijón in 1982, they failed to advance beyond the group stages. After that summer's capitulation, Watford manager Graham Taylor publicly berated the team's stoic playing style. "Possession and patience are myths," he said. "Goals come from mistakes."

* * *

After graduating from McGill, Pollard moved back to London. He got married and had a bunch of kids, so the family bought a house up in Watford, a pleasant commuter town about 15 miles north of London. There was a soccer team, but it wasn't much, having never reached England's first division. In fact, they'd spent only three total seasons in the *second* division. Watford were just filler for the football pyramid—a nice way to spend a Saturday or a Sunday for a few fans, a launching pad for talented young players and coaches who were destined for bigger and better things, or a permanent home for players who were too good to be full-time amateurs, but not good enough to be competing against the likes of Liverpool. The club shared its stadium, Vicarage Road, with a greyhound-racing track.

Pollard would go to Watford FC games here and there, but unless you were from the area or you accidentally got the dog-racing times mixed up, you didn't have much of a reason to keep coming back. Pollard, though, eventually found one. One day, he noticed that the soccer he was seeing had started to change. The sideways passing that, in his mind, plagued the various levels of English soccer had been replaced by a frantic, vertical, aerial style. Watford were suddenly moving the ball up field as quickly as possible, thumping passes toward the opposition goal as soon as they could. They were unconcerned with keeping possession and instead focused on forcing the ball into the other team's defensive third. It was beautiful. It was Reep.

Now, if there was one particularly notable thing about the first 90 or so years of Watford FC, it was that the club had somehow managed to rope Elton John in as a supporter. The Rocket Man grew up near Watford, went to games as a kid, and became a lifelong fan of the club. By the mid-'70s, he'd also become one of the most famous people on the planet, and so he decided to do what every sports fan with comical levels of disposable income wants to do: buy his favorite team. He became the Watford chairman in 1976 and his mission was to turn the Hornets from a brick at the bottom of the English soccer pyramid to the capstone at the top. In 1977, he hired 32-year-old Graham Taylor to manage the club. It was just Taylor's second professional gig, and although Watford were stuck in the fourth division at the time, Sir Elton told his new manager that he expected to eventually see the team competing for European silverware. (Soon after Taylor arrived, they removed the greyhound track. The last dog to win a race at Vicarage Road was named "Chad Supreme.")

As Pollard watched Watford thump the ball forward and chase after it, he realized that Taylor had come to the same conclusions as Reep: They both believed that the right way to play was to force the ball toward the opposition goal, over and over and over again. This man needed to meet Charles Reep. Taylor's approach could be fine-tuned with Reep's data, and Taylor was a kindred spirit who would put Reep's evidence-based philosophies into full use.

Pollard told Reep he needed to get in touch with Taylor, that *this* was the way he could truly put his ideas into practice. The correspondence began with Pollard himself attending matches, writing up his own form of Reepian statistical analyses, and then sending copies to both Taylor and Reep. After enough time, Taylor became convinced that math would help him win matches.

"He must have worked out by himself without any recordings that this was the correct way to play," Pollard said. "He saw Reep as validating everything that he believed. And then Reep convinced him that by recording games and looking at the numbers from the games, he could improve what he was doing, and he did for several seasons. But Taylor certainly wasn't doing any recording when we started with him."

Taylor hired Reep and wanted to hire Pollard, too, but as much fun as sorting through data during a dreary English winter might be, Fiji still sounded a lot better. Although he moved 10,000 miles away, he continued to trade letters back and forth with Reep. As he trashed the Fijian national team in the local paper, the same methods he advocated for began to propel Watford up the ladder. They were promoted to the third division in 1978, and to the second division in 1979, and finally reached the first division in 1982. And then, in their first-ever season in the top flight, they somehow finished in second place, one spot above Manchester United and one below Liverpool. But the following season there were warning signs that this style of play might not truly be the right way. By finishing second, Watford achieved Sir Elton's goal of qualifying for Europe; they made the UEFA Cup, a tournament that at the time included all of the best teams in Europe who *didn't* win their domestic leagues. After cruising past German club Kaiserslautern in the first round and taking down Bulgarian side Levski Sofia in extra time in the second, they were clobbered by Sparta Prague. The problem, as Taylor noted postgame, was that Czechs could pass and Watford didn't want to: "It was men against boys. When you gave the ball away, they didn't give it back to you."

However, Reep and Taylor's domestic success led to a meeting at Taylor's house with Charles Hughes, who would soon become the English Football

Association's director of coaching and development. From his perch, Hughes got to decide how every promising young British soccer player would be molded—what kind of game they would learn how to play. "The strategy of direct play is far preferable to that of possession based football," Hughes wrote in *The Winning Formula*, the FA's unofficial coaching textbook. "The facts are irrefutable and the evidence overwhelming."

According to Pollard, Reep would write to the FA every couple of years to reveal his latest findings and offer his services to the national team. "They hated him," Pollard said. "The only person in the FA that thought Reep was of any use at all was Hughes. And he stole a lot of Reep's ideas without giving him credit."

Hughes claimed that he came to his ideas independently of Reep, while Taylor claims to have influenced Hughes during one of his first jobs, a brief stint as manager of the England under-18 national team. That initial meeting seemed to hold so much potential for the trio; Reep described it in a "very enthusiastic" 10-page letter to Pollard. But instead, those few hours ended up being the peak of their collective promise, and Taylor eventually became the face of a nation's collective failure.

On the back of his success at Watford, Taylor was appointed manager of the English national team in 1990. The team lost only once in his first 23 games in charge. But after that hot start, England struggled to qualify for the 1992 European Championships, needing a late goal against Poland from striker Gary Lineker to secure a spot in the competition. Then, once there, they drew their opening two group-stage matches, 0–0. Needing a win in the final match against Sweden, they succumbed 2–1 and went home early. The day after the match, British tabloid the *Sun* ran the headline "Swedes 2 Turnips 1" with a picture of Taylor's face photoshopped onto a vegetable.

But at least they'd qualified. Taylor's side then missed out completely on the 1994 World Cup. In UEFA, the top two teams advanced from each qualifying group. The Netherlands, at the tail end of a golden generation of some of the best players in the world, unsurprisingly took the top slot in England's group. And then, there was—incredibly, coincidentally, hysterically, impossibly—Norway.

"I'd met [Norway manager] Egil Olsen at a conference and I suddenly realized that Norway were playing, not exactly Reep's style, but extremely directly in the 1990s," Pollard said. "And I wrote to him and said, 'Would you like me to take you down and see Charles Reep?'" After leaving Fiji in 1987, Pollard was between teaching jobs in Bulgaria and Malawi and was spending the intervening months near his parents, who lived in Cambridge. "And he said, 'yes,' and he got the next plane from Oslo to London Airport, Heathrow, and I met him at Heathrow and drove him straight down to Reep's house. He spent a couple of days there and he and Reep got on like a house on fire. They really enjoyed each other's company, because they were convinced that performance analysis was the way to go in soccer. Although Norway were playing a somewhat different style from Reep's Watford and the other teams, they both believed you should always be going forward and not tapping these square passes around all the time."

Olsen, too, developed his theory on the right way to play by looking at data. The key difference between Olsen and Reep, though, was the former's flexibility. Olsen's core belief was that the location of the ball was more important than who had possession—and how exactly you controlled the field was less important than just simply ensuring that you did it. "There is no definitive answer in football," he said, "but there is probably some kind efficiency threshold." He believed that teams that tended to pass the ball forward more often tended to win. When his side famously upset defending champs Brazil at the 1998 World Cup, he suggested that if the Brazilians had just focused on playing more forward passes, then his team wouldn't have stood a chance.

In their two matches against England in qualifying for the 1994 World Cup, Norway drew 1–1 at Wembley and then won 2–0 in Oslo to all but clinch qualification for their first World Cup since 1938. The Norwegian FA even invited Reep himself to attend the home match. "It was very ironic that having offered his services to the FA for the last 40 years, he was completely ignored," Pollard said. "Then it was Norway that finally took [Reep] seriously and then beat England."

Taylor resigned from his post in 1993, while Hughes made a point to publicly blame the team's failure not on its approach but on the manager's selection of players. The long-ball game—and the use of data, by association—became anathema. "This slam-bang-wallop stuff will be the death of football," said Allen Wade, who preceded Hughes at the FA. "Football in which players are controlled by off-pitch Svengalis, backed up by batteries of statisticians and analysts, will never hold the magical appeal of what Pelé called the beautiful game." The legendary Brian Clough, who won back-to-back European Cups as manager of Nottingham Forest in 1979 and 1980, wasn't a fan, either: "I want to establish without any shadow of a doubt that Charles Hughes is totally wrong in his approach to football. He believes that footballs should come down with icicles on them."

Reep's influence within the game peaked right around then, too. He kept doing research and writing papers, but the man was born in 1904. He was in his 80s by the time he finally got Taylor's ear. He passed away in February of 2002 at the age of 97. And in the years since his death, his legacy has taken a beating. Wilson's *Inverting the Pyramid* was published in 2008, and it pulled no punches when it comes to Reep. In 2012, Barney Ronay wrote a piece for the magazine *When Saturday Comes*, titled "Grim Reep." "He is the national game's deep dark secret," Ronay writes. "We know he's bad for us, but we just can't help ourselves." A number of other books concerning data and soccer—such as *The Numbers Game* and *Soccernomics*—raise Reep's pigheadedness up for a light roasting. And in 2016, the website FiveThirtyEight squared the circle. Not only was Reep despised by the soccer intelligentsia for attempting to boil the game down to a science; now the numbers guys were coming for him, too. The title of the piece, written by Joe Sykes and Neil Paine: "How One Man's Bad Math Helped Ruin Decades of English Soccer."

* * *

That's where I thought the story ended, too. Growing up in the United States in the 1990s, I was bombarded with awful English soccer coaches who taught me their own version of area bombing. At the time, it seemed like anyone with an accent could convince suburban parents to fork over money for an "authentic" lesson in "football." In particular there was an organization called NOGA (short for "No Other Game Around"), which would hold camps and clinics all across Long Island. My main memory from these NOGA sessions was practicing "diving headers," where someone would lob a ball into the box and you'd try to direct it into the goal by, well, diving and then hitting it with your head. It was fun—I vividly remember one of the coaches telling my parents that I scored a "peach of a goal"—and useless. I was 10 or 11 at the time, and I should've been learning how to control the ball with both feet, how to receive a pass under pressure, how to play a pass out of pressure—the kind of bedrock skills that are necessary to access some of the finer aspects of the game. In the 10 years of competitive play after those training sessions, I might've scored a diving header once.

As I learned about Reep when I was older, I was able to connect him to my upbringing. *Of course* these unqualified doofuses were obsessed with crossing and heading the ball. If they were old enough to coach in the late '90s, then they'd grown up in the England of Taylor, Hughes, and Reep. American soccer foolishly tried to chase after the English model despite the proof very clearly not being in the pudding. The kick-and-run style jibed with the way we played our other sports: strong and fast and always at 110 percent. The US national team is only now finally producing the kinds of players who are able to play at a number of different speeds and feel comfortable with the ball at their feet at the highest level. If part of my own soccer journey was waylaid by a soccer structure that didn't seem to value the things I was particularly good at, now I finally had some people to blame.

But then I came across a paper titled, "Invalid Interpretation of Passing Sequence Data to Assess Team Performance in Football: Repairing the Tarnished Legacy of Charles Reep." It was written by Richard Pollard.

Pollard claimed that the findings—popularized in Wilson's book but first published in a paper by researchers Mike Hughes and Ian Franks—regarding the successes of different lengths of passing moves had been misinterpreted. "Successful eight pass moves probably are more likely to produce the goal than a successful one pass move," he said. "But the thing about short pass moves—two pass, three pass, four pass—most of those are going to be from teams that are trying to build up longer passing moves. They can't really be a proxy for direct football."

The paper doesn't disclose the relationship that Reep and Pollard had, which seems like a bit of a tell and certainly a publishing oversight. There is a "Conflict of Interest" section in which Pollard claims no conflict of interest. I wasn't swayed by his argument; at best it suggests we still don't actually know whether short passing is better. But I was intrigued by the fact that anyone was making the argument at all. It seemed like most people who knew about Charles Reep were in agreement about his oversight, and yet here was someone writing the following words: "The way in which the paper by Hughes and Franks has been used by others to discredit Reep, while at the same time claiming definitive proof that direct football is less effective than keeping possession, is a salutary warning as to how easily false information can disseminate itself."

Those words sound dangerously close to the popular phrasings used in some of the more conspiracy-happy corners of the Internet. But then I spoke to Pollard and found a sweet, thoughtful man who was just about to go for his first dose of the COVID-19 vaccine. Pollard is defensive about his old friend, and he's still got strong opinions about the efficacy of their methods and the importance of swift, quick play. But that's not the interesting part.

No, when I first spoke to Pollard, I had this strange experience, where he'd tell me he'd researched something 25 or 30 years ago, and it would immediately remind me of something that exists today. He's 78 years old and first told me that he barely watches soccer anymore. When I started to talk about how the top teams play today, he interrupted me, as if this was all something he'd heard before. "Teams like Manchester City and Barcelona can just buy up the world's best players and it doesn't really matter what sort of style they're going to play," he said. "They're going to be good."

But that wasn't my point. As we discussed the kerfuffle over counting passes, he suggested to me that it was only one metric of an assortment used to objectively quantify performance: "That wasn't the main thrust of Reep's analyses. He had dozens of other measures that he would record in games. It's much more meaningful for the number of times you regained position in the opponent's third of the field, the number of times you got the ball up there."

Current Liverpool manager Jürgen Klopp employs an aggressive system known in German as *gegenpressing*, where his attackers attempt to win the ball back as soon as they lose it, instead of dropping back and protecting their own goal. "*Gegenpressing* lets you win back the ball nearer to the goal," Klopp said. "It's only one pass away from a really good opportunity. No playmaker in the world can be as good as a good *gegenpressing* situation, and that's why it's so important." That strategy led Liverpool to two of the four highest point totals in league history, their first-ever title since the Premier League became the Premier League, and another European Cup. And it's straight out of Reep's playbook. "I didn't realize that's what he advocated," Pollard said.

Another Reepian belief, according to Pollard, concerned the guy with the gloves: "The goalkeeper is extremely important in Reep's play. Goalkeepers that get possession of the ball can immediately hit the ball into the opponent's penalty area if they've got a good kick. So goalkeepers were one of his main attacking positions on the field."

Who adopted the same thing? Pep Guardiola—the king of the short pass. At Manchester City, Guardiola signed the Brazilian keeper Ederson, who in addition to his shot-stopping ability can kick the ball farther, with accuracy, than just about anyone in the world. His ability to play the ball long prevents City's opponents from pressuring them too high up the field, and it essentially allows City to play with 11 players against the opponent's 10 outfield defenders. "With his feet, he is the best," Guardiola said of Ederson. Pollard was especially shocked by this: "They do? They must have . . . They certainly didn't when I was watching them a few years ago. I'll have to start watching again."

Then, I asked Pollard if he was familiar with the concept of expected goals.

"Yes, I started using that about 50 years ago." He went on: "I did a PhD on all this performance analysis of soccer in 1989, I think. One of the things I used was what I called 'expected goals.' And 30 years later, they're getting all excited about it now. I've got a paper published on this in 1995. My whole analysis and my thesis is based on the concept of expected goals."

He's not lying, either. Once we were both vaccinated, I visited Pollard at his house on the west side of Los Angeles. There's shrubbery and overgrowth shielding the front of the house from the street, and a big wooden front door with no windows and an ornate knocker instead of a doorbell. After I smacked the handle against the door a few times, Pollard appeared. He maintains the look of a very particular, elderly LA man: shaggy, long hair, an even longer beard, coupled with a long sleeve T-shirt, cargo shorts, and hiking boots. He led me through the house, a sort of mixed tribute to waterside villas everywhere—massive windows, maroon and yellow walls, and an outgrowth of potted plants competing with a large collection of Southeast Asian and African artwork. We went out through a back patio that wouldn't have been out of place in the Mediterranean, dipped through the garage, and entered a musty backroom that doubles as what is essentially the world's only Museum of the History of Soccer Analytics.

Incredibly, Pollard has saved *everything*. He has copies of just about every article Reep ever published, in addition to a manuscript of a book that Reep wrote in 1973 that was never published because no one wanted to publish it. It's called *League Championship Winning Soccer and the Random Effect: The Anatomy of Soccer Under the Microscope*. It's essentially Reep's theory of the game—not just a plea for passing moves but an analysis of through balls, a breakdown of how probabilities can improve our perception of results, what kinds of crosses are most likely to lead to goals, and lots more. There's an interview in a short-lived Scottish magazine called *The Punter* with Stan Cullis, who defends Reep's methods and echoes some of the sentiments you still hear today: "You won't get very many managers who will admit that somebody like Charles Reep will be of benefit to them. Since the advent of 4-4-2 and 4-3-3, managers like to give the impression that football is more scientific, and a game that only people at the professional level can understand. They like to keep the myth going to convince other people that football managers have infallible wisdom which other people can't have. They like to think that football is so scientific and that Charles Reep's methods are just 'kick and rush.'"

Pollard kept just about everything he's ever written or analyzed, too. He showed me various letters he received from Graham Taylor over the course of their correspondence. There's one written on Watford letterhead, addressed to a Mr R Pollard in Suva, Fiji. There's also a mention from Taylor about the possibility of raising one of Pollard's ideas with the team owner: "I do speak with Elton John from time to time, but not on a regular basis. However, when we next make contact with one another I will raise your proposition with him, although I think it most unlikely that he will involve himself." Taylor even briefly wrote to Pollard while he was England manager. The top of the letter is stamped with the England Football Association badge, right above which reads, "Patron: HER MAJESTY THE QUEEN."

Pollard also kept copies of everything he wrote for the *Fiji Sun*, and it is more advanced than almost anything you'll see in a British newspaper today. He would write his own shot maps, marking an "x" where both teams took their attempts from. Sometimes, he'd even create his own touch maps, marking every spot on the field where a player touched the ball. In May of 1985, Newcastle United traveled to Fiji to play a pair of exhibition matches against the Fijian national team as part of their preseason. Although Newcastle's roster included the likes of England national-team stars Peter Beardsley and Paul Gascoigne, they lost the first match, 3–0. After the second match—a 2–0 win for the visitors—Pollard wrote up a detailed statistical breakdown of the game, including the number of shots in the box, the number of attacks that reached what he classified as "shooting range," and the number of attacks that began within "shooting range." Alongside each one, he included a brief breakdown of why those stats mattered and what they portended for both sides: "Although Newcastle's total was only one better than Fiji's, the shots were more accurate and from closer range. On average, 10 shots are needed to score a goal. Unless Fiji can make a drastic improvement in both the quantity and quality of their shots, they are heading for trouble in New Zealand." It's clear, concise, contextualized information—a model of statistical analysis designed to be consumed by the general public.

* * *

In 1968, Reep cowrote a paper with Bernard Benjamin for the *Journal of the Royal Statistical Society*, titled "Skill and Chance in Association." Using Reep's pen-and-pad notation, they analyzed 101 different professional matches. Given that it was produced without a computer, it's an incredible document, and it truly does seem like the first step toward something like an objective, unified analysis of the best way to play the game. Some of their findings:

- Fifty percent of goals come from moves beginning in what they referred to as "shooting areas," or the final quarter of the field.
- Fifteen percent of attacks that reached the final quarter led to shots on goal, but 22 percent of attacks that *began* in the final quarter led to shots on goal.
- Fifty percent of goals conceded by a team occur from moves when they lose possession in their own half.
- Ten percent of shots led to a goal.

That last point is essentially the first and most-crude expected-goals model on record. Every shot was worth 0.10 xG. But more importantly, the data seemed to establish the bedrock principle upon which all soccer analysis needs to be based: It's random as hell. "The observation that there is a stochastic element in the number of goals arising from a particular number of shots in one match (as well as a near-constant proportion over a larger series of matches) is easy for a statistician to accept; indeed he would be surprised if it were otherwise," they wrote. "It indicates, of course, that an excess of shots by one team does not mean that, by chance, the other side will not get more goals and thus win the match. All this is so far removed from current soccer beliefs and tactics that general acceptance of the random element has been inhibited (though one of us, [Charles Reep], has shown that a successful style of play can be built upon it). It seems, however, that chance does dominate the game and probably most similar ball games."

There's a note of empirical humility in there. For one to accept that a game is defined by a significant degree of uncontrollable and immeasurable events, there has to be. But Reep's public writing and his handful of public appearances never offered that; no, this was a man who either thought he had all the answers or wanted others to *think* that he did. Forget that Reep's math wasn't quite right, or that these conclusions have been disproven by the fact that in every Premier League season over the past 10 years there's been a *negative* correlation between the number of long balls a team plays and how many points they win in a season. People are wrong all the time; frequently being wrong is the life of any scientist. And this was a scientific pursuit. No, what I see as Reep's biggest fault is his failure to comprehend the complexity and dynamic nature of the sport. He never seemed to consider that he was measuring aggregates and that certain ways of playing wouldn't work against certain opponents or with certain players or in certain weather conditions or as the talent profile of the professional athlete changed. It's incredible, really, how Reep moved so quickly from his first attempts at measuring a sport that had never been measured before to claiming that he basically had it all figured out. Sixty years later, no one is even close to figuring it all out.

"I've changed my mind about him as I've learned more about his work and re-reading biographical details," said Mark Thompson, a data scientist at the data company Twenty3, who wrote his own critical reassessment of Reep's legacy. "My main memory of what he'd done was that 'early data collector, bad analyst' two-dimensional figure that I think he's been flattened into. Learning that he'd coauthored proper research papers was really interesting to me, although I don't know what part he played in them—I wouldn't be surprised if he'd mainly supplied the data and some small insights and his coauthors had taken the data and applied more thorough statistical analysis to it. Having read *World Sport*, I suspect it is correct that he misinterpreted his data around long ball football, but on the other hand, everything I read about him from people who knew him was really defensive of him and said he was far more intelligent than that."

In these same debates in other sports, the onus always falls on the outsiders—the people trying to use math, trying to suggest a new way of thinking—to be the humble ones in awe of the revered traditions of the game, while the insiders get to keep doing things the way they've always done them. If Joe Morgan sounded bad, then just imagine what it must've been like for Reep to try to bring match analysis into the soccer world of the 1960s.

"He was made fun of more than anything else," Pollard said. "And a lot of coaches used to downgrade him all the time. *Weird, weird old retired wing commander with a hat and a pencil and paper.* The thought that he could have anything to offer at all was considered ridiculous by most people in soccer, particularly the media, who were terrible in England."

Perhaps Reep had to be steadfast in his claims in order to find purchase within the game, to eventually earn the trust of someone like Taylor. It's not like the traditional figures within the soccer world were constantly rethinking their own ideas. And well, the main reason his ideas gained any traction was that there were lots of other coaches who believed what he'd thought he'd found. His data paid proof to that early British ideal of soccer as a game that was decided by who was bigger, faster, stronger, and tougher. To this day, Reep remains *the most* influential analyst in the history of the sport. No other single individual has influenced the actual tactics and strategy of the way multiple top teams played more than Reep did some 50 years ago.

The last published paper with Reep's name on it—"Measuring the Effectiveness of Playing Strategies at Soccer"—came out in 1997 in a journal called *The Statistician.* He was 93. However, Reep had nothing to do with the production of the paper; Pollard just included his name as coauthor as a tribute to his mentor. In the paper, Pollard aimed to provide a crude goal-scoring probability for every possession at the 1986 World Cup—even if the possession didn't lead to a goal.

"At the end of each passing movement, I would give it a value, which I would call the yield," Pollard said. "You didn't even need to apply it to shots, 'cause shots are part of your passing moves anyway. So for every passing move in a game, I would give it a yield, which could be termed the expected number of goals you would get from using that passing move in that position." He was attempting to take expected goals beyond shots—before anyone else had even begun looking at shot-based expected goals. Pollard recorded the characteristics of a given possession—where it started, where it ended, what kind of passes it included—and then figured out how often a possession with those same characteristics would result in a goal. That was the yield, and he hoped it could be used to inform tactical strategy.

The paper also includes an image of what today might be called an "expected-goals map," which cordoned off the attacking area based on the probability that a goal would be scored from a shot from a bucket of locations by a player less than one yard from the nearest opponent:

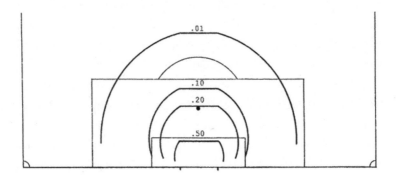

Pollard concludes the paper by saying, "With a few notable exceptions, our experience has been that soccer coaches, players, fans and the media are deeply sceptical and often suspicious, to the point of paranoia, at the suggestion that a statistician might have something useful to offer in the way of tactical analysis. Perhaps it is understandable that the preservation of a soccer mystique is something that those professionally involved in the game would want to maintain." It doesn't end there, though: "Nevertheless, because of the overwhelming importance of winning, anything that might give a coach an additional advantage might at least be expected to be worthy of investigation."

There's no dogma, no "three passes are better than four or more passes." It's just an offer: Here's what we found, and here's how it could help. If you open your mind, you might find that there's an even better way.

* * *

When he left Fiji, Pollard first took a job as a statistics professor at California Polytechnic State University, San Luis Obispo, but soon lost his job thanks to the recession in the early '90s. He then took his family with him to Bulgaria; the "fall of communism" had just happened, as he puts it, and professors were needed to staff up the newly opened American University there. He continued to analyze games for his own enjoyment, keeping the same stats he kept for the

Fiji Sun, but he didn't work for anyone. Then, since Bulgaria was awful—he had to teach his kids algebra because there was nowhere for them to go to school—he moved to Malawi, where an English-language medical school had just opened. He was a fit because of his background in medical statistics, but he also worked for the Malawian soccer federation as an analyst *and* wrote for the local paper about the team he was analyzing. After a 3–0 loss to Zambia in which the Malawians were also outshot 11–4, Pollard pulled no punches: "There is something drastically wrong with a team that can manage only 4 shots at goal in the entire game. Since it takes on average 10 shots to produce one goal, Malawi's performance was totally inadequate."

The Pollards didn't last long in Malawi and eventually made their way back to California's central coast. There, Richard started to analyze games for the University of California Santa Barbara's men's soccer team under coach Andy Kuenzli. At this point, Pollard had started to add what, at the time, he referred to as "goals earned from shots," which was just xG by another name. He'd award a conversion probability to each shot based on whether or not it was inside the box, and then sum them up to come up with the total. For an October 1989 match against the University of Nevada, Las Vegas, UCSB earned 1.2 goals, while UNLV earned just 0.2. Pollard searched for the final score on his analysis sheet and once he found it, we both started laughing. Regulation ended 1–1 because of course it did. Soccer is silly like that.

Beyond employing statistical analyses more advanced than those of 99 percent of the best European soccer clubs at a collegiate soccer program in a country that hadn't been to a World Cup in 40 years, the other notable part of Pollard's work with UCSB is that it was the first time he'd ever been paid to analyze soccer games. He did his initial work for Watford for free, and most of his other stuff was academic. In Fiji, as part of visa requirements, he couldn't be paid by the *Fiji Sun*, so they'd basically send him on frequent "vacations" to the other side of the island, which the paper would cover as a "work expense." It seems important to remember here that Pollard wasn't only analyzing his own data, he was recording all of it, too. He showed me notebooks filled with the shorthand he'd developed: random markings and letters, scattered seemingly haphazardly across the pages. It would be completely unintelligible to every person on this planet other than Richard

Pollard. But he said that all he needed to do was to look at those pages and he could "see the game."

As he said this, I looked up from where we were standing—over the stacks of boxes filled with the early history of the ideas that would ultimately revolutionize the way the world's most popular sport was played. The shelves in this cramped backroom were filled with various pieces of African art: wooden carvings, masks, sticks, chains, you name it. Suddenly, I felt like I was sitting in Frasier Crane's storage closet.

Then, I remembered that Pollard hadn't mentioned how he'd been compensated by the Malawian federation. Since he had an official title and worked directly with the manager, I figured he'd just forgotten that they, too, had given him money for his services. He'd led a long and wild life; it'd be an easy thing to lose track of. I asked him about it, and then he pointed to all the carvings. They couldn't pay him with actual money for his analysis. Instead, they gave him thousands of dollars' worth of traditional Malawian artwork.

CHAPTER SIX

SET PIECES

"Science" is one of those words that has lost nearly all of its meaning. On the campaign trail in 2016, the Democratic presidential candidate Hillary Clinton said, "I believe in science." In 2020, a popular yard sign among Democratic voters featured a number of phrases, including "science is real." During the COVID-19 pandemic, President Joe Biden earned plenty of headlines for simply saying, "I trust scientists." Signaling your support for "science" has become an act of political posturing, an utterly banal statement turned supposed marker of enlightenment.

But what *is* "science"? This "science" sounds like it should have a capital "S"—as if there's one big global group called "Science," who get together in their labs, do their experiments behind closed doors, and then emerge with consensus opinions about the world's most pressing issues. Except, these scientists often get things wrong, like when they authenticated the field of "eugenics" and led to it being taught at the likes of Harvard and the Massachusetts Institute of Technology in the early 20th century. While getting things that badly wrong is unforgivable, assuming you're wrong is the essence of the science espoused by Ernst Mayr, the father of evolutionary biology. "All interpretations made by a scientist are hypotheses, and all hypotheses are tentative," he wrote. "They must forever be tested and they must be revised if found to be unsatisfactory.

Hence, a change of mind in a scientist, and particularly in a great scientist, is not only not a sign of weakness but rather evidence for continuing attention to the respective problem and an ability to test the hypothesis again and again."

In the broadest sense, "science" is the creation of a hypothesis and the testing—and testing and testing; and OK, now go test it again—of said hypothesis. You come up with a question, suggest an answer, and then try to prove yourself wrong, over and over again. If you made it through elementary school, you, of course, know this—or you at least *knew* it at some point in your life. It's the idea behind the scientific method. And when you learned the scientific method, you learned about the importance of "control groups." If you wanted to test, say, the effect of direct sunlight on the growth of a houseplant, you couldn't just put a plant in direct sunlight, watch it grow, and then claim that sunlight causes house plants to grow at whatever rate your plant grew at. No, you'd also need to measure the growth of a plant that *wasn't* put in direct sunlight, and then compare the two. On top of that, you'd also need to make sure that everything else about the two plants—soil, watering, pot size, and so on—is as close to equal as possible in order to prevent any other variables from affecting your result. Even an experiment as basic as that sounds like a huge pain in the ass, doesn't it?

Well, now imagine trying to apply the same process to a soccer game, where you have 22 different players of varying levels of skill and fitness and mental preparation all trying to kick a ball across a field that, from game to game, varies in size and grass length and flatness. The fans change every match, the managerial instructions differ from week to week, the referee almost never repeats, the balls are never inflated exactly the same, and the weather shifts from day to day and sometimes even from half to half.

Expected goals provides a nice example of the issue. While Michael Caley and other model-builders are constantly updating their models and are well aware of their imperfections—they've been able to test the data across a big enough historical sample to at least know that xG is a better predictor of performance than any of the rudimentary statistics available in a league table or a "match summary" graphic on TV—there is still an unanswered question within all of it. The ability to get lots of great shots is the key differentiating factor between all strikers at the highest level of the game, rather than the ability to convert those shots. But that doesn't necessarily mean that kicking the ball into the net isn't an important and requisite skill at the highest level. For all we know, there really could be certain players who possess the movement skill and anticipatory instincts of Cristiano Ronaldo who are just completely incapable of accurately redirecting a soccer ball with any of the International Football Association Board–approved body parts. If those players exist, they would likely have been filtered out somewhere along the line. Unless he wants to get fired, a coach isn't going to play a player who can't shoot, and so if these players exist, they wouldn't appear in the dataset that then creates the expected-goals model.

The institutional pressures of the game at the highest level and the structure of the sport itself have made soccer incredibly resistant to any kind of scientific-seeming experimentation across the major leagues in England, Spain, Italy, Germany, and France. If you want to find anything remotely resembling a science experiment, you have to fly to Copenhagen, take the E20 west, then hop on Route 18 north to Ejstrupholmvej in Brande. Then take exit 11-Brande Ø from Route 18, jump on the Dørslundvej/Klinkhøjvej to Brandevej until you get to Stadion Alle in Ikast.

* * *

In 1999, everyone in Herning was angry. The tiny Danish city (population just over 50,000) had two major professional soccer clubs: Ikast FS and Herning Fremad. The clubs were huge rivals, although they had one major thing in common: They both sucked. Each club appeared to be stranded in the Danish second division, with no real hope of ever going much higher. Such is the life of a pair of soccer clubs in the 11th-largest city in the 25th-largest country in Europe.

Hopeless situations often require heretical solutions—and a local carpenter and a Mercedes dealer eventually came up with one. The carpenter, Johnny Rune, was the chairman of Ikast, while Herning were chaired by luxury-car salesman Steen Hessel. Both of their teams had just lost, and both men were sick of watching terrible soccer week after week, so Rune and Hessel decided it was time to employ the nuclear option. They called an emergency weekend meeting, they sketched out the details on the back of a napkin, and come Monday they were sitting in front of TV cameras, announcing the creation of FC Midtjylland: a super-club formed by the merger of Ikast and Herning.

It was a little awkward at first. The team suddenly had two coaches and too many players. They had more stadiums than a second-tier Danish soccer club could ever reasonably need. And their uniforms didn't match, either. But once they got the details sorted—socks from one club, shirts from another—the merger became an immediate success. Not only did FC Midtjylland get promoted in the club's first-ever season; they smashed the competition, losing just twice in 30 games and producing a goal differential—78 scored, 17 against—that was more than twice as high as the next best total. Their first decade in the Danish top tier was a competitive success—a bunch of top-four finishes that earned them qualification to the UEFA Cup/Europa League, the European competition for all the teams not quite good enough to qualify for the Champions League.

However, the unsustainable economics of European soccer eventually caught up with them. Spending begets success begets higher revenues begets higher spending begets even more success. Once in the first division, the club had to pay its players more money in order to stay competitive. Established in the Europa League, the club had to pay its players even more money in order to stay competitive. The ultimate windfall would have come from the revenue distributed to teams that qualify for the Champions League. Playing against the best teams in the world is the ultimate vindication—from a competitive perspective, but also from a financial one. The payouts are so big that they make up for all the money a team typically has to spend in order to get there. You spent *that* money to make *this* money. Except, in Denmark, only the first-place team qualifies for the next season's Champions League—and without those revenues, Midtjylland's operating costs eventually plunged the club into debt. In 2014, just 15 years into its existence, the club was on the verge of bankruptcy.

Rasmus Ankersen was born in Herning and grew up playing for Midtjylland. He captained its youth teams and was one of the nascent club's most promising prospects. At just 19, he earned his first call up to the senior team, and in his first match with the big boys he . . . suffered a knee injury that essentially ended his career. Feeling like his own gift had been taken away from him, Ankersen became obsessed with talent: where it comes from, why it exists, how it's cultivated. After taking a six-month hiatus to backpack across Asia—soccer players: they're just like you wanted to be when you were 20—Ankersen returned to Midtjylland and became an assistant coach for the same youth teams he'd just played for. Without any real history, money, or an especially vibrant location to offer potential players, the club had decided it would dedicate itself to producing better youth players than everyone else. Their main trick, according to

Ankersen? Have the kids train seven days a week instead of three. Ankersen's teams included the likes of Winston Reid and Simon Kjaer, a pair of center backs who would each go on to play more than 190 matches for teams across Europe's five biggest leagues.

"They developed one of the best football academies in Europe, and it's really counterintuitive that should happen in a place in the middle of nowhere where there's very few people living," Ankersen said. "There was a good culture for innovation already because it was a young club."

Equipped with both coaching and playing experience at a young age, Ankersen decided to write a book, *DNA of a Winner*. It was successful enough that he quit his job at Midtjylland, moved to Copenhagen, and started working as a performance coach of sorts with individual athletes. He wrote two more books, *Leadership DNA* and *The Gold Mine Effect*, and they were successful enough that he decided to move to London to find an English publisher. Once it was published in translation, *The Gold Mine Effect* caught the eye of Matthew Benham, a former hedge-fund manager who made even more money when he launched Smartodds, a sports-betting syndicate that was frequently more successful at predicting the outcomes of soccer matches than the betting markets were. Benham became convinced that the knowledge he'd cultivated in determining what wins games could be applied to running a club. First, he pulled an Elton John and bought his boyhood club, AFC Brentford, a tiny London side that was playing in the third division. It would be a long slog to the top of the English pyramid, and there was so much money and cultural baggage to overcome. Ankersen told Benham that he knew of an even better place to test out his hypothesis. He had a club that (a) didn't have any of the historic inertia, (b) was already competing in Europe, and (c) was desperate for anyone to save it.

In the summer of 2014, Benham became the majority shareholder of FC Midtjylland. "I am convinced that we can create a sound and sustainable top club," he said at the time, "not by outspending other clubs but by outthinking them and by being more effective." In 2015, Benham appointed Ankersen as the chairman of FCM. The experiment had begun: Can you successfully run a first-division soccer club with a top-down mandate to use numbers and employ evidence-based decision-making?

* * *

The answer was obvious almost immediately. In its first season under Benham's ownership, Midtjylland won its first-ever first-division title. They finished four points ahead of FC Copenhagen, the Danish giants who played their home matches in front of twice as many fans as Midtjylland. They've won two more league titles since then and haven't finished lower than fourth since Benham took over. In 2016, they beat Manchester United, 2–1, in the first leg of their Round-of-32 matchup in the Europa League. (They lost the second leg, 5–1, and were eliminated.) And in 2020, they qualified for the Champions League group stages for the first time, which earned the club lucrative matches against multi-time European Cup winners Liverpool and Ajax. Though they were eliminated after the group stages, they tied one game with Liverpool and another with the Italian club Atalanta. This was a long way from the dour final days of Herning and Ilkast.

According to the website Off the Pitch, Midtjylland made €14.5 million for the 2018–19 season. Their wage bill was €12.6 million, and their transfer-fee spend was €4 million. Qualification for the group stages alone was worth around €15 million, with another €1 million for each of their draws. Infused with all this new income, Midtjylland has since publicly stated that its goal is to become one of the top 50 clubs in the world by 2025 according to the UEFA coefficient, which ranks clubs based on their performance in European competition over a five-year span.

How do they plan on getting there? It all starts with Stefan Szymanski's law. "Everything we do points to creating a larger player budget," said team president Claus Steinlein in a press release outlining the club's new ambitions. "If we are successful in Europe, it increases the player budget, we sell a player for a large amount, it increases the budget, and so it is with the commercial revenue. If we increase earnings, it gives us the opportunity to raise the player budget, and all studies show that 75–85 percent of the explanation for sporting results is about the money you can put in the first-team squad." They understand how this works, and they're not afraid to tell you about it, either.

When Ankersen and Benham took over the club, one of the first things they did was stop focusing on standings. *We're not looking at the league table.* From the outside, it might appear to be a radical step: *Don't you guys, uh, care about winning?* But within the context of what people like Michael Caley had discovered about how goal-scoring works, it made perfect sense. They stopped looking at the table because they believed it didn't provide an accurate representation of how well their team, and all the other teams across the league, had performed. It was way too noisy, and even glancing at it could cause you to start asking the wrong questions. Instead, they used what Ankersen referred to as "the table of justice," which is essentially an expected-goals leaderboard that uses the club's in-house rating system, which is based on Benham's work with Smartodds. "We make it clear to our head coach that the primary way of measuring the progress you make with the team is the on-the-line rating change," he said. "There's so much randomness that the same performance can swing you 15 points one way or the other. So we don't work with that league table. We don't look at it much."

The same kind of thinking applies to the club's long-term goals. Before the season begins, they don't ask themselves: How do we win the league or make it to the knockout rounds of the Champions League? They know they can't *really* control that, so instead they focus on what they *can* control: how their model rates their team's underlying performance.

"We're asking a question: How much does our rating have to improve to increase the probability of achieving automatic promotion?" Ankersen said. "And then we discuss where those rating improvements are going to come from. We feel we're measuring the coach on something he can actually affect and control. Then you can discuss how much a head coach can affect those numbers, and it's less than people think. But that's what he's being measured on, so he knows that—if we didn't win the first of eight games but our performances were tremendous both statistically and with your eyes when you watch the games."

What separates Midtjylland from other clubs isn't just how they judge their manager but how much power they give him. He exists within the team's hierarchy, and his performance is judged just like anyone else's. His main job is to improve the team's performance in areas he can control, as measured by their model, and perhaps in hitting some other softer benchmarks, like playing younger players. In England, the managerial job still often works differently. Managers are usually judged on results, so they're constantly scrambling to attempt to control things that no one, in the history of the sport, has been able to fully control. But they're also given power in what players the team acquires and in what style the team plays.

Take the example of Tottenham Hotspur. In fall 2019, they fired manager Mauricio Pochettino, who oversaw the team's run to the 2019 Champions

League final and had helped establish the club as a perennial top-four finisher despite revenues that suggested they should be only sixth or seventh.
Pochettino's teams played an aggressive attacking style and pressured the
ball high up the field. The roster was built with that idea in mind: younger,
athletic players who were more comfortable in the opposition half than in
their own. The chosen replacement for Pochettino? The infamously reactive
José Mourinho, who preferred for his teams to stay organized behind the ball
and then try to counterattack into the space that teams like the one he was
now taking over tended to concede. Mourinho was allowed to sign a handful
of players to fit his preferred style but ultimately had to ask a majority of the
roster to play in a completely new way that didn't fit their strengths. It didn't
work, and Mourinho was fired in April 2021, lasting just 17 months. Spurs
were left with all kinds of waste: a mishmash roster of players brought in for
two polar-opposite managers who were no longer coaching the team, plus
millions of dollars in severance pay owed to Pochettino *and* Mourinho.

"In England there's a structure in most clubs which I believe stops loads of
clubs from progressing because the average life span of a manager is maybe 14,
16 months," Ankersen said. "So you basically have a guy who on average has the
job no more than 16 months. And he's gotta make decisions about long-term
strategy; that's doomed to fail. Then one week it's all about him not losing next
week's games because he might get the sack."

Since Benham purchased Midtjylland, the average managerial tenure
has lasted for more than two years—but even when a manager's stay has been
shorter, as was the case with Kenneth Andersen, who lasted for one season and
now works for the club's academy, there was no institutional upheaval as a result.
Midtjylland hire managers who fit their approach—not the other way around.

So, what, exactly, *is* the Midtjylland approach? Being smarter about hiring
managers and judging their performance is great—and it *does* provide an edge
compared to the traditional inefficiencies that still plague European soccer. But
that can take you only so far. How do you improve the team's performance in
the eyes of the all-important model?

Ankersen, unsurprisingly, wouldn't reveal what goes into their system, but
it's safe to assume it's something like Caley's xG model with a couple of other
key performance indicators baked in. One clear way to get better at things like
creating and suppressing good chances is to, you know, acquire better players.

But at the start, the club learned that data could tell them only so much about which players were actually any good.

"In the early days we probably overestimated the benefits of data on identifying the next players we were going to sign," Ankersen said. "We didn't see the limitations of the quality of the data available, and we also realized that the data ended up identifying similar players with similar problems. For example, the way it should work—expected goals is a great measure to judge whether a striker is truly good or if he's just lucky. It's a great way of identifying undervalued strikers, but if you have a good expected-goals model that's kind of the first step. Assuming you have a good expected-goals model, then you can use that to find undervalued talent, but you still always want to look at all the clips. You see this player who's really high on expected goals but not that high on actual goals, so that's quite interesting. You assume the market undervalues the player like that. But then you watch all the clips, you get to see how all these shots might be a problem."

In other words, they were thwarted by soccer's suboptimal science. Since Midtjylland weren't recruiting players from the Big Five leagues, they were recruiting players whose outputs weren't being used as inputs in the calibration of the average xG model. They kept finding players who did, in fact, have all the skills necessary to get the shots but none of the skills needed to turn them into goals. "In the early days we had a tendency maybe to rely too much on what the data said and not digging behind those stats to see: What are the reasons for this? What are our eyes actually telling us? That balance between objectivity and subjectivity is really important to get right," Ankersen said.

Based on the UEFA rankings, the Danish league is the 18th-strongest league in Europe, one spot behind Norway and one ahead of Croatia. Beyond the obvious disadvantages that come from having less money than other teams in other leagues, Midtjylland face a number of problems that stem from their spot on the European-football food chain. Although they're certainly not coming close to exhausting the possibilities in this area, a Premier League team could build out a full analytics operation for less than the cost of one starting player. It's a no-brainer; there's basically nothing to lose. But even though Midtjylland make only a fraction of what a mid-table Premier League team make per year, they have to pay the same amount of money for the data—if not more. Most big clubs are scouting from within the Big Five leagues or from the clubs just outside that orbit—second divisions in their own countries, the Portuguese league, the Dutch league—and so the data is both relatively accurate *and* readily available. While Midtjylland will occasionally sign a player from a bigger league, they're frequently acquiring players from the second divisions of other Scandinavian countries, South America, or Eastern Europe. When the data is more expensive and less reliable, the value of investing in the process doesn't have a clear payoff.

"It's not totally obvious to me that it's a great investment if you're a small team," Luke Bornn said. "Let's say you have a $2 million-a-year player budget, you're like a Finnish team or something. So we need to do two things. We need to hire someone that can deal with this data, and we need to buy data. And we need to warehouse it. You're probably talking $200,000 of investment. Right? And if that's 10 percent of your player budget, that's insane."

According to Bornn, most NBA teams are spending around 0.5 percent of their revenues on analytics, and some are even closer to 0.1 percent. For NBA or MLB or NFL teams, who are all spending hundreds of millions of dollars on players, the benefit of investing in something that will make you better at identifying players is obvious. As long as you think that the investment in data is giving you a small edge—even, say, 5 percent—on your competitors, then an investment of 0.5 percent of your revenue is an easy call to make. In that case, even if it turns out that your edge is 10 times less effective than you thought, you'd still break even.

"If you're a soccer team, you think, 'OK, analytics is even arguably harder, and we're going to get less information about players,'" Bornn said. "So maybe it's not a 5 percent edge, maybe it's a 2 percent edge. Well, then we should really be spending to make sure that we're getting an edge, so we should be spending less than 0.5 percent." For this theoretical Finnish team, that would equate to spending something like $20,000 to $30,000 of the budget. What would you get for that? "Nothing," according to Bornn.

If you're an owner that doesn't have the guaranteed millions of the Premier League TV deal every season and you're working in a sport that's still resistant to the use of numbers, there are all kinds of reasons—some good, some bad—not to make a sizable investment in the incorporation of data into your team's decision-making process.

"It's really unclear," Bornn said. "If you're in a league where player salaries are $30,000 a year or something, why would you want to sacrifice two players for one analyst? I'm not saying that teams shouldn't be incorporating data more into their process. I just think where the economic argument for it is super obvious in North American sports, and maybe you could say the same for the top few leagues around Europe, but it's not uniformly true across the sport. Even though I think basketball seems like it should absolutely be making every decision based on data, I would not go to my local D3 college program and say, 'You need to be totally data driven.' It doesn't make sense."

One way to get around this problem: be owned by a wealthy sports bettor who has already spent years gathering this data and understanding how to use it. Plus, the implementation of this new way of thinking wasn't as painful (or expensive) at Midtjylland because the club was only 15 years old. Unlike at Brentford, there was no real institutional inertia to beat back—coaches to argue with, lifelong scouts who couldn't be replaced—and even if there was, the club was desperate. If a bunch of nerds had to save the club, at least the club was being saved by *someone*.

"People were quite open to whatever it took to save the club from bankruptcy," Ankersen said. "So there was an openness to those ideas that was quite situational because of the financial conditions at the time."

While Midtjylland were able to overcome the cultural issues that prevent evidence-based decision-making from permeating the big clubs and the financial issues that prevent smaller clubs from doing the same, they haven't solved the sport by any means. In fact, they haven't really come close.

"The game has a lot more complexity and randomness than most other sports," Ankersen said. "It doesn't mean we shouldn't pursue ways of measuring players' contributions more accurately, but in our pursuit to develop those methods, it's important to understand the limitations. And we have some simple—but we believe very powerful—tools and analytical models to identify the type of players that we want, but for every model there is a risk that the model overlooks something or undervalues something. Knowing the risk of the model—it's not what you see, it's often what you *don't* see that decides whether a player will be successful or not."

Midtjylland, in other words, try to control only what they know they can control.

* * *

In 2019, Massimiliano Allegri gave one of the most revealing interviews you'll ever read from a still-practicing coach. Allegri won a Serie A title as manager of AC Milan in 2011, and then he won an incredible five-straight titles from 2015 through 2019 while managing Juventus. The club also reached the Champions League final twice under Allegri's watch. He left Juventus in 2019 and then didn't get hired for another job until Juve rehired him in 2021. The interview he did with the journalist James Horncastle for ESPN helps to explain why a guy coming off five-straight league titles couldn't find a new job.

The headline quote from the story is "In my ignorance I don't even have a computer." But the more revealing tidbit comes a bit later in Horncastle's piece, when Allegri explains his grand theory of coaching. "I have to put the other players in a position to get the ball to [the best players], and once they have the ball they decide what to do with it, what the best decision is," Allegri said. "My son is 8, and every now and then we go on YouTube and watch the great players, the amazing things they do in attack and in defence, because football is art. In Italy, the tactics, schemes, they're all bull—. Football is art and the artists are the world-class players. You don't have to teach them anything, you just admire them. All you need to do is put them in the best condition to do well."

It's tempting to point out that, yes, here is an unemployed coach making the case that coaching really isn't that hard or even that important. But in a way, Allegri is making the same point that various people have been making throughout this book: Soccer is a mystery. All of this stuff happens between the lines, the ball moves forward and backward, and all 22 players react, some of it matters, some of it is repeatable, some of it is random, and beyond the players who make the goals happen—the artists—we don't really know what's going on. Allegri is also validating the point that Stefan Szymanski made to me. Allegri himself is supposed to be the "general"—the man who organizes his troops and gives them "the play" and inspires them to execute it to the best of their abilities—and yet he's saying, *Me, a general? No, no, no. I'm an art curator.*

However, there *are* moments when soccer very clearly becomes much more of a science than an art. Whenever the ball goes out of bounds or someone commits a foul, the beautiful game becomes the pre-planned game—or at least it could.

Soccer has a complicated relationship with set pieces—the moments when the game stops, the defense has to stand at least 10 yards away from the ball, and the offense can actually discuss and then decide how they're going to try to score. "There's this whole perception that scoring from set pieces is almost cheating," Paul Power said. "You know, it's not part of the beautiful game."

During the 2013–14 season, Power was a consultant for Everton, Liverpool's eternal rivals and one of the biggest clubs in England. They'd just hired the Spanish manager Roberto Martínez, who had guided tiny Wigan to an FA Cup victory and a multi-year stint in the Premier League. What was remarkable about Martínez's time at Wigan—and why a club like Everton decided to hire him despite the fact that Wigan were ultimately relegated under Martínez's watch—is that his team always possessed the ball. At the time, garnering more than 50 percent possession over the course of the season was still seen as the province of the richest clubs, the ones with the most expensive players who could monopolize control of the ball and create an overwhelming number of chances. Yet, despite one of the cheapest rosters in the Premier League, Martínez's Wigan broke the 50 percent mark in each of their seasons in the top flight. It was an impressive and bold approach that eventually crashed up against the limitations of its personnel: The team's attackers weren't very good, so they didn't create high-quality opportunities with their possession, and since their defenders were very bad, they gave up goals whenever they lost the ball. While most other smaller clubs played a similar version of the same game—pack as many bodies into your own defensive third as you can, try to score goals on the occasional counterattack—Martínez took the opposite approach. Not only did it work for a few years; it also made him a candidate for a top job. Just imagine what he could do with attackers who could turn all that possession into goals and defenders who could deal with all the counterattacks that would inevitably come whenever they lost the ball.

Martínez was even amenable to using data to help fine-tune his approach. According to Power, he wanted to see how analysts could measure the synchronization between his players. He wanted to know how his team could create space with the ball, what kind of movements from his attackers would create space against the packed-in defenses they would inevitably face. He obsessed over every aspect of attacking play—except for set pieces. "There was no interest,"

Power said. "This still kind of plagues soccer, from top to bottom. Teams are scared—or maybe that's players, I don't know. They don't want to put in the work and reap the rewards from the set-piece systems and routines."

One inherent problem with set-piece practice is that it's boring as hell. Other than the few players involved in the direct execution of the play, everyone else just kind of stands around, and it's easy to lose focus. That's what the experience was like for me in college, and although I wasn't getting paid to pay attention, I've been told many professionals have had the same experience. And so set-piece practice becomes perfunctory.

"Teams will practice for 10 minutes on a Friday—why?" Bornn said. "There's all this research about how teams can score more goals from set pieces. It's like a basketball team not practicing free throws."

Just how many goals might the likes of Roberto Martínez be leaving on the table?

"If you have a very good set-piece regime, that's basically the equivalent, in terms of goals, as spending £80 million on a striker," Power said. "If you get it done really well, you could score anywhere between 15 and 25 goals a season. If you're a small market team, even if you're a big market team—if I can save myself £60 million, £80 million, that's remarkable. Just from working on something on the training ground."

This century, most of the teams that relied on set-piece scoring seemed to do it out of desperation. Two of the more infamous examples are Stoke City in the late aughts and early 2010s and West Bromwich Albion for a couple of years in the mid-2010s—two teams that were, uncoincidentally, coached by a stern-faced Welshman with a taste for tracksuits and brand-name hats who once head-butted one of his own players while completely naked.

Tony Pulis took over at Stoke while they were in the Championship in 2005, and he had them promoted to the Premier League by 2007. Pulis quickly turned the club into a Premier League mainstay and then a Europa League qualifier by, for lack of a better term, beating the shit out of his opponents. Pulis built a roster of gigantic, comparatively unskilled players that attempted to play a version of the game that Charles Reep and Richard Pollard envisioned: They packed bodies in their own third and then tried to move the ball up field as quickly as possible via passes in the air. Much of it was grim stuff; the ball was in play, on average, for less than 60 minutes of the matches Stoke played under Pulis. A soccer game, of course, lasts for 90 minutes and change. His approach was maybe not as extreme when he was at West Brom, but the style was roughly the same.

Despite their success, Pulis's teams were constantly criticized by commentators, coaches, and players alike, and Pulis could rarely resist fighting back. He loved to claim that the criticism didn't bother him—and then immediately list a bunch of reasons why the criticism bothered him. In one of his first games in charge at Liverpool in December 2015, Jürgen Klopp's team drew 2–2 with Pulis's West Brom. After the match, Klopp suggested that their opponents "only played long balls," which might just seem like a simple statement of fact. But in the soccer world, it's a grave accusation of aesthetic fraudulence. Pulis responded by pointing out that statistics from the match showed that his team played only three more long balls than Klopp's side. "So as a football club we apologize to Liverpool for playing three more longer passes than they did," Pulis said. "There's always a bit of spin put on things these days. But if I had a team that was worth £200m, playing against a team that was worth less than £20m and we never won that game, I'd be doing my best to divert it away from the fact that I had 10 times more value on the pitch than my opposition and couldn't win. I'm not annoyed—I'm just stating the facts."

Despite the, let's say, "industrial" nature of their play, there *was* a method to their madness and a brilliance behind their brawn. At both Stoke and West Brom, Pulis's teams were always near the top of the league in set-piece goals scored despite the fact that they were never anywhere near the top of the league in total goals scored. At Stoke, they scored an incredible number of goals via throw-ins, thanks to the long-range laser beams produced by the Irishman Rory Delap. Stoke have scored 24 Premier League goals from throw-in situations since 2008—by far the most in the league despite the fact that they haven't even been in the league since 2018. West Brom, meanwhile, scored 10 percent of their goals from corner kicks in the 2016–17 season; since 2008, no other team in any of Europe's major leagues has broken nine percent.

"He was actually a magician at creating goals from set pieces," Power said of Pulis. As he showed me a couple of West Brom's corner routines, Power was legitimately giddy, as if he'd just watched *Vertigo* for the first time or something. There were clear, pre-planned movements among the West Brom players that created space inside the six-yard box for the ball to be delivered into. "I actually get goosebumps looking at that," Power said. "It's so perfectly choreographed."

Despite the obvious success of Pulis's dead-ball routines, the theory of the case was that the turgid open-play approach was inextricable from the set-piece proficiency. For starters, the thinking went, Pulis's sides were able to be so successful at set plays *because* they signed big dudes who weren't good with their feet. (If there was a big dude who *was* good with his feet, Stoke and West Brom wouldn't have been able to afford him.) At the managerial level, coaches would constantly tell people like Power that they just didn't have the training time to work on set plays. No, they needed to practice their open-play movements and their passing patterns and their defensive shape. Any time spent working on set plays would, in theory, make the team less effective in open play. This also helped to explain why Pulis's teams seemed so elementary when the ball was in play; they never practiced passing!

Given that somewhere between 70 and 75 percent of goals typically come from open play, the theory that training time was zero-sum—that you couldn't get really good at set pieces without sacrificing your performance in open-play—appeared to be a sound one. That is, until Midtjylland and the rest of Denmark proved it wrong.

* * *

In their inaugural title-winning year of 2014–15, FC Midtjylland scored 25 goals from set pieces. Only three other teams in the Danish first division even hit double digits, and no one else got higher than 11. A goal is typically worth roughly one marginal point in the league table, and Midtjylland finished four points clear of second-place FC Copenhagen, who only scored nine goals from set plays. Viewed from one angle, Midtjylland won the league because of their proficiency outside of possession play.

Ted Knutson, himself a former sports bettor and soccer blogger, was hired by Benham to be the head of player analytics at Midtjylland and Brentford. Knutson's first job was to watch as many set plays as he could, discern the patterns that typically led to goals, and create a guide for how Midtjylland could get better at them. He figured out what worked, and then one of the team's assistants, Brian Priske, who would eventually go on to become the manager that led FCM to the Champions League, implemented the ideas in practice during the week.

It worked better than anyone could have imagined, but then something weird happened. Some people at Midtjylland started *talking* about it. Rather than protecting their edge and continuing to exploit it, someone with the club decided that it was time to start telling everyone how good they were at set pieces and how important these valuable set pieces were to the club. Perhaps it was a mistake, perhaps they were so confident in their own methods and the anti-innovation inertia across Europe that they didn't care, or perhaps it was a PR move to distract attention away from the fact that Brentford weren't having the same kind of success as Midtjylland. Whatever the reason, the rest of Denmark eventually caught on.

"It was almost an unintentional economics experiment," Knutson said. "Other teams in the league immediately started paying more attention to this phase of the game, and most of the teams in the league started scoring more goals—in some cases *a lot* more goals—because of it."

In 2017–18, Midtjylland won the league again while once again scoring 25 goals from set plays. But they weren't the only ones to bang 'em in from dead balls this time around. Two other teams broke the 20-goal mark, and eight more cracked double digits. Now, for the objections: The league had expanded from 12 to 14 teams, which of course increases the number of teams that can score a lot of set-piece goals and could also dilute the quality of the league. On top of that, who cares how many set-piece goals you score? All goals count the same.

Well, the Danish league inadvertently disproved one of the managerial theories for ignoring set plays. If spending increased practice time on corner kicks, throw-ins, and free kicks took away from valuable possession-play practice, we'd expect to see an increase in set-play goals but *not* an increase in overall goal scoring. In 2014–15, teams in Denmark averaged 0.55 set-piece goals per game, and that increased to 0.75 in 2017–18. However, *total* goal-scoring increased, too: from 2.41 per game in 2014–15 to 2.91 in 2017–18. It was as close to a controlled experiment as you could get across an entire soccer league, and the conclusion suggested that practicing set pieces would only add to a team's total goal tally.

"Critics initially suggested that FCM only scored as much as they did on set pieces because Danish teams were bad at defending them, but the Danes were fine at defending them *before* we found an edge," Knutson said. "And it's not like the whole league could become bad at defending one phase of the game at the same time."

Midtjylland has brought in former NFL and NBA coaches to discuss play design. And for all of its immeasurable dynamism, when the ball does stop moving, the sport really does start to resemble the average NFL play or NBA out-of-bounds play. Unlike in possession play, which is pretty much determined by general managerial direction and the on-the-fly decisions of the players, when there's a set play, the team decides what to do, how they're going to try to score. The taker attempts to serve the ball to a certain area—with a specific foot, spin, and trajectory—while the other players make a series of predetermined runs in an attempt to open up space.

Knowing the value they can create from these moments, Midtjylland even hired a "kicking coach" to improve the way certain players deliver the ball into the penalty area. They also hired a "throw-in coach." Traditionally, things like "kicking" and "throwing" were taken for granted. You weren't playing professional soccer if you couldn't kick a ball or take a throw-in. *What's next? A coach to teach them how to tie their cleats?* But Midtjylland's set-piece program was so successful that their throw-in coach, Thomas Grønnemark, was hired by Liverpool right after FCM won the Champions League. Andy Gray, a voice of the old-school establishment (who lost his job as a commentator at Sky Sports after making sexist comments about a female assistant-referee), didn't handle the news well. "Here is a lesson," he said during a broadcast for his new employer, beIN Sports. "Pick the ball up, take it behind your head, throw it to a teammate and keep both feet on the ground. I have got a new one. I want to be the first kick-off coach." Liverpool proceeded to win their first-ever Premier League title during Grønnemark's first season with the club.

"There are normally between 40 and 60 throw-ins in a match," Grønnemark said. "So, there'll be like 15 to 20 minutes in the match that are affected by the things you're doing with the throw-ins. For me, that's not marginal gains. It's more like a big part of the game that has just been underestimated." He added, "Most of the teams have a really low quality on the throw-in, and the reason why is a lack of knowledge." According to Knutson, employing a coach like Grønnemark pays for itself. "Say you *only* create additional set-piece goals from implementing a long-throw program, and you create five new goals per season. That would equate to around £15 million in additional value per season off a phase of the game where most teams get nothing."

* * *

If you're searching for soccer's cutting edge, the international game is no longer the place to look—unless you're looking when the ball stops moving. The best coaches are attracted to the club game for two reasons: (1) The jobs typically pay more, and (2) you can actually coach. In international soccer, teams gather just a handful of times a year, during FIFA-mandated breaks in the club calendar, and they rarely ever play more than 20 matches over a 365-day stretch. This makes it all but impossible for managers to institute any kind of cohesive and effective playing style because there's barely any practice time and the players just don't have enough time to develop any kind of on-field chemistry. On top of this, club teams can pick from a much larger pool of players than a national team, making it easier to find better players or players who better fit the team's preferred approach. The technical and tactical precision on display in a given weekend in the Premier League or a weekday in the Champions League now dwarfs what you see every four years at the World Cup or the European Championship.

However, scarcity has bred at least one form of innovation. Perhaps because they know they can't implement any kind of beautiful, free-flowing attacking structure with their limited practice time, international managers have been less wed to the faulty theorem that training set pieces will make you worse at everything else. At the 2018 World Cup, 70 set-piece goals were scored—43 percent of all the goals at the tournament, making up the biggest share since 1966. (For the 2020–21 season, just 29 percent of all the goals in Europe's Big Five leagues came from dead-ball situations.) England manager Gareth Southgate studied NFL and NBA play-design before the tournament, and the Three Lions scored nine set-piece goals in Russia, more than any team since 1966. Then, at the Euro 2020 in 2021 (the pandemic did some weird things to naming conventions) surprise semifinalists Denmark and champions Italy both employed set-piece coaches who had previously worked for Matthew Benham.

Ultimately, only about 1.8 percent of set pieces lead to goals, while corner kicks in particular are converted around 2.5 percent of the time. Some clubs and coaches will also look at those numbers and conclude, *Nah, not worth our time*. Except, that's wrong for two reasons. The first: "This is the problem that arises when people do studies on the effectiveness of set pieces," said Euan Dewar, an analyst who has performed a significant amount of public work on set plays. "A lot of teams (most, even) could be doing better, so using them as the basis for how useful set pieces could possibly be is going to lead you astray." And the second: The average open-play possession leads to a goal only

1.1 percent of the time. So, even with un-optimal execution across the world, set plays are still significantly more likely to create a goal than your average settled possession.

While throw-ins and free kicks can essentially occur anywhere on the field and require different movements and skillsets to be deemed a success, all corner kicks take place in the same spot. And barring some late-game situations where a side wants to waste time, the team that's attempting the corner is trying to score. This also provides a somewhat controlled environment for study. What kinds of corners work best? And if you're watching a game at home, how might you tell if you're watching a team that understands the value of these situations?

Power and Dewar agree that in-swinging corners, balls that are curving back toward the goal and thus taken by a lefty from the right corner, and vice versa, are preferable to out-swingers. In-swingers end up in the net 2.7 percent of the time, out-swingers 2.2, according to Power's research. There's a mental trick in there, though. The average out-swinger leads to a *shot* more often (20.9 percent of the time, compared to 18.6 percent for in-swingers) and that might fool a coach into thinking it's the better option. Since an out-swinger is bending *away* from the goal, it's bending toward the attackers. That makes it easier for them to get to the ball first, but it leads to attempts that are significantly farther away from the goal than when an attacker connects from an in-swinger.

These aren't hard-and-fast rules, but in general, it's also preferable to aim for the near post rather than the far post. The theory behind it is easy to follow: The farther the ball travels, the more defenders it has to clear and the more time the defenders have to react to its movement. The other benefit of a corner to the near post is the potential for a flick-on, where an attacker runs across the face of the defense—into the space they're not worried about defending—and then slightly redirects the angle of the ball to an on-rushing teammate elsewhere in the box. From Power's research, 4.8 percent of flick-ons lead to goals, as opposed to just two percent from direct shots. In fact, shots from any second ball are more likely to lead to goals (2.5 percent) than a shot directly from the pass from the corner.

Given the likelihood of a goal from a scramble, a flick-on, or a cleared ball pumped back into the box, the short corner—when two players go over to the corner flag and one passes the ball to the other as if to resume a posses-sion sequence resembling open play—is the bane of Power's existence. "I'm a complete advocate against using short corners," he said. "They are a waste of time." Dewar disagrees. At least, he thinks it's worth sending two men over to the flag: "Short-corners are somewhat underrated. You have the possibility to take a defender out of the box and/or create a 2v1 outside the box. There's lots of potential there." The crude math checks out. If a player is taking a corner by himself, there's no one marking him. If two players stand by the corner and only one defender follows, they could use that numerical advantage to create an opportunity from closer to the goal. And if *two* defenders follow the two attackers to prevent that 2-on-1 situation, then you've shifted the numbers inside the box in your favor.

One reason why some teams just opt to play the ball short and keep possession is that they don't want the *other* team to clear the ball and go score at the other end. You think you're close to going up a goal and then *bam, counterattack*. Fifteen seconds later, you're the one that's losing. Moments like that feel incredibly demoralizing, but much like, say, going for it on fourth and short and failing to convert, the math makes it worth it. Teams concede goals from their *own* corners only 0.2 percent of the time—one goal for every 500 corners. "Genuinely less than 1 percent of all corners result in a *shot* for the other team, not a goal," Power said. "It's insanity to be worried about conceding a goal from your own set piece."

Defending corners is also riddled by these perceptive biases. When a team scores from a corner with a shot that sneaks in at the post, there's one obvious solution to the problem: Have a defender standing on both posts. Except, Power found that teams that put players on both posts conceded goals more often (2.8 percent of the time) than if they had only one or zero players resting against the woodwork. Fewer players on the posts means more players to defend the corner means fewer goals conceded. "It's all about that spacing," Power said. "So when you have more players on the posts, there's more space in the box to exploit."

And if you've watched, say, 10 or more soccer games at some point over the past decade, you've probably seen a team score from a corner at least once and you've probably heard an announcer bemoan the idea of "zonal marking" at least once. For most of the sport's history, teams defended corners via man-to-man marking—pick an attacker, follow him around, beat him to the ball. But over the past 15 or 20 years, some sides have employed a zonal strategy, whereby defenders guard the space, rather than players. That occasionally leads to an attacker scoring a goal without a defender near him. Seems bad! But it ignores the other times a zonal system prevented a goal that a man-marking system might've allowed. Except, this isn't a case of the new school triumphing over the old. Overall, there's zero statistical difference whatsoever between using zonal or man-to-man marking.

* * *

If you're an aspiring analyst, it's in your best interest to say that soccer clubs are stupid and need to hire people who can make them smarter. If you work for a consultancy, then you're not necessarily going to be in the business of pointing out the *limitations* of applying data-based analysis if you're running a team. If you've created a new stat, conducted a study, or whipped up some kind of unique data-visualization, you're probably not going to spend your time questioning whether or not the thing you've created actually has any real-life applications that would help a soccer team play better soccer. The person writing this book has his own incentives, too. If soccer was just purely following the *Moneyball* narrative—a stodgy, ancient institution ignoring clear, obvious, and actionable evidence of a better way to do things—on a 20-year delay, this would be a lot simpler. *Everyone who works in soccer is blinded by tradition. Let us now praise these brave disruptors!* It is, of course, not that simple.

Every time I've spoken to him, Luke Bornn has made a point of pointing this out. "People who are analysts have very clear incentives to say everyone should be using data because they want to grow their space," he said. "They want to sell more product, they want to make themselves more hirable."

It's certainly not bad for business that Rasmus Ankersen is quoted in newspaper stories and books about his team's alternative approach to soccer and how well it's worked. That's, you know, the kind of symbiotic writer-source relationship that sports journalism was built on. But when I asked him why he was willing to talk to me about what Midtjylland were doing, he pointed to two specific things.

"Part of the reason why I'm talking is to attract talent to the club," Ankersen said. "I know that I can't know every analytical talent or every talent that has a great idea. I know a lot of these great ideas in football, they develop in the underground environments, someone who's done a really interesting study in his bedroom for two years could come up with something that can actually have a big impact and I would never know. I want to get in touch with talent, so partly I'm telling this story to connect with those guys."

In addition to marketing for the club, Ankersen and Midtjylland simply don't think anyone else can do it as well as them. They're not wrong, either; in addition to all of Midtjylland's success, Brentford was promoted to the Premier League in 2021. And we'll soon find out if Ankersen's ideas scale up, beyond Benham's brand. He left Brentford and Midtjylland in December to create Sport Republic, an investment firm that purchased Premier League club Southampton with the backing of Serbian telecoms billionaire Dragan Šolak. Ankersen will serve as club chairman, and he'll once again face the challenge he had to overcome in Denmark: It's one thing to have these new ideas about how soccer should work and how to win games, but actually implementing them at a club and getting your employees and coaches and players to buy in is a totally different challenge that requires a totally different set of skills.

"There are the IQ guys and the EQ guys," he said. "The IQ guys are the geeks that crunch the data and then you have the EQ guys, who are traditional football people who've been in the game for a long time and trust that gut feeling and the experience, the intuition. There's a big gap between those two—and there's a lot of arrogance on both sides of the table. There's a lot of arrogance from the traditional football guys because they're not open enough to new ways of evaluating players, using data as an integrated part of the football operation. But there's also a lot of arrogance on the other side of the table because they tend to overvalue what stats and analytics can tell you. They end up answering questions that no one else has asked. You need to have someone managing that process that understands the strengths of both worlds and then connects it. We've been successful because we have a respect for the traditional side of things and also for what the eyes and the ears actually can bring." He continued: "The media wants a sharp, clear story and yes we've been radical in some ways compared to how traditional football acts, but it's not that we are all about stats and we don't do any of the other stuff. We do. But nothing we've developed over the past few years happens without a better understanding of how to balance subjective methods with objective methods."

The ideas and the models, which Ankersen would *not* reveal, aren't the hard part.

"It's not easy to copy an idea really well," Ankersen said. "A lot of things we do? It's not rocket science. It's not something that you need 10 PhDs to come up with, but implementation is really difficult. Getting people behind an idea and creating buy-in and ownership across the full football corporation is difficult. That's not about stats. That's about human relationships. How do you make people feel part of the strategy? If you don't have that buy-in, then it won't happen, and you won't be successful."

You can try to replicate the experiment. But good luck getting the same results.

CHAPTER SEVEN

BIG TED

About 4,000 people live in De Motte, Indiana, and about 3,840 of them are white. It's one of those midwestern towns that exists for no reason other than "it's been a while since the last stop, let's put a railroad station here." The town was named after Mark De Motte, a colonel in the Union army and a one-term US congressman. Every year, the town celebrates something called "Touch of Dutch," your standard small-town parade-plus-festival, just with some miniature windmills and wooden shoes added in. Ted Knutson remembers people talking about how his hometown once held the Guinness World Record for the most churches per capita, but I have been unable to confirm that fact. "We're out in the cornfields, and you don't have a lot of choice," he said. As for soccer? "We didn't have it."

In Paris, they have plenty of it. Were someone able to figure out a way to codify the idea, the Île-de-France, as Greater Paris is known, would probably hold the Guinness World Record for world-class soccer players per capita. At the 2018 World Cup in Russia, 15 of the players on the French squad were from Paris, while other cities produced no more than 10 for their respective countries. Per an analysis by the sociologist Darko Dukić, the estimated transfer value of those Parisian players was €483 million; players from Buenos Aires were next at €180 million. Across the five World Cups from 2002 through 2018, 60 of the players were Parisians—10 more than were from Buenos Aires.

Except, this is a relatively new phenomenon—both within France and within the history of European soccer. While there are all kinds of socialistic methods to maintain competition and redistribute wealth and talent across the major American sports, the best teams still tend to be the ones in the biggest and richest cities. Across the NBA, MLB, NFL, NHL, and MLS, the city with the most championships is New York, followed by Boston, Los Angeles, and Chicago. Boston is the outlier, perhaps, but New York, Los Angeles, and Chicago are the three biggest cities in the country. Drafts, salary caps, equal distributions of TV revenue? They haven't prevented the talent from trickling toward the biggest markets.

Given that European soccer has no draft, distributes TV revenue unequally, and limits spending only as a percentage of overall revenue, you might expect the list of champions to read like a list of the richest cities on the continent: Paris, London, Moscow. Yet, those three cities have combined for only two Champions League titles—and the first one didn't come until 2008. Throw in the likes of Rome, Istanbul, and Berlin, and the number stays stuck at two. Meanwhile, the city of Liverpool has five, Manchester has three, Porto and Nottingham each have two, while Birmingham, Rotterdam, and Dortmund each have one. Not quite De Motte, Iowa, but not quite the fashion or economic capitals of Europe, either. Remember how the best early English clubs sprang up around factories? This happened all throughout Europe, in smaller industrial towns. The presence of a soccer club gave people in these towns an identity that cities like London didn't need. And so these teams from these secondary European cities were much more successful as soccer was first codified into a professional game and eventually unified across Europe. And a lot of them are still holding on to that advantage. "Manchester United became arguably the most popular club on earth largely because Manchester had been the first industrial city on earth," Joshua Kuper and Stefan Szymanski write in *Soccernomics*. "The club is only the biggest local soccer relic of that era."

For someone with trillions of dollars, this would be a clear inefficiency to exploit. What handsome, fit, 20-something soccer star *wouldn't* want to live in Paris? In the richest and most talented soccer city in the world, the biggest club wasn't founded until 1970. Paris Saint-Germain didn't win their first league title until 1986, and over the following 25 years, they won only once more. Up until about 10 years ago, they were a middling club—at best. And then came the Qataris. In 2011, the now-ruler of Qatar, Tamim bin Hamad Al Thani, purchased a 70 percent stake in PSG through Qatar Sports Investments, a subsidiary of the state's $300-billion sovereign wealth fund. A year later, QSI bought out the remaining 30 percent of the club. This is the part of the story where European soccer becomes a shell game for power politics in the Middle East. The Qataris didn't buy PSG to make money; whatever revenues are produced by the club aren't even a drop in the bucket of the hundreds of billions of dollars they're working from. No, they bought the team to give the world a better picture of Qatar, a country where forced labor of immigrants is the norm and same-sex relations are subject to capital punishment (although there have been no recorded cases of such). "Our aim is to make the club an institution respected around the world," PSG chairman Nasser Al-Khelaifi said in 2017. "If we are going to make that happen, we have to win the Champions League."

The only constraints on QSI's spending were UEFA's Financial Fair Play (FFP) regulations, which say that a club can spend only a certain amount in excess of its revenues. The rules were theoretically designed to prevent smaller clubs from overspending and then going bust, but for legacy teams, like Manchester United and Liverpool, they had the added benefit of preventing more hyper-speed takeovers like PSG's, Manchester City's, and Chelsea's. However, these are only "rules" in the most loosely defined sense of the word. Documents obtained by the Portuguese whistle-blower Rui Pinto, a collection known colloquially as "Football Leaks," suggest that Abu Dhabi and Qatar artificially increased Manchester City's and PSG's revenues by more than $1 billion through things like state-based sponsorship deals where the club owner was essentially paying the club in order to sponsor the club it already owned. However, neither club has suffered any serious consequences. And within a year, PSG had won its first title of the QSI era—and then they won six of the next eight. They acquired big-name talents like Zlatan Ibrahimović and Thiago Silva from AC Milan, and they had as much money as anyone, but they still seemed to exist in a tier below the likes of Real Madrid, Bayern Munich, and Barcelona—the three super-clubs that dominated European soccer in the second decade of the 21st century. With France being the "poorest" of Europe's five major leagues, domestic titles became a fait accompli, but the team never advanced beyond the quarterfinals of the Champions League.

Then, in the summer of 2017, PSG shocked the world. First, they acquired Brazilian superstar Neymar from Barcelona for €222 million, which was more than double the previous transfer record of €105 million, paid by Manchester United in 2016 to acquire midfielder Paul Pogba from Italian club Juventus. Beyond the sheer sticker shock, this move disrupted the established food chain: Barcelona bought *your* players; you didn't buy theirs. Neymar was seen as the heir apparent to the best player in the world, his Barcelona teammate Lionel Messi. But PSG didn't stop there. A couple of days later they bought the next-next-best player in the world—also shattering the previous transfer record (€180 million) to acquire the then-18-year-old Paris-born striker Kylian Mbappé, who'd just led Monaco to a shocking first-place finish ahead of PSG thanks to an astonishing 15 goals and 7 assists in just 17 league starts. (Don't worry, the expected-goals data backed it up, too.) If you can't beat 'em, buy 'em.

With Neymar and Mbappé in tow, PSG easily reclaimed the Ligue 1 title, but things didn't get any better in Europe. Despite winning their group with a plus-21 goal differential over six matches, they didn't even reach the quarters this time, losing 5–2 across two games to the two-time defending champs Real Madrid. Even worse than the result was how it happened: Neymar, purchased for the sole competitive reason of winning this tournament, missed the second match—basically, the only match that mattered for PSG that season—due to injury. It was a lesson in the dangers of building a soccer team around two players; sometimes they get hurt or have a bad game, and *poof*, your season's over. So, the following summer—after Mbappé and his six fellow Parisians led France to a World Cup victory in Russia—PSG went after another superstar. They brought in Ted Knutson.

* * *

When Knutson first left De Motte, he ended up in Norman, Oklahoma. He'd scored well enough on his exams to earn a National Merit Scholarship, awarded by a nonprofit program that started in 1955 with the goal of essentially identifying the highest-achieving high schoolers in the United States and ensuring they could afford to attend whatever school they wanted. Past winners include multiple Nobel Prize winners, two US Supreme Court justices, that angry money guy from CNBC, Bill Gates, Jeff Bezos, and the author of the *Twilight* series. But amid the deregulated, no-rules-just-vibes, free-market good times of the 1990s, there was one catch: To actually get the full scholarship, you needed to find a corporate sponsor. De Motte didn't have many of those, so Knutson enrolled in the University of Oklahoma, where school officials made a point of recruiting and sponsoring National Merit Scholars who were unable to find a corporate sponsor.

OU launched its women's soccer program while Knutson was there, but the school has never had a men's program. It was and still is a football school and a football state. But Knutson fell into soccer in the same way that so many Americans did in the late '90s and early 2000s: through World Cups and video games.

"I really started paying attention at World Cup 1998," he said. "I was finishing up my degree and working for UPS at night. I was on the ten thirty to two thirty A.M. shift loading trucks, and then during the daytime you'd be like, 'Well, I got nothing to do,' and it was like, 'Well the World Cup's on,' and that was an awesome World Cup. And then we picked up *International Superstar Soccer* in '98 on the Nintendo 64 and that combination of two things locked me in."

Although you might think someone who won a Merit Scholarship and worked the night shift while in school was industrious, Knutson likes to tell a different story about his college years. He started out as a biochemistry major, but he didn't understand why he wasn't getting credit for all the extra lab work; he'd get the credits for three hours' worth of class like you would across any discipline, but then he was spending 15 extra hours in a lab and getting no credit in return. English majors weren't doing that!

"There's a common thread from me: Up to a certain point I was very lazy," he said. "At that time, I should have switched to computer science, which I kind of knew, but it would have taken me an extra year to finish school, and again: lazy. But it was obvious, and I was like, 'Yeah but I could also finish school and switch to something else.' So I switched to politics and economics, and I got a scholarship to Emory University for PhD work to do international political economy."

Once he left OU, Knutson's life entered that kind of turn-of-the-century phase that doesn't seem possible anymore: manic slackerism. As we spoke, his brain rattled back and forth from job to job, major life decision to major life decision, city to city—a crackling stream of consciousness of just, *you know, whatever, man.* He dropped out of Emory after a year "partly because I

was depressed, and partly because my ex was at Harvard Div[inity School]."
This was during the tech boom, so Knutson got a job doing tech support for a
company called Peachtree Software, and then quickly transitioned into doing
more technical work: building and administering databases. "At that point, I
was already making more than the professor who was teaching me," he said.
Of course, then his ex got into a PhD program at the University of Virginia,
and "I was like, Charlottesville's pretty cool, I'm up for this." He got a job at a
pharmaceutical company with a "crazy boss," so he eventually quit. Then, *boom*,
the tech crash. No jobs. So he started delivering pizzas and worked for a little
while at a community theater, and after months spent cleaning and organizing
to the tunes of *The Magic Flute* and *South Pacific*, he got the first job that really
set him off on the path to where he is today: managing a website that focused
on a fantasy card game called *Magic: The Gathering*.

To the uninitiated, *Magic* might look like the kind of game for which you
need to own at least one cape in order to play. Every player takes the role of what's
called a "Planeswalker," and they battle the other Planeswalkers by casting spells,
summoning creatures, and transcending various realms. The game is played with
dice and cards. Among the 20,000-plus cards that have been developed since
Magic was founded in the early 1990s, you've got the likes of the Demonic Tutor,
Jace the Mind Sculptor, and Deathrite Shaman. There's a card called "Recurring
Nightmare" and then my personal favorite: the Ashen Ghoul.

To be clear, you absolutely *can* wear a cape to play *Magic: The Gathering*,
and the fantasy-lore aspect of the cards has certainly played a role in the game's
global popularity. Estimates put the number of worldwide *Magic* players in the
tens of millions. But being able to summon a glowing angel or a putrid-looking
snake-beast isn't what drew Knutson to the game.

"Some people think of it as the best strategic game ever invented," he said.
"It's got elements of chess in the tactical elements, but it changes all the time,
and you get to choose the things that are in and out of your deck. Most people
are at least a little familiar with a Pokémon or a Hearthstone these days, but
back in the day it'd be like chess with Dungeons and Dragons mixed into it."

Magic was invented by a PhD in combined mathematics named Richard
Garfield for a company called Wizards of the Coast, which was owned by a
systems analyst at Boeing. The game was very clearly *engineered*, with the fantasy
aspect serving as nothing more than the narrative trappings for the functionality

of the pure game that sits at its core. Each participant brings their own deck of cards to the game. You'd buy them in packs, like sports cards, or you could trade or go to a shop and pay a premium for specific desirable cards. Players then play their cards in turn, as they attempt to kill all 20 of their opponent's lives. Some of the cards, however, allowed you to *change* the rules of the game as you played, which served two reinforcing purposes: (1) It meant every single *Magic* match was its own unique series of events, and (2) it drove people to buy more cards so they could change the rules in a new way.

"*Magic* is really good at training people to play poker, because it's a more complicated version of poker, with slightly less human reading," Knutson said. "Plenty of the people who were great *Magic* players have gone on to run hedge funds. And now you look at it 20 years on, many of them are major players in the biggest adjustable market of entertainment that exists: computer gaming. The other thing it's really good at it is teaching you to do professional gambling, including sports betting."

Choosing a team? Managing your pre-set tactics? Adapting to an ever-changing infrastructural fluidity as you make your decisions? Sounds like another game, too.

* * *

Gambling on sports, it turns out, is more lucrative than casting spells—or at least it was. *Magic* led Knutson first to a sports-betting syndicate, where he and two other guys would make a living by outsmarting the betting markets. In the early to mid-aughts it was still easy to make a number of sizable bets through one of the various offshore Internet sportsbooks. Knutson and his partners found their biggest edge not by discovering new knowledge about the way sports worked but by uncovering some bad math from the bookies and hammering away at it as often as they could. In the NFL and NBA, every game has at least a spread, a money line, and a total. The spread represents how much the market expects a team to win by, the money line represents the score-agnostic probability of a team winning, and the total represents the combined number of points the teams are expected to score. In a sound market, those three numbers have a nearly airtight relationship: The amount a team is expected to win by when compared to the overall number of points expected to be scored in a game is just another way of representing their overall probability of winning.

"The world was just wrong about the equivalent values of all sorts of things," Knutson said. "One classic example is 'What should the money line equal based off of this spread and this total in the NBA?' It's basic probabilities really: How likely is this team to win outright based on the more important number? The spread has five times the volume the money line does."

Since more people bet on the spread, that line eventually moved toward a high degree of accuracy thanks to the wonder of the wisdom of the crowds, but the money line wouldn't always react along with it. So Knutson and his partners would use that information to figure out which side was being undervalued on the money line and then bet away. They used the market to beat the market. They also figured out that markets weren't accounting for the randomness inherent in higher-scoring games. "The higher the total, the more likely there could be other variants inside it because that's the way the sport works," he said.

The house, of course, eventually wins. On October 13, 2006, President George W. Bush signed into law the "Unlawful Internet Gambling Enforcement Act." It was tacked onto a larger bill, called the "SAFE Port Act," which sought to prevent the sale of US-owned ports to foreign entities. The Gambling Act was mainly in response to the poker boom in the US; essentially, it prevented institutions in states where gambling wasn't legal from accepting money from Internet-based, gambling-related businesses. It's a strange bill that tried to prevent a thing from happening without punishing anyone. If you won money on the Internet from playing poker or betting on the Toronto Blue Jays, that was OK. You just had no way of bringing those winnings back into your bank account.

At the time, Knutson had already been doing some consulting work with Pinnacle, a popular sportsbook located in Curaçao. So, a year after the bill was passed, he decided it was time to become the house. The sportsbook hired him, essentially, to close the loopholes he'd been exploiting for the past few years. They also gave him the keys to the sport he'd been mystified by since he picked up that Nintendo 64 controller back at OU. He'd mastered making markets for all the major American sports with their complex rules and high-scoring results, so soccer, where the main rule was you couldn't use your hands and there were only four goals in a match if you were lucky, would be simple.

Or not.

Knutson's job—and the job of any line-maker—is to both attract bets and win money. It's a tricky line to walk because, as logic suggests, one way to attract bets is to offer bettors favorable lines that will then make *them* money and not you.

"In soccer, Asia was in control of the markets. They had way more information than us and we got absolutely killed in the first two months. My first day at work I lost $68,000, which at the time was the entirety of a year's income at any other job that I'd ever had. I think I went home and played [the soccer simulation game] *Football Manager* for eight hours before I went to bed, and then the next day too, because I thought I was not able to handle this."

After a rough couple of months, one of Knutson's bosses straightened him out. The new task: Learn how these markets work—what wins games, how likely a draw is, and how it all affects the total—and focus on not *losing* any money. Rather than trying to totally outsmart whatever was going on in Asia, Pinnacle focused on attracting bettors by adding more options, allowing bettors to place moneyline bets on specific scorelines or totals for a single half. And by creating more options, they were creating new markets where they were suddenly the ones with the deepest knowledge of how things worked. Essentially, Knutson had created the same situation that existed for him when he was the one trying to beat the house; he'd just flipped it inside out.

As he explains: "Say you've got a game where Manchester United are at home to somebody good, say Chelsea, and they are exactly 50 percent to win at home. What are they to win at one goal? Or a minus-one handicap? There are all these equivalences inside of that, probabilistic ways that this can happen, and as the total moves, that changes things. The lower the total, the more likely a draw is to happen. There's real mathematical complexity inside of trading this sport now, and you have to build models around it looking at the past way that this has gone, but you also have to have people who are pretty smart on top of it saying, 'Actually, things are changing on the ground and what should we do when these situations happen?' So we were able to start learning that and putting all these things together into a more comprehensive package and that really helped the product to grow. That also helped us win against everybody else that was a little bit wrong about these equivalences, which was the same stuff we had done in the American sports."

While learning to properly value the probability of a 2–1 win for Tottenham against Arsenal didn't quite reveal anything new about the inner workings of the Beautiful Game, Knutson did start to understand the outsize value of particular players. It takes only about five minutes of viewing to figure out that Neymar is quite valuable to whatever team he's employed by, but you can't necessarily say the same thing about Ron Vlaar. Well, you don't even really need to watch Ron Vlaar play soccer to know what kind of soccer player he is. Just say his name out loud a couple of times and you'll understand: Ron. Vlaar. All thuds, little nuance. He played a handful of seasons for Aston Villa in the Premier League, where fans referred to him as "Concrete Ron." It was a double-sided nickname: You couldn't run through the guy, but you could pretty easily just run around him. "Ron Vlaar" is a name you might say when you were bored on a Saturday afternoon and you were trying to list off as many random Premier League players from the mid-2010s as you could. *Remember Ron Vlaar? Yeah! But also not really!*

Knutson certainly remembers him, though, because there was a brief stretch of time where Ron Vlaar was one of the most valuable players in the Premier League.

"There was a period where Aston Villa was pretty good," he said. "They used to finish fifth, sixth, regularly, but they could never quite make it up into the Champions League. They were also a bit fragile. And Ron Vlaar was quite a thoughtful and important center back to them. And when Ron Vlaar wasn't in, they just seemed to fall apart. When Vlaar was out, Villa would crumble, and they would be worth so much less than they would be otherwise. And it was weird to find out that a center back could be that valuable."

This wasn't just some back-of-the-napkin math; this was a major sportsbook with a ton of money on the line, adjusting their lines because they were scared of how bad Aston Villa might be without Ron freaking Vlaar. Knutson soon became aware of similar situations across the league. Other bettors found "that a right back or a defensive midfielder can be as valuable as any of the forwards, depending on game style or what the backups look like."

Unlike baseball, soccer is nowhere near achieving a universal kind of value judgment for players—in part because every team is different, both in how they play and in how they're built. If a team wants to play on the counterattack, then the value of a great passer is different to them than it would be to a team that tries to keep the ball for the majority of the match. Meanwhile, a big club like Manchester City might have a roster with stars, two deep, at every position. While Aston Villa will have a much more lopsided distribution of talent.

"Depth is a real issue, and quality depth is a real issue. Sometimes it's sussing out these teams that have young kids. The replacement player looks like they're an 18-year-old nothing—and then turns out to be [Barcelona star] Pedri."

* * *

It's not *quite* accurate to say that a *Magic: The Gathering* blog written by a professional bookmaker would eventually change the way we think about soccer, but something that *was* a *Magic: The Gathering* blog did eventually change the way we think about soccer. The first post on *Mixed kNuts* was a re-post of something Knutson posted on Facebook: an open letter pleading for various *Magic* pros to start acting like adults. Here's how it began: "Look, I like most of you. You're smart, you are probably funny, and many of my best friends were once just like you. That said, some of you made monstrously stupid choices in 2010." His first bullet point of advice: "Grow the fuck up." The post ends with Knutson signing off as "Teddy Card Game" and then urging any readers of the piece to contact him via America Online's Instant Messenger username: cryos23. It's a beautiful, earnest relic of the early Web 2.0 era.

For the first year or so—2011, while he was still working at Pinnacle—the blog remained *Magic*-focused with the occasional post delving into whatever the hell was on Knutson's mind. Slowly, though, soccer started to creep into Knutson's head. He started to pick at whatever numbers he could find, and people on the Internet seemed interested in whatever he had to say about Arsenal's center-forward depth, so the blog gradually shifted toward a balance of something like half-soccer, half-*Magic*. There's an energy to the posts—of someone with a lot of thoughts, a lot of big ideas, but nowhere to put them other than on a WordPress site.

In late 2012, Knutson was diagnosed with testicular cancer. He underwent an initial surgery right around Thanksgiving and began chemotherapy at the start of the new year. Contemplating his own mortality took up only so much of each day, and he didn't know what to do with all of his newfound free time.

"[Pinnacle] wouldn't let me work, which was smart of them," he said. "They should not have let me work. But I didn't know what the fuck to do with myself. And you start having these existential questions around your health. I had two very young children at that point, and so I used it as a way to really start taking my mind off of things but also to dig into some questions, which as you can see had been lingering for a long time. And I finally had the opportunity to begin examining them. At that point, I opened back up into the way you could use these stats, if you were betting. And then, I started to apply *Moneyball* to soccer."

From the beginning of 2013 on, *Mixed kNuts* became a soccer blog. Right around this time, the website WhoScored started publishing a set of very basic team and player stats for most of Europe's top leagues. It wasn't much—shots, tackles, passes, and a few other things—but it was more than enough for savvy modelers and thinkers like Knutson to sink their teeth into. After a half-year of attempting to analyze soccer through the lens of *Moneyball*, he wrote a post summing up what he'd learned. First: "crossing is bad." While David Beckham may have turned bending a perfectly timed ball onto a striker's forehead into a reverential form of pop art, the vast majority of crosses—about 80 percent— didn't even find an attacker. Even the best crossers found a teammate only about 30 percent of the time. Second, and not unrelated: "headers are bad." Although his analysis at the time found that 12 percent of headed shots led to goals, compared to 9 percent of all shots, once you controlled for the location of the shots, a shot with a foot was way more likely to end up in the net.

This might sound obvious. *Wow, kicking the ball into a crowd of opponents, one of whom can use his hands, is a bad idea? And smashing a round ball with a round part of your body that is* above *your eyes doesn't work as well as redirecting it with a body part that you can actually see? No way!* But most of the analytical breakthroughs across sports *are* obvious. In England in particular, wingers and strikers played traditional roles. The wingers tried to dribble past defenders, then they tried to cross the ball into the penalty area so their strikers could score the goals. It was the way things were done because it was the way things were done—and yet here was a guy with a blog, upending multiple decades' worth of orthodoxy.

However, the piece ends on a note of epistemological humility. Another thing that Knutson learned from that half-year: "Football is inherently about percentages." As he wrote, "It's true, and the game does not give a damn whether people care about this or not, because it is imposed as one of the basic structures of playing football. I know that's statty/geeky as hell, but it is a simple, obvious truth. The sooner this is accepted, the sooner people can go about applying the principles to make their teams better." And in order to make the percentages work in your favor, you still have to cross the ball sometimes, still have to hit it with your head, too. "All those things listed above are bad, but . . . you can't just play it on the ground all the time, or your team becomes predictable and easier to stop," he wrote. "Mixed strategies aren't just recommended, they are vital when it comes to success."

At this point, Knutson realized he was on to something. He had a knack for thinking about soccer at a high level. He knew that the use of data and the reversal of tradition had turned the other American sports on their heads; it was almost like he'd been given a peek into the future: Data was going to come for soccer at some point, too, so why shouldn't he be the one to lead the way?

In the summer of 2013, he launched a website called StatsBomb with Benjamin Pugsley. When Knutson started delving into the world of soccer analytics, he'd often stumble across pieces he enjoyed, stuff that slightly shifted the lens through which he viewed the game, but the community was disparate. Anyone could start a blog; not everyone could start a blog that was easy to find. Michael Caley was writing for a Tottenham website. Pugsley was blogging about Manchester City. The cutting-edge analysis wasn't hidden in a Fijian newspaper anymore, but it remained ad hoc; anyone who had new ideas about the sport became a node in a barely connected, undesigned system. The ideas would interact by chance, and anyone who wanted to read the latest analytics piece had to have a comprehensive knowledge of the soccer-data blogosphere. With StatsBomb, Knutson sought to solve that problem.

"For starters, it's going to be a place for analysts to publish their work on a website with a bigger, more regular traffic footprint than their personal blog," Knutson wrote in the site's introductory post. "It's also going to be a place where fans who are interested in this stuff can come every day for useful writing, info, modified league and player tables, etc. At some point in the coming months, we're going to add a forum to the site, and hopefully that will become a bit of [a] community hub in the process. The organization of some of the site will also change pretty regularly as we go along and discover better ways to display and update the information readers are interested in across the various leagues.

"We're going to start with football, but I don't see us as limited to that sport. Cricket will be a natural fit, as will basketball and hockey. And I don't see us limited to just stats either. If the site grows and fans respond, I see StatsBomb growing into a place you can come to for good, thoughtful writing about sports and/or numbers. At the very least, it's a home for at least Ben Pugsley and I to dump all the stuff we've been working on that doesn't live anywhere else. This includes my player analytics work, and Ben's extremely useful stats transforms. At the very best, it could become something special."

* * *

Over its first year, StatsBomb was a lot of the things Knutson hoped it would be. While the site remained relatively low-fi and never came to include the kinds of searchable stats databases that really drive traffic and keep curious minds on the site, it was the only public-facing, English-language publication that sought to question everything we thought we knew about soccer. They'd break down transfers. They'd suggest transfers. They'd write about the weekend's games. They'd criticize lazy writing from elsewhere. And they'd ask questions: How do players age? How important is the placement of a shot on the goal frame? How does home field advantage differ in MLS, where players are traveling more miles and not on chartered flights, compared to the major European leagues? How do goals change the way teams approach the rest of the match? What does it mean to be a "good" passer?

StatsBomb published something close to an article per day that first year. There was a demand in both directions: writers and analysts who wanted to think about the game differently, and readers who wanted to learn and hear something new. The site was an immediate success, but it eventually raised a familiar problem: What do I do now? Knutson was working on StatsBomb while employed at Pinnacle. Could StatsBomb remain a hobby? It seemed likely to get only more and more popular. Could he quit his job and do the site full-time? Neither possibility seemed like a good option. And then came Cesc.

Knutson is an Arsenal fan. Like all Arsenal fans, he hates his team but also has an undying faith that the good old days still might one day return. Arsène Wenger vaulted Arsenal to the top of the Premier League by focusing on three different things: He signed players who weren't English, he forced his players to stop eating pizza and drinking so much beer, and he encouraged them to pass the ball. It must be getting annoying at this point, but I'll say it again: Though incredibly basic today, all three ideas were unheard of at the time. Thanks to Wenger's innovations, Arsenal fans got to root for a special collection of continental players who played a thrilling, new type of soccer. However, as Wenger insisted on never overpaying to acquire players, the club got left in the dust by the old money of Manchester United and the new money of Chelsea and Manchester City. Soon, everyone was doing the things Wenger did, but they were doing them better and with more money. In the 2003–04 season, Arsenal became the first and only team to go undefeated across a 38-game Premier League season. They're known as "The Invincibles"—and they haven't won a Premier League title since.

The following year, a 17-year-old Spaniard named Cesc Fàbregas became a full-time starter for the Gunners. This was one of Wenger's final innovations. After just winning the league, he handed the keys of his midfield—at the time, still the province of bruising, athletic types—to a slight, skillful foreigner. Cesc quickly became one of the best players in the league. He played seven seasons for Arsenal before moving back to the club he played for at the youth level: Barcelona. He posted a trio of statistically impressive seasons at the Catalan club—nine non-penalty goals and seven assists, 11 and 12, and 8 and 14—but he also had the misfortune of joining right after arguably the most impressive three-year stretch in the modern history of the sport, when Barca won three La Liga titles in a row and two out of three Champions Leagues. With Cesc back at the club, they won just one league title and no Champions Leagues, so he became an easy target within the fanbase and the club hierarchy. In a bizarre post on the club's website announcing Cesc's departure, Barcelona wrote: "Despite glowing starts to each campaign, Cesc's contributions to the cause gradually decreased as each season drew to a close. From being someone who joined in with the attack, supplying and scoring goals, the magic tended to fade later on in each season. He only scored one, six, and one goals in the last 24 games of each season. For some reason, he was never as good in the second half of a season as in the first."

Fàbregas and his people knew he wasn't the problem, despite what some press releases might say. But they knew he needed to leave Barcelona if he wanted to remain a consistent starter through the tail end of his prime. Goals and assists, though, didn't seem to be enough to convince his current employer of his value, and so Cesc Fàbregas needed someone who could convince the world of just how good Cesc Fàbregas still was.

"He was coming out of Barcelona and it was World Cup time," Knutson said. "I worked with his people to put together an explanatory package: that he's going to be really quite good when he comes back, and these are all the reasons he's going to be quite good. He ended up at Chelsea. It was fun to see the media leaks and rumors that you knew were lies because you knew that he did not have that meeting or that conversation."

In June of 2014, Chelsea gave Cesc a five-year deal, which paid off almost immediately. In his first season with the club, Fàbregas recorded what was then the second-most assists in Premier League history (18) and Chelsea won the Premier League by nine points. They then won the league again, two years later. That season, Fàbregas averaged 0.81 assists per 90 minutes; no one else in the league was above 0.53.

While clubs have remained slow to adopt evidence-based decision-making processes, players haven't had the same problem. Getting an entire organization to start believing in expected goals requires buy-in from, well, everyone. When it comes to contract negotiations for players, no such friction exists. If fancy stats suggest that a player should be paid more money, then why wouldn't the player want to bring those fancy stats to the bargaining table? Players have continued to approach Knutson about similar work: Show me the numbers that show me that I'm great. In his latest contract negotiations with Manchester City, Kevin De Bruyne eschewed a traditional agent and instead employed the service of data consultancies to show City how he compared to the best players in Europe at his position and how his potential departure would affect the team's odds of winning the Premier League. His teammate Raheem Sterling did the same when he was at Liverpool. In his age-18 season, Sterling broke out with nine non-penalty goals and five assists. Those are impressive numbers on their own—0.57 goals+assists per 90 minutes, where 0.5 or more is above average—but the list of players who have done that at age 18 doubles as a list of the best players in the world. It's people like Lionel Messi and Neymar. Liverpool wanted to continue paying Sterling like a promising teenager; the numbers showed Sterling what he really was: already a star, on the verge of exploding into superstardom. City bought Sterling for $70 million in summer 2015. He's become one of the best players in the world, and City have won the Premier League title in four of his eight seasons at the club.

"Players are now looking at this stuff and wanting to understand more about their perceived value in the market and also to give themselves comparisons," Knutson said. "Can I find out information about how some of the best center backs play? Because I'm pretty sure I'm one of them. Can you tell me if I'm one of them? And what should I get paid based off of that information?"

If this all happened in the US, 15 years earlier, and with a different sport, Knutson likely would've been scooped up by a professional team. Provided he didn't piss anyone off too much, he likely would've gradually made his way up the front-office ranks as the team hired more and more people who thought like him. The other thing that would've happened: StatsBomb would've been scrubbed from the Internet. Knutson's employer would've made sure that his knowledge would be useful only to them. RIP *Mixed kNuts*, too.

Soon after the Cesc deal went through, Knutson *was* hired by a team. That's when Matthew Benham brought him in to serve as head of player analytics for both Brentford and Midtjylland. One of Knutson's requirements, however, was that StatsBomb continue to exist and its archives remain in place. The site slowed down for a couple of months while Knutson was gone, but then an amateur analyst named James Yorke came in to revive the site. The quality and the quantity were roughly the same; there was just no Ted.

Knutson lasted in the club game for two years before returning to StatsBomb. Mainstream English soccer culture did not take kindly to the brash, number-crunching University of Oklahoma grad invading their world. "Brentford's analysis department is one of the best in English football, yet Knutson had been imposed on it, above an existing structure," wrote the journalist Michael Calvin in his book *Living on the Volcano: The Secrets of Surviving as a Football Manager.* "He was so unversed in the ways of football that on a rare visit to the training ground he created a stir by choosing to lean against a goalpost to watch a practice match. To players and coaches, that lapse in protocol is the equivalent of mooning the Queen."

It's not that Knutson necessarily wanted to stop mooning the Queen. He just realized it was a lot easier to do it if you weren't inside Buckingham Palace.

* * *

After leaving Benham's employ, Knutson went back to StatsBomb and turned the site into a consultancy. The blog remained, but it served as a marketing arm of sorts—a précis for StatsBomb's way of thinking, a brief glimpse into what you could pay them to do for you. In a sense, Midtjylland and Brentford were the worst places for Knutson to work; their processes were already established; out of any club in the world, those two were the ones who would least benefit from having his brain in the room.

In addition to his work with players, coaches had begun to approach Knutson about his writing, too. Thomas Tuchel, who was in between jobs in Germany and would go on to take Paris Saint-Germain to the Champions League final in 2020 and then win the whole thing with Chelsea in 2021, was fascinated by the idea of creating higher-probability chances and figuring out how to do it. You can see it in the way his teams play now, too: Tuchel's sides tend to attempt fewer shots than Europe's other big clubs, but the shots themselves are almost always of a higher quality. Roger Schmidt, formerly the coach of Bayer Leverkusen in Germany, was also interested in Knutson's work. His team played arguably the most frenetic style of any modern team in a major European league. They fired off shots at will, quickly shifting the ball upfield or even shooting directly from a turnover. They paired that with an aggressive pressing approach that attempted to quickly win the ball back in the opposition half so they could shoot some more. Michael Caley wrote an analysis of Schmidt's team, in which he discovered the rough value of a pressing system. While the average possession led to a shot just 2 out of 100 times, possessions that began with a turnover near midfield in the center of the opposition half were *10 times* more likely to lead to a shot. "I showed Roger that, and he got really excited about it," Knutson said. In 2015, Knutson discussed set-play strategy with then New York Red Bulls coach Jesse Marsch. "The year after we talked about that, Sacha Kljestan had 20 assists or something absurd in MLS, and they scored infinite set-piece goals."

Even if you couldn't convince an entire organization to adopt your philosophy and even if the soccer world as a whole was boulder-like in its resistance to change, there were still curious people everywhere, at every club, at every team. A consultancy was the way to reach them—and a way to get them to give you money. With the help of Yorke and some others, Knutson pretty quickly started working with clubs across the world—giving them advice on whom to sign and what coaches to consider hiring. Most people ignored them, some listened, and even fewer acted on their advice. One MLS club asked StatsBomb to do an analysis of three players they were considering signing. StatsBomb wrote up their analyses and sent back the same verdict on each guy: Don't sign him. Except, that's not what the club wanted. You see, they'd already signed all three players, and they didn't *really* want an honest assessment of their abilities. No, they just wanted some numbers that would make their new signings look good. *Could you guys make that happen, please?*

Along the way, Knutson continued to develop the broad outlines of his theory for the right way to play the game. To start, get good at set plays. "If you don't show up prepared for set pieces, that's criminal negligence for your job and you should be fired," Knutson said. "You're just really dumb, and that's not the way to do this." And when you're not attempting to flummox a defense with pre-set patterns and precise dead-ball passing, you should run, run, and run. Unlike a coach who, as Luke Bornn pointed out, may have developed his theory for how to win games from a succession of random events that caused goals to be scored, Knutson developed his theories with an open mind. He wanted to know what won games so people could pay him to tell *them* what won games. And based on what he's seen, pressing the opposition in their defensive third is the way to go. The advantages are twofold: (1) If you win the ball back, you're winning it against a formation of players who are aligned to attack and not defend. It creates gaps in the defensive structure that wouldn't be there otherwise. And (2) it keeps the action far away from your goal, where bad things can happen.

"We're pretty sure that pressing is the most high expected-value system, but it's got the highest costs and you have to be willing to either enforce that across your whole club and say, 'This is our ethos,' or you have to have a fallback, a second alternative," he said. "I think this is actually pretty important in seasons where you have a ton of games and you don't have much rest. Even if you find the best system, you can't always employ that system because the costs are too high."

Some coaches shy away from a pressing approach for the same reasons coaches shy away from everything: They're scared. When you push your whole team up in an attempt to win the ball back, you're bound to give up some bad-looking goals, when the opposition breaks free and the opposing striker gets a 35-yard breakaway. When it goes bad, it looks *real* bad, but the positives greatly outweigh the negatives if you stick to it for the long haul. There's an added benefit, too, for smaller clubs that play a more aggressive style.

"If you're not super concerned about getting promoted right now and you play a higher tempo, a higher tempo will increase goal stats which will increase your players' rankings in the league," Knutson said. "*That's interesting. Oh, maybe we should buy that guy.* Almost none of the people working in this sport seven or eight years ago were looking at it through this lens. But if you come from a gaming background, you start to realize this stuff. How can I sell someone my goods at a higher price than he may be willing to pay otherwise?" Another way to do that: "Your forwards should be taking penalties because they're going to show up on the goal stats and not everybody takes them out," Knutson said.

During this time, StatsBomb's biggest challenge was figuring out how to talk to people within the game. Having ideas about conversion rates, expected-goals overperformance, and set-piece execution is great, but you still have to convince the executives and the coaches that what you're doing can add value.

"We basically spent a whole year trying to figure out things coaches cared about in terms of players or roles, and we did it with archetypes. It was like, 'OK, coach, for this role, tell me any superstar that would be the perfect epitome of what you want that role to do. Give us three or four. Who would fit that? Who could we sort of find in the data?' And then: 'What do they do? Describe what they do. What are the things they must do, and what are nice to have?' We may or may not want to play your system, but tell us who these dudes are so we can find them and give them to you. That first year inside of football was figuring out how to talk to these guys and trying to find ways to get buy-in—partly linguistically but also giving them ways to succeed pretty quickly so that they then would want to do it more often."

The logical endpoint of any great consultant should be self-negation. Your ideas will prove so successful and so widespread that your services will no longer be needed. You'll master the language, everyone will eventually be pressing, everyone will realize that penalty goals don't tell you much more than "this player was chosen to take penalties."

"I think there are three phases where data comes and disrupts sport," Knutson said, "and the first phase is the natural *Moneyball* phase. Basically, how do we find better players? And that happens in every sport because that's kind of the biggest cost center. If you can crack that, you get a big edge early on. That edge is actually fairly maintainable if you start getting better data or better ways to analyze stuff or whatever. So that's phase one. The second phase: How do we play the sport better, in a more efficient or winnable way? And that's threes and drives and stuff like that in basketball, or it's finding out that velocity and launch angle are pretty interesting in baseball. But then the third wave is always, all right, we've kind of got an efficient market around players now, and we understand how to play the game in the best way we currently know—although those edges can change over time as we get more and better information, we get better technology we'll apply—so the third phase is: How do we train the players better? I think soccer is a million miles away from that one right now. Can I teach someone to strike the ball like Messi? If I do, I can have a lot of extra goals a year just off free kicks because he's so absurd."

While soccer still struggles with the first two phases, Knutson didn't want to become the victim of his own success, so in 2018 StatsBomb entered its next phase of evolution. First, it was a *Magic: The Gathering* blog. Then it was a way to pass the time during chemotherapy. Then it became a centralized hub for amateur analytics. Then it became a consultancy. And now, it's a data company.

* * *

Expected goals isn't reality. It's a collection of decisions made by an individual or a group of individuals that is attempting to mimic reality. And most expected-goals models aren't trying to mimic reality in the moment; they're trying to mimic it over the long haul. Michael Caley's model—and all other early models—work in aggregates. They compare every shot to multiple previous seasons of shots to calculate how often a shot with a certain set of characteristics was converted into a goal. However, every individual attempt is unique, and the true likelihood of it being converted—were it possible to ever figure that out—is different from what the model says. The differences are usually small and it's rare that a team or player will be constantly creating or conceding chances that defy the historical signifiers on a consistent basis. But it can happen, and the volatility of the stat over a small sample makes it questionable when assessing the precise quality of a single shot. Even for a single game, there's a gap between what the models suggest and what reality is.

The main way that xG models attempt to deal with this issue—and exacerbate it at the same time—is something called the "Big Chance." For all the algorithmic complication and high-powered data computation behind these models, there's an in-the-moment decision at the heart of most of them. Given that the input for the models is just a number of attacking indicators—type of pass, body part used, location of the shot—you could have a situation where a player is on a breakaway, with no keeper or defender in sight, and he rolls the ball into the goal from the top of the penalty area. A basic model would see a shot from the top of the box, with a foot, and it'd see what kind of pass led to the shot. It wouldn't know that there were no defenders or a goalkeeper near the ball, and it'd treat the attempt like the vast majority of attempts with those stylistic tags. To avoid this situation, Stats Perform has its coders tag certain attempts as Big Chances, which they define as "A situation where a player should reasonably be expected to score, usually in a one-on-one scenario or from very close range when the ball has a clear path to goal and there is low to moderate pressure on the shooter." The Big Chance tag immediately increased the xG value of the shot, and it also increased the predictive power of the stat while destroying its micro-precision.

Remember that conversation Paul Power had with Gordon Strachan? Imagine it going a step further.

Aye, so here's a good attacking move from us that created a lot of space for a shot. How does this thing decide what number that one was worth?

Well, so there's someone sitting in an office somewhere who decides . . .

What? Who?

I don't know. They're freelancers, usually just out of university.

Jesus, man. What the hell?

Knutson himself had many of these same conversations over the years—most vividly with former US Men's National Team coach Bob Bradley, who was being interviewed for the Midtjylland job when Knutson was still with the club. Creating a better xG model would not only give StatsBomb a tool to get buy-in from the traditional soccer crowd and therefore make more money, it would also shine a little more light into the darkness.

In mid-2018, StatsBomb launched its data-collection arm and by September 2018 it had announced its highest-profile client: Paris Saint-Germain. At the center of the information PSG were now paying for was a new way to think about expected goals. The StatsBomb model did away with Big Chances and, instead, included a handful of new factors that were aided by the use of computer vision. Computer vision is exactly what it sounds like: using a computer to identify objects in a digital image. At the moment a shot is logged by one of StatsBomb's coders, the computer takes a picture of the broadcast video. It then determines what kind of pressure is on the ball: How far away is the nearest defender? And that's followed by the structure of the defense: How many defenders are behind the shot and how are they positioned? And lastly, it also accounts for the positioning of the goalkeeper: Where is he standing in relation to the shooter's sight at goal? These factors captured some of the basic intuitive details around what most coaches—and most people—think of when they assess the quality of a chance. They made the model more accurate when it came to individual chances and game-by-game performance, and according to an independent analysis by a mathematician named Lars Maurath, those factors also made the model significantly better at predicting future performance than the first-generation type of xG model.

One of the main ways the model improved on the data that came before it is that it integrated one of the things Knutson believes is central to the most efficient way of playing the game: pressure. The effectiveness of a teamwide press was first quantified in 2014 by the analyst Colin Trainor, who created a metric called PPDA (passes per defensive action) in a post for StatsBomb. Trainor's stat took the number of opponent passes in their defensive three-fifths of the field and divided it by a team's number of defensive actions (tackles, interceptions, failed tackles, and fouls) in the same area of the field. It's a great, descriptive metric, but it was a proxy (measuring one thing as an indicator of another thing) and it couldn't be applied to individual players. Although tackles and interceptions had been recorded for a while, they told you only about the moment an individual player won back possession of the ball. Coaches valued ball-winners but more important was a player's ability to force an opponent into a decision, ideally a less optimal decision. Pressuring made up the majority of the active, individual defensive actions players undertook, but it was nowhere to be seen in the data that was being collected until StatsBomb created its own. For the 2020–21 Premier League season, the league leader in tackles and interceptions registered 174 such actions. The league leader in pressures did so 807 times. Another flicker amid the darkness.

With the new data, StatsBomb also provided a new framework for assessing goalkeeper performance. If there's one position in the sport that lends itself to something closer to an isolated value-added analysis, it's the goalkeeper. But for a long time, the necessary stats didn't exist. The number of saves a keeper made had more to do with how bad his defense was than with how good he was at saving a ball. Save percentage was a slightly better indicator: How many shots on target does he save? But it still didn't take into account the kinds of shots he was facing. Rather than acknowledging any of that, the Premier League itself has just decided to shrug and give out an award to whichever keeper posted the most shutouts. And yes, even if you didn't face a single shot on target over the course of a match, it still counted toward your tally.

While there are small edges to be gleaned from other skills—claiming a cross into the box, charging out of the box and clearing a potential breakaway, reliable passing when your team is in possession—a goalkeeper's main job is to stop shots from ending up in the back of the net. The only way to know how good a keeper is at doing that is to watch every single shot they've faced. The potential pitfalls of *not* doing that call to mind a statement by Bill James, the father of baseball's analytical tradition: "One absolutely cannot tell, by watching, the difference between a .300 hitter and a .275 hitter. The difference is one hit every two weeks. . . . The difference between a good and an average hitter is simply not visible—it is a matter of record." Even the best-trained human eyes struggle to process all of the factors that go into good goalkeeping. There are some keepers who make obviously great saves fairly often, but they may be doing so because they're out of position. They might also concede goals that look impossible to save but might've been reachable with better positioning. Then there are others who are always in the right position, so the majority of their saves look routine. On a game-to-game basis, the former would appear to be the better keeper, and only a long-term analysis of a large sample of shots would reveal the value of the latter. The difference between a good and an average shot-stopper, too, might be a matter of record.

In the summer of 2018, Chelsea paid £71.6 million in order to acquire 23-year-old Kepa Arrizabalaga from Athletic Bilbao, breaking the world-record transfer fee for a goalkeeper. He was young, tall, handsome, and athletic, and he'd already become the starter for the Spanish national team. Yes, it was a *lot* of money, but who cares? Chelsea were owned by a Russian oligarch. Most mainstream press praised the move. Not StatsBomb, though. Equipped with the company's new tools, StatsBomb data scientist Derrick Yam decided to take them for a test drive on Kepa. By considering the velocity of the attempt and the placement of it on the goal frame for 95 percent of the shots Kepa and other La Liga keepers had faced in the 2017–18 season, he was able to determine how often the average keeper would concede a goal. Based on the shots he faced, Yam determined that Kepa's save percentage was actually four percentage points lower than you'd expect from the average keeper. More importantly, he conceded 37 goals from 126 shots on target, while the average keeper would have conceded about 31. In other words, Chelsea paid a record-breaking fee for a player who was below average at the main thing goalkeepers are supposed to do.

In his first season with the club, Kepa conceded 1.8 more goals than expected, per the StatsBomb data, but on a game-to-game basis, that kind of performance is completely undetectable to the naked eye. Your brain can't understand what it means to allow an extra 0.05 goals per game. And so, the move continued to live on as a success. At the end of 2019, ESPN named Kepa the seventh-best keeper in the world: "The world's most expensive goalkeeper of all time has been worth every penny for Chelsea since joining from Athletic Bilbao in 2018." But when that was written, Kepa was in the midst of a debacle that would eventually become impossible to ignore. For the 2019–20 season, he allowed 9.5 goals more than average; anyone can tell the difference between a .100 hitter and a .300 hitter. The following year, Chelsea replaced Kepa with Édouard Mendy, a roughly average shot-stopper for his career, and they went on to win the Champions League. Meanwhile, shortly after writing the article, Derrick Yam was hired by the Baltimore Ravens.

* * *

One of the big differences between the early days of baseball's analytics movements and the early days of soccer's is the availability of data. Other than what Charles Reep and Richard Pollard were scribbling down in their notebooks, there is no comprehensive event data for matches in Europe's Big Five leagues prior to 2008, which is as far back as Stats Perform's database goes. For matches before then, you're lucky if you can find accurate goal scorer totals, let alone assists or shot numbers. Despite its initial consternation about newfangled advanced stats, baseball has a long history of record-keeping. There is at least partial box-score data that is publicly available for professional baseball going all the way back to 1876—thanks to Sean Forman.

While he was writing his dissertation in microbiology at the University of Iowa, Forman figured it might be fun to launch a website that gathered up all of this information. As he described it: "I just thought, 'Hey, you know, a baseball encyclopedia on the computer would be really cool.' You could be on Mickey Mantle's page. You could go to the 1962 New York Yankees and see their stats all in one fell swoop instead of having to lug around a 12-pound book. At that point it was technically feasible to do, and I was a graduate student, so I had some free time and I decided to do it."

Launched in 2000 as a hobby, Baseball-Reference.com has grown into a full-blown company—Sports Reference—with 20 employees and millions of monthly users. And it's not just baseball now, either. There's a basketball site, a football site, a hockey site, and as of 2018, a soccer site called FBref.com. The site for every sport except soccer is filled with lovably low-fi tables and player pages that track just about every statistic imaginable over the modern history of the major American sports. If you want to know how many total bases Honus Wagner recorded in 1901 or who led the NFC East in yard-per-rush in 1984 or who attempted the most full-court heaves for the 2007–08 New York Knicks, you can find the answers at one of Sean Forman's sites. Incredibly, it's all free. The initial plan was for the soccer site to one day resemble in scale and scope the other sites in the Sports Reference family, but the data just doesn't exist.

"It's far, far, far behind it," Forman said, comparing the availability of soccer data to the availability of data about the major American sports. "Nothing was tracked other than top level stuff for very long. La Liga doesn't care what Premier League stats look like, and vice versa. So there's no real standardization terms of how even assists are counted across the leagues and things like that. In baseball, we have play-by-play accounts of like 98 percent of all the games back to the '50s. That's 70 years of play-by-play accounts of the games, where Opta got going with their stuff in the mid-2000s. And, you know, Opta is not exactly cheap or public."

Before being acquired by Stats Perform, Opta had been protective of its data, licensing out some of its basic numbers to a handful of terribly designed websites like WhoScored and Squawka. For a couple of years, the only publicly available source of expected-goals data was a shady-looking website called Understat. The data itself, according to some people I know who had access to Opta's xG numbers, was very similar to what the Opta xG model produced. But there was no published methodology, and no one knew who created the site. There was a Russian IP address, and the only reason I know that is because the site was temporarily blocked by the IT team at the studio lot our office was on when I worked at the website The Ringer. The television show *Scandal* was filmed on the same lot; there were vital secrets that needed protecting.

Why does any of this matter, when most professional clubs can easily afford to pay the cost of whatever Opta or any other data provider offers them? The more people with access to data, the more likely someone is to discover something new about the sport. Bill James, whose insights into what actually leads teams to score runs formed the basis of early analytical theory in baseball, was an amateur analyst, coming up with these ideas when he was working as the nightwatchman at a cannery in Lawrence, Kansas. In the late 2000s, a handful of amateur analysts figured out a way to scrape granular pitching data from Major League Baseball's media site. The data—called PITCHf/x, from a company called Sportvision—included the exact speed, type, and location of every pitch. Three different bloggers used the data to discover something they called "pitch framing"—certain catchers turned pitches that were balls into strikes, and vice versa, more often. For a long time, managers thought catchers had this kind of "skill," an ability to fool umpires with how they received a pitch. The data confirmed it—to an unthinkable degree. The amateur researchers found that the difference between the best and the worst framers was worth upward of 30 runs per season, or multiple wins. They'd discovered tons of value and they upended the way most analysts, who had written off catcher as a less valuable position, understood the sport. All three were soon hired by MLB teams.

"Bill James started it, but there were others beyond him," Forman said. "You look at all the first kind of wave of people that were hired by MLB teams. There were people from sites like Baseball Prospectus and FanGraphs who had done public research." He added, "You don't see as much publicly available data in other sports as you do in baseball. Baseball is just all about data, so there's that, but Bill James and the Society of American Baseball Research have all been pushing for more publicly available data over a very long time period. That's where you see that benefit come out."

Publicly available also means the data is available to more people: Anyone with an Internet connection and a computer can work with the numbers. As you may have noticed by now, while most of the leading figures in soccer's fledgling analytics movement took circuitous routes to get to where they are now, almost all of them are white and almost all of them are men. More data available to more people could, theoretically, change that, though that hasn't been the case in baseball with its Ivy League GM club, nor has it been true in basketball. ESPN analyst and former NBA player Jalen Rose has suggested that the league's increasing reliance on data has crowded out Black candidates for front-office positions in a majority Black sport. "There are many people that feel like it has a cultural overtone to it that basically suggests that, even though I may not have played and you did, I am smarter than you, and I know some things that you don't know, and the numbers support me, not you," he told *The New Yorker*. In the Premier League, analytics isn't crowding out minority candidates because it's nowhere near achieving widespread top-down use—and also because there's no one to crowd out. Despite a player pool that's roughly 30 percent non-white, the Premier League began the 2021–22 season with one Black coach and just a handful of non-white club executives, the most prominent of which is Manchester City chairman Khaldoon Al Mubarak, the Tufts-educated CEO of the UAE's sovereign wealth fund.

While it's probably naive to think that this new era of soccer could birth a new, diverse non-playing workforce, it also can't really make things any worse. Plus, although most of the same patterns that occurred in baseball and basketball are slowly repeating themselves in the soccer world, the context is different; racial equality and equity is a way more prominent issue now than it was when the nerds took over the other sports. If soccer teams really want to look outside the typical in-club pool, they can. In 2019, the Scottish club Dundee United hired a 17-year-old Indian student named Ashwin Raman who lived with his parents and posted analyses on his blog and Twitter account. He lived in Bangalore, where he worked as a part-time analyst and scout for the club.

Raman did much of his pre-Dundee work with scantily available public data. That is, before FBref and StatsBomb hooked up. In 2019, in an effort to scale up their process, StatsBomb acquired ArqamFC, a sports-data-collection company located in Cairo, Egypt, with more than 100 employees. The company's way of collecting data is similar to Stats Perform's—coders watch the game and mark down whatever things StatsBomb wants to be marked down, usually around 3,400 events per match—but their process is aided by computer vision. Now, StatsBomb collects advanced data for more than 80 global leagues. And in 2019, they started providing some of it to FBref for the Big Five leagues, the Champions and Europa Leagues, *and* the World Cup and the Euros. Forman's team decides which stats to display, how to display them, and even what stats to create. Access to the StatsBomb data for the FBref team led to a basic-seeming-but-very-useful statistic called "shot-creating actions," which gives credit to any player who was involved in either of the two actions—passes, dribbles, a shot that leads to another shot, or drawing a foul—prior to a shot. By looking at these numbers over the long run, you get a better sense of which players are involved in the possessions that, you guessed it, create shots. In addition to shot-creating actions, FBref offers StatsBomb's xG data, pressure statistics, and all kinds of dribbling and passing info, too. Want to know how far Christian Pulisic carried the ball against Burnley in October 2019? You can know even more than that; he carried it 320 yards, but only 244 of those yards were toward the opposition goal.

Given the global popularity of the sport and the twice-a-year, foaming-at-the-mouth fervor over potential player transfers, Forman figured creating a soccer version of the other Sports Reference sites was a no-brainer. This is a world where fans frequently track flight details across Europe in the hopes of connecting them with the transfer of a player, mark the progress of unmarked Mercedes vans through the city streets, and flood the comments sections of their favorite team's social-media posts with the phrase "Announce [X Player I Want You to Sign]." Nowhere else on the Internet could Manchester United fans go to get detailed, granular, match-by-match info about the new defensive midfielder they just signed. Plus, there's nothing soccer fans on the Internet like to do more than argue, and now they had all this free data that they could use—and more often, *misuse*—to win their arguments. That still hasn't happened, though. "Our audience is not as big as I'd hoped it would be at this point," Forman said. "It's still our smallest site—smaller even than our college basketball and college football sites, which has surprised me a little bit."

Forman chalks some of it up to the black magic of search engine optimization, and he also said that a lot of new users—their biggest audience comes from the United Kingdom, second-biggest from the States—complain about the way the site looks, almost as if they're offended that an encyclopedia of soccer stats would look like an encyclopedia. Most American fans were introduced to the Sports Reference sites back when everything on the Internet looked a little bit worse, so they're used to it. But beyond those reasons, the subset of fans who want to know these things—who care to see how their team's xG totals look or which of their midfielders is progressing the ball up the field most often—remains relatively tiny. And then there's also a group of fans who remain offended by the very idea of the existence of a site like FBref.

"I can't remember some of the derogatory terms that I've seen people use for people who use FBref," Forman said, noting that in baseball, "the number of people who make fun of Wins Above Replacement is shrinking. I don't know if soccer will eventually get to that point. I don't know if it should, but I would have to think with the billions of people who follow soccer that, you know, there's gotta be a hundred million of them maybe would like to look at the analytics? Fifty million? But we haven't gotten there, so if you have any ideas, I'd love to hear."

* * *

The line between data company and marketing company quickly gets blurry. In a sense, it has to. StatsBomb sells their data to FBref, and they also get the benefit of seeing their name associated with the Sports Reference sites. They've released free StatsBomb data for every match Lionel Messi ever played for Barcelona—along with some other, previously unrecorded competitions. They also offer various courses—one on set-piece coaching, one on scouting and recruitment, and another, more general class about using analytics to improve your team. The costs range from about $80 to north of $650, and classes have included representatives from a number of top clubs throughout the world. StatsBomb doesn't aim to break even from these courses, according to Knutson, but increasing the number of analytics-friendly coaches in the world will also increase the number of clubs that might be interested in purchasing the data necessary to employ those analytical strategies.

StatsBomb also popularized the much-maligned radar plot. It's essentially a circle with 11 equidistant points aligned along the edge. Each point represents a statistic, and then inside the circle, there are 11 more points. Their distance from the center of the circle is determined by the player's percentile rank in that particular stat. The points are then connected by lines, producing an off-kilter polygon. It's difficult to describe, but intuitive to look at: the more of the circle that's filled in, the better player is. Sometimes, they'll make Christian Pulisic look like he's as good as Lionel Messi.

Except, the radar suggests that all stats are equally valuable on first glance, and the shape is in large part determined by *where* each stat is positioned around the circle. Luke Bornn hates them, and even Daryl Morey came out against the plots, tweeting, "No analytics person worth his salt uses radar plots or pie charts or 2 Y axis. Probably more if I think on it. All super misleading." It's more marketing—easy to share on social media, easy to look at, easy to argue about—than it is a device moving us toward a more enlightened understanding of the sport. Same goes for some of the visualizations StatsBomb and others

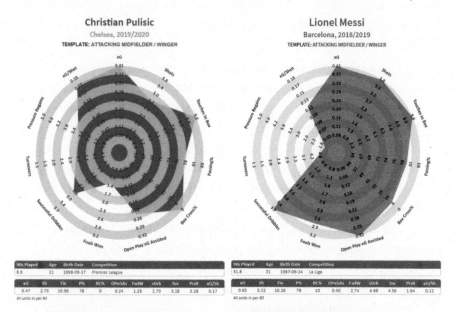

Christian Pulisic
Chelsea, 2019/2020
TEMPLATE: ATTACKING MIDFIELDER / WINGER

90s Played	Age	Birth Date	Competition						
8.8	21	1998-09-17	Premier League						

xG	Sh	TiB	P%	BC%	OPxGAs	FwlW	sDrb	Tov	PrsR	xG/Sh
0.47	2.75	10.56	78	0	0.24	1.25	2.75	3.18	3.18	0.17

All units in per 90

STATSBOMB

Lionel Messi
Barcelona, 2018/2019
TEMPLATE: ATTACKING MIDFIELDER / WINGER

90s Played	Age	Birth Date	Competition						
51.8	31	1987-06-24	La Liga						

xG	Sh	TiB	P%	BC%	OPxGAs	FwlW	sDrb	Tov	PrsR	xG/Sh
0.65	5.22	10.26	79	10	0.40	2.74	4.69	4.56	1.64	0.12

All units in per 90

STATSBOMB

produce. You'll see a slick black background with various fire-colored vectors shooting off in all different directions, with slight variations to each line—a squiggle in the middle, a different shape on the end—to signify the different kind of action the line is representing. It's like if Jackson Pollock was a graphic designer who cared only about soccer. I'll find myself marveling at the detail and the design before butting up against an intellectual wall: What does this actually tell me? How am I learning anything here beyond "This player or this team sure did a lot of stuff"? And then I realize I'm not; it's a display of the company's computing power, a call to convince more clients to sign up.

And more and more do because beyond the radars and the splatter-charts, there are wins to be gained and millions of dollars to be saved by figuring out what the data StatsBomb supplies can tell you. It's not just PSG anymore; Knutson's company has clients in just about every major league in the world. They provided data and analysis for the Belgian national team when they were atop the FIFA world rankings. They designed the set-piece program for Sweden ahead of Euro 2020. And in mid-2021, Liverpool announced they'd be using the company's data, too. While very few—if any—high-level clubs are willing to give Knutson the keys to the operation, more and more are realizing that they need to at least listen to what he's selling.

Soon enough, he's hoping to sell the other football on it, too. He spent the fall of 2021 embedded with the University of Miami football team to lean on some goalposts, figure out how coaches speak, and learn the same best practices he's developed for soccer. Ultimately, Knutson wants to develop StatsBomb's abilities to deliver accurate and insightful data and consulting to American football teams, both in the NFL and at the college level. They've also hired Seth Partnow, former director of basketball research with the Milwaukee Bucks, to help expand the company into the NBA one day, too.

Given that soccer is still in such an early phase of adoption, trying to tackle the NFL—pun absolutely intended—might seem like a ton of extra, unnecessary work. But that might not be true. Knutson's prediction for the next phase of evolution in soccer is that it becomes more like its American counterparts: more organization and more plays.

"I was breaking down some tactical stuff around Manchester City and looking at their little midfield rotation they were doing with [former manager] Manuel Pellegrini," Knutson said. "One guy would come get the ball, either David Silva or Yaya Touré, and they would have one or two little route patterns they would trigger and they would look for that. If not, they would either recycle the midfield, or Sergio Agüero would be surprisingly good at posting up. This guy is five foot seven, but he's so strong that center backs had a real problem moving him. If he's able to post up, one of the things City would do all the time is they would have [right fullback] Pablo Zabaleta come in on that overlapping run, and he would then do pullbacks for the midfielders. I was like, 'This is interesting. This is just a set play.' In basketball, it goes into the post, you have one or two runs, maybe you kick it out to a pick-and-roll, maybe you have a three-point shot; this is sort of around that concept. I think that's the next area. As teams get into a sort of final-third set, or the equivalent, that's what you'll start to see happen in the next wave of tactical evolution. They'll all have their little playbooks based off of that."

Perhaps that's the key, the way to create a flashlight that's big enough to see almost everything. Stop chasing the dynamic, unstructured mess that currently makes up a 90-minute soccer match, and instead change the way the game is played. Make it work in a way that's easier to measure.

CHAPTER EIGHT

THE MIDDLE FIELD

Anyone can watch LeBron James elegantly barrel down the court and understand that what they're seeing is something that maybe seven other living human beings are capable of doing. It's not hard to see that Barry Bonds just hit a baseball that was curving and moving at 95 miles an hour 450 feet in the other direction with the flick of his wrist. Randy Moss? Yeah, the human body isn't supposed to be that tall and move that fast without constantly and seriously injuring itself.

The whole point of American sports as they currently exist—multi-billion-dollar industries centered on games that have been around for only a tiny speck of human history and have no essential role in the functioning of society—is that they're easy entertainment. The rules governing the sports have become increasingly byzantine—an ouroboros in search of fairness that's impossible to achieve; but you can take any game—Cleveland Cavaliers vs. the Houston Rockets in mid-March, New York Jets vs. . . . OK, maybe not the Jets—watch for five minutes and see multiple people do incredible things with their bodies. The novelist Jonathan Franzen referred to a Sunday-night game between the Baltimore Ravens and the Kansas City Chiefs as "high, high entertainment."

However, each sport carries with it a kind of secret code—little indicators that you, in fact, know ball. Sure, the casuals get that LeBron is better than all of his peers, but you *really* got basketball only if you could appreciate the subtleties of Jrue Holiday playing defense. All those Aaron Rodgers Hail Marys were cool, but they never would've happened if his left tackle David Bakhtiari didn't have the footwork of a ballerina. And yes, Mike Trout has three MVPs and his own Subway commercial, but there were a couple of seasons there where Andrelton Simmons's positioning at shortstop made him a more valuable player.

For soccer, it's Sergio Busquets. Busquets served as a gangly, unathletic six-foot-two litmus test for the savviness of a generation of soccer-watchers. It was too easy to see the brilliance of Lionel Messi in any Barcelona match. But if you'd erected a small altar in your closet to Busi's play over the past decade—his simple sideways passing out of impossible pressure, his savvy shoulder feints to create space, and his intelligent defensive positioning—then you were a worthy student of the game.

As Barcelona won La Liga title after La Liga title and three Champions League trophies in seven years, Messi got most of the plaudits. He won the Ballon d'Or, the award (theoretically) given to the best soccer player in the world, seven times, more than any other player in the history of the sport. Alongside Messi in the attacking trio, Barca cycled through a collection of beloved world superstars, ranging from the cool Frenchman Thierry Henry to the psychotic Uruguayan Luis Suárez. Behind them were perhaps the two most feted midfielders of their generation, Andrés Iniesta and Xavi—both of whom finished in the top three of the Ballon d'Or voting multiple times. At right back, there was Dani Alves, simply the best right back of his generation. And then at the center of defense was the punk-rock punishment being delivered by Carles Puyol and the stately calm of Shakira's husband, Gerard Piqué.

But everyone at Barcelona would tell anyone who was listening that Busquets was the real reason for all their success. Born in Sabadell, a small Catalonian industrial city just north of Barcelona, Busquets never popped as a prospect. His father, Carles, was a backup goalkeeper for Barcelona, spending more than 10 years at the club and winning the Champions League with Johan Cruyff's team in 1992. A converted striker, the elder Busquets was known more for his skill with his feet than for his ability to save shots. The French newspaper *L'Équipe* called him "the goalkeeper with no hands." Given his size, Sergio also started off as a striker, as he cycled through the youth teams at a number of clubs on the outskirts of Barcelona. At 17, he finally joined Barcelona's famed academy system, La Masia. Two years later, he graduated to Barcelona B—a Triple-A team of sorts for the club that plays in one of Spain's lower divisions. La Masia had recently produced the likes of Messi, Piqué, and Fàbregas, so this was a time when every decent prospect at the club spent some time being considered the Next Big Thing. Not Busquets, though. No one was talking about the awkward guy with the long legs and bad haircut as a future star.

His break finally came in 2008. His coach at Barca B—Pep Guardiola—had just been promoted to the manager of the first team, and seemed to see some of himself in Sergio Busquets. Even still, Guardiola didn't call Busquets up to Barcelona's first team at the beginning of the 2008–09 season. He got his first start on September 13, replacing Yaya Touré in the lineup, as Barcelona drew with Racing Santander, 1–1. At the time, it seemed absurd. Touré was a rangy, domineering midfielder—able to carry the ball through traffic, play passes through pressure, and pick out the upper corners with his cannon of a right foot. And yet Guardiola wanted . . . this? Touré would go on to become one of the most dominant midfielders in the Premier League with Manchester City—scoring 20 goals and adding nine assists during their 2013–14 title win—but this was basically the end of his time in Barcelona. Guardiola stuck with Busquets for the next match, and Barcelona won, 6–1. The rest was history. They'd win the league and the Champions League, and they'd go on to do it all, again and again and again. Busquets has made more than 450 appearances for Barcelona and 100 for the Spanish national team. His coaches and teamates talk about him almost as if he's some kind of mystic.

Messi's take: "When there will be trouble, he will be there." Guardiola got weirder: "If I could come back and play as any player, it would be Sergio Busquets." During that first season, Cruyff couldn't contain his excitement, either: "The speed of his passing is perfect and he is the kind of player you don't need to explain anything to. You just put him in his position, and he performs." Xavi, who played with Busquets and coached him after being appointed as Barcelona manager in late 2021, made the point that all of your soccer-loving friends were making every weekend: "Those watching from afar may not appreciate or see everything Busi does on the pitch, but those who play with him know he is unique. He improves everything around him, he made me a better footballer."

While it wasn't easy to see his impact, Busquets was a constant at both the best club and best national teams this century. He clearly contributed to winning at an elite level—or did he? Your favorite player's favorite player has spent his entire professional career waging his battles at a new frontier. Through the eye of the modern analyst, midfield remains a mystery.

* * *

Omar Chaudhuri has one big question for the soccer world. He thinks it can change the way everything works—how clubs make decisions, how analysts measure statistics, how managers move their players around, how players move the ball. The question: So what?

Before getting there, though, Chaudhuri thought he wanted to be, well, me.

"Like any good South Asian son, I studied economics at university," he said. "Both my parents studied economics, and it's kind of the obvious choice, but I never really had ambitions to go work in the city. I actually wanted to kind of have the job that you have. I also majored in sports media, so I did a lot of student radio and a lot of writing and that kind of thing."

He studied at the University of Warwick, on the outskirts of Coventry, about as close as you can get to the dead center of the UK. About two hours southeast, a straight shot on the M40, were the BBC studios, where twice every weekend during the Premier League season, they'd film *Match of the Day*. It was and still is appointment viewing for most British fans—either an extended high-light show or an abbreviated match edit, depending on how you want to look at it. Every weekend, they show an edited version of every match—key moments stitched together with only the in-game commentary—and sandwich the games with bits of studio analysis on both sides. The show is especially popular because, unlike in the United States, fans can't watch every Premier League game. In the 1960s, Bob Lord, then-chairman of Burnley FC, convinced the league that games taking place from 2:45 through 5:15 P.M. on Saturdays should not be aired on television, so as not to discourage fans of lower-league teams from attending matches in person. This was, of course, before billions of dollars in TV revenue; Lord was concerned with protecting ticket revenue, his and most other clubs' primary source of income at the time. Despite just about everything changing since then, the rule remains in place to this day. For 2.5 hours every Saturday, there is no English soccer on TV in the United Kingdom So, *Match of the Day* remains the first place to go if you want to see extended highlights of what happened in all the matches across a given Saturday. This lends a special power to the commentators who work the show. They can drive the national conversation about the sport in a way few American commentators are capable of doing. And a decade ago, they were driving the conversation into the ground.

In 2010, Newcastle United signed a 23-year-old French winger named Hatem Ben Arfa. On *Match of the Day*, Alan Shearer, the former Newcastle striker and the all-time leading scorer in Premier League history, appeared confused by the move, saying, "No one really knows a great deal of him." Except, Ben Arfa had already made 127 appearances in Ligue 1, he'd won the Ligue 1 title five times, and he'd made multiple appearances for the French national team. There was plenty to know if you just put in the tiniest effort to find out.

"How on earth have we got pundits on TV that are talking that way about football"? Chaudhuri said. "So I started writing a blog that was kind of challenging the existing narratives that existed in football and so on. Because I was doing economics, I naturally took a data slant on things, and collected data from wherever." The blog was called *5 Added Minutes*—a wink at the idea that Manchester United always got more injury time added on when they weren't winning—and Chaudhuri's goal for it was pretty clear: "Trying to position myself as a different thinker in football."

It certainly worked. First, he interned at a data company called Decision Technology, which led to a full-time gig at another data company, Prozone, which led to where he is today, chief intelligence officer at the consultancy 21st Group. Initially called 21st Club, the company was founded by Omar's boss at Prozone, Blake Wooster, and, yes, Rasmus Ankersen. The ethos of the company existed within the name: "If we were the '21st club' in the league, how would we achieve an edge?" They attempted all different kinds of research to figure out what factors affect winning: Things like "Does playing more young players lead to worse results?" (No.) And: "Is there a difference between winning 3–2 or 1–0?" (Actually, yes. They found that when a game includes more goals, the better team—the one that creates the better chances—is more likely to win.) If StatsBomb is now focused more on the granular inner workings of the sport, 21st Group wants to look at the game from a higher level. Using these findings, they work with clubs and even leagues to help improve their decision-making. The name has shifted over time because it's not just soccer anymore. They also launched 15th Club, their golf arm, in 2013. (Why the name? There are 14 clubs allowed in a golf bag.) Most famously, they worked with the 2018 European Ryder Cup team, who dominated their much more talented American counterparts. After the tournament, Europe's captain, Thomas Bjorn, tweeted about 15th Club, "Stick to the plan!!! These guys played a vital role. Thanks for your hard work." In early 2021, they merged their disparate operations under the 21st Group umbrella.

Of course, the existence and success of a consultancy that fancies itself as smarter than the 20 clubs in the Premier League suggests that most of the 20 Premier League clubs are not, in fact, all that smart. Chaudhuri started off as a data scientist with the company, but he now serves as "a bit of a kind of bridge, translator between those two worlds" of data and sport. In his experience, most clubs at least *acknowledge* the existence of data now. He just doesn't think that most stats are worth a damn.

"Whenever I look at a stat, there's just so much context that sits around it," he said. "There are very few stats that I'd go, 'Wow, that's really interesting. That tells you a lot about a thing.' If you look at progressive passes per game, you know that's going to be influenced by the quality of the team that the player played for, the number of times that their teammates passed them the ball, the position that they played. All these kinds of things, and so it's very hard for me to look at something like that and draw much meaning from it. Of course, once you do, once you do some benchmarking, you begin to get some of the way there. But I think the big leap, or the big question that isn't asked enough of data, certainly in football and probably in a lot of sports, is the so what? When you look at something, *So what, why should I care?* That's why when we do a lot of our strategy consulting work, we never have a slide where there isn't a takeaway or action point or conclusion you might draw from it. I think that's probably why you wouldn't see many teams really hang their hat on any positions based on data, because I think a lot of them instinctively feel that they wouldn't be able to go, 'This thing tells me this.' And so that's why you still have data playing a much more supporting role rather than a concurrent role with subjective decision making."

Like others, Chaudhuri described the majority of Premier League clubs as committed to hiring "analytics" people but not to empowering those people to drive decision-making. And when clubs do use objective information as a bigger slice of the pie, it tends to come on the player-acquisition side, not on the coaching end of things.

"The reason you see data having greater influence in the sphere of recruitment rather than tactics is because in recruitment roles you're more likely to end up with someone that comes from a non-football sporting background, whereas coaching, 99 and close to 100 percent of coaches will come from a playing background or non-academic background," he said. "In other countries it's slightly different. But just the way that sports are divvied up in England, football tends to come from more working-class backgrounds, which means you don't tend to have people who have university degrees in economics or maths or whatever."

One of Chaudhuri's favorite parts of his job is trying to convince skeptics within soccer clubs about the efficacy of untraditional ideas: walking into a room and challenging the conventional wisdom about how the game works. And that's gotten easier over time. "I hesitate to say it's all an old boys' club and mass anti-intellectualism in the game. I don't think that really is the case as much anymore. Ten years back when I started in the industry, that was much more the case, but I think it's a lot less now." But rather than trying to revolutionize the way the game is played or understand what wins matches to a more precise degree, he thinks that the easiest way for clubs to improve performance is to just hire new people.

"You mentioned that half of the baseball GMs come from Ivy League institutions," he said. "That's certainly not the case in football, and I think hiring a really high caliber of people within your management team in a football club is a massive edge that you can take without a huge additional cost on top of what clubs are already paying." Given soccer's popularity, Chaudhuri thinks clubs should be able to attract all kinds of interesting thinkers with diverse backgrounds who could help improve performance for way less than it costs to acquire and then pay a new striker. Instead, most clubs still limit their search to people who have worked in the sport before.

The thing that's always appealed to me about Chaudhuri's work is that it doesn't strive for complexity for complexity's sake. As he describes it, "We tend to look at the kind of basic stuff first, and actually get sort of 80 percent of the way there, rather than trying to muddle through lots of sophisticated stuff to try to get 100 percent of the way there, but maybe fall 50 percent of the way short."

Take the transfer market. Given how hard it is to judge player performance amid the changing context of coaches, opponents, and game-to-game strategy, how could you ever realistically judge the true success of a player acquisition? There are plenty of complicated ways to attempt to model the problem, and then there's one simple way of looking at it: Did the player this club spent tens or hundreds of millions of dollars on get a lot of playing time? It won't get you all the way there, but it reveals an overarching truth: Teams suck at signing players.

"On average, record signings play 50 percent of minutes at their club," he said. "Half of them become bench players. It's kind of staggering. If the market was perfectly efficient, you'd have a one-to-one relationship between how much clubs spend on transfers and where they finish in the league. And that clearly isn't the case."

When Manchester United signed French midfielder Paul Pogba in the summer of 2016, the transaction stood out for a number of reasons. The first was that Pogba had started with the club but left after his contract ran out. At age 19, he immediately became a starter for his new team, Italian champions Juventus. Letting Pogba go ended up being a roughly €105 million mistake, as United had to break the transfer-fee record in order to reacquire him. But that wasn't the strangest part of the deal. No, that was Pogba's position. He was a central midfielder, and the previous record fee for a player at that position was just €38.3 million, set all the way back in 2001, when Manchester United acquired Argentine Juan Sebastián Verón, from Lazio.

By Chaudhuri's metric, the Verón deal was a failure. He played 55 percent of the available Premier League minutes over two seasons with United before moving to Chelsea. While he's starred at a World Cup for France, Pogba hasn't fared much better than Verón at United. He's played fewer than two-thirds of the available Premier League minutes since rejoining the club. If you're paying more than €100 million just for the ability to sign a player to a contract, you'd think you'd want that player to be on the field more than just 60 percent of the time.

Pogba is no Busquets. He's a physical and aesthetic marvel—thudding, field-shrinking athleticism combined with superb close control and Bolshoi-level balance. Across a single game, he'll do at least one thing that no other player in the world is capable of doing. To watch Pogba is to be awed—or, for some members of the British media, to be mad that he's not awing you more often.

But across every sport there exists a kind of positional spectrum—players who are inherently more valuable than others simply because of the position or role they're able to play. In football, a quarterback is more valuable than a punter, and all of the other roles slot in somewhere between. While basketball has moved toward a more fluid positional approach, wing players—those who can create their own shots and create shots for others—hold more value than big men. And in baseball, well, baseball obviously already has this all figured out. In WAR calculations, there's a positional adjustment baked into the numbers: Catchers get the biggest boost, followed by shortstops. Second basemen, third basemen, and center fielders all get smaller positive bumps. And then, corner outfielders, first basemen, and designated hitters all get significantly dinged because of the comparative ease of occupying those roles.

Chaudhuri wonders if the same kind of idea shouldn't apply to soccer, too. Once again, it's simple. Soccer is such a low-scoring game that goals—and the players who can score them and create them—*should* have outsize value compared to the other players on the field. Plus, execution in the final third requires a much higher degree of precision than anywhere else on the field. To score a goal, you need to be able to find slivers of space in areas already filled with defenders and then place a ball in one of the few pockets of the goal frame not blocked by the opposing keeper. The pass to set up the goal has to be accurate, too—both right at the player and at a specific height and speed that allows him to attempt a shot. Meanwhile, when a defender clears a ball, the precision doesn't really matter; he just has to clear it toward a general area. In the midfield, passes can be a little more lax, and when a player receives a ball, there's a lot more space for him to control it into.

This idea, however, goes against soccer lore. The best youth players end up playing central midfield because it's the position where you touch the ball the most. It's the thinking man's favorite position—the one who pulls the strings. One theory suggests that midfielders make the best managers because they have to be aware of everything happening on the field, on a 360-degree spectrum. The theory is certainly not disproven by the fact that Pep Guardiola, the most successful coach of the 21st century, was a midfielder. Midfielders tend to give the best quotes, too. "I'm always looking. All day, all day," Xavi told the *Guardian*. "Here? No. There? No. People who haven't played don't always realize how hard that is. Space, space, space. It's like being on the PlayStation. I think shit, the defender's here, play it there. I see the space and pass. That's what I do."

As a former midfielder myself, I've struggled to come to terms with this idea. I prided my game on my positioning, my ability to get out of pressure, receive passes away from the pressure, and make the pass before the pass before the pass that leads to a shot. There are few things I enjoy more than watching an elegant center mid, gliding through traffic and playing pass after pass, just a microsecond before the 21 other players even recognize its possibility. But when I shut off my romantic brain and try to dial into sporting efficiency, I'm left with the nagging possibility of this: *Sure, it might be hard and it might look cool, but midfielders are secondary actors! They play too far away from the goal.*

"By that logic, the better players should be playing in more dangerous areas," Chaudhuri said. "When Pogba was constantly playing in central midfield, it always felt to me, 'Why be spraying passes from the center circle out to the wing?' Like, get him in more dangerous areas." Perhaps not uncoincidentally, Pogba's best stretch of time at United came in early 2019 under former manager Ole Gunnar Solskjaer, who played him as more of an attacker than a midfielder. That season, his fellow players selected him for the Premier League team of the year.

The market tends to agree with the idea. In addition to Pogba, Barcelona's Frenkie de Jong is the only other midfielder in the top 30 of the most expensive players of all time. And according to Chaudhuri, coaches verify the idea, too. "Even if you just look at the way players are selected, it seems like coaches either consciously or subconsciously kind of agree with our hypothesis," he said. "When attacking players move to better clubs, or get older, they tend to move backward on the field, not forward." The best example of this is Victor Moses, who was a winger for a number of mid-table clubs and then became a starter for Chelsea when they won the Premier League in 2016–17—only after he started playing as a wing defender. "He'll maximize his earnings at Chelsea so playing a more defensive role makes more sense," Chaudhuri said.

I suggested to Chaudhuri that perhaps this is something akin to Luke Bornn's slam-dunk problem—if we know only how to measure dunks, then we're going to think that the people who don't know how to dunk aren't as important. Expected goals and expected assists put numbers on just how much of an effect attackers are having on a team; could it be that we just haven't figured out a good way to measure how midfielders drive winning? "I certainly think there's things we aren't quantifying in midfield," he said, "but I'm not sure even if we could quantify them they'd make them more valuable than attacking players."

Sergio Busquets did, after all, start off as a striker.

* * *

"It was something new and foreign to me," Tim Sparv said. "I was bought because of stats and data."

It would not be wrong to call Sparv the Sergio Busquets of Finland. He's a year older and two inches taller than the Spaniard, but they play the same role at the base of midfield. At six foot four, he's all gangly arms and legs, intense eyes, and an intimidatingly dense beard. He moved to England at age 16 to join the academy of Premier League club Southampton, where he was teammates with the likes of Champions League winner Gareth Bale and England internationals Theo Walcott and Adam Lallana. Sparv never made an appearance with Southampton's senior team, though he didn't expect to: "I don't think I was ever thinking that I was good enough to play for Southampton's first team," he said. He left in 2007 and has since played in Sweden, the Netherlands, Germany, Denmark, Greece, and Finland.

Where you might have seen him: playing for the Finnish national team. After all, you can't miss him, the bearded beanstalk with the neon-colored armband. As the captain of Finland's national team, Sparv did something no other Finn has done before: led the country to its first-ever major tournament. At Euro 2020, however, the greatest moment in Finland's footballing history—a 1–0 win in their first match—coincided with the near tragedy of Denmark's Christian Eriksen collapsing on the field and going into cardiac arrest. After the match, Sparv, in particular, spoke thoughtfully, not just about the difficulty of finishing the game and his concern for Eriksen's health, but about the shock that everyone else had experienced, too. "You start thinking about your family, for me it's my girlfriend and five-month-old daughter," he told the *Guardian*. "I contacted them immediately after what happened to Eriksen and told them how we were feeling. Seeing it up close, the kids in the stadium, kids watching on TV, it can be a very traumatic experience. I hope anyone who needs it will get the help to deal with this."

Seven years prior, Sparv had just joined Greuther Fürth, a small German club in northern Bavaria. Fürth, the town, was first mentioned in the year 1001, in a document written by Henry II, the 15th emperor of the Holy Roman Empire. The club was founded about 900 years later and won German championships in 1914, 1926, and 1929. Then, the rise of Adolf Hitler, World War II, and the subsequent partitioning of the nation threw the German-soccer landscape into disarray. Whatever organizational structures and competitive advantages had been built up before the war were completely erased. Greuther Fürth didn't make it back to the first division until 2012—only to be relegated right back down the following season, which is when Sparv arrived.

In 2013–14, Greuther Fürth finished in third place in the German second division. This earned them a two-game playoff with the 16th-place team from the first division, Hamburg, for the final spot in the first division the following year. They drew the first match, 0–0. The second game was also a draw, but this one ended, 1–1, and the match was in Fürth. You know how this goes now: The tiebreaker was away goals, so the result kept Hamburg in the Bundesliga. A moderately successful season for Greuther Fürth had ended in failure, and no one outside of Nürnberg would care. At least, that's what Sparv thought.

The folks at Midtjylland did care. Their model thought that, based on their underlying performance, Greuther Fürth were better than just the third-best team in the German second division. No, it saw them as equivalent in quality to a lower-level *Premier League* side. They, of course, couldn't prove this, but there was enough cross-pollination between countries in the Champions League and in the Europa League that the model could make estimates the club was confident in. From there, they decided to take another leap. The club wanted to acquire a central midfielder, and they saw that Sparv played more minutes than any other central midfielder for this team they thought was much better than anyone realized.

"They were looking for a central midfielder," Sparv said. "In their eyes, the league was undervalued compared to others, so they felt like, 'OK, we can find some gems in this league.' We were doing really well back then. I was playing and doing fine myself. They could see, 'OK, this is someone we like,' and also that when I was in the team, we were winning more than when I was not playing."

Rather than trying to solve the mystery of midfield or write it off as a position that wouldn't move the needle, Midtjylland decided to simplify things. Greuther Fürth were a good team. Tim Sparv played a lot for Greuther Fürth. Therefore, Tim Sparv must be doing things that help make Greuther Fürth a good team. On July 3, 2014—the day before the quarterfinals of the World Cup in Brazil began—Midtjylland purchased Sparv from Greuther Fürth for $330,000. "Back then, statistics for me was like goals, assists, possession and stuff like this," Sparv said. "So I was not sure what they were talking about. It's a different, very inspiring approach."

It quickly became clear that it was the right move, for both sides. In Sparv's first season with the club, Midtjylland won their first-ever Danish title. In his second season, Sparv played every minute of the team's eight Europa League matches, captaining Midtjylland in that famous 2–1 victory against Manchester United. Across Sparv's six seasons in Denmark, he played more than 10,000 minutes and appeared in 140 games. He was signed for little reason other than an assumption based on some readings spit out by an algorithm: Tim Sparv makes his team more likely to win. And the results are hard to argue against. With Tim Sparv on their team, Midtjylland won the league title in three out of six seasons.

Sparv, meanwhile, became fascinated with the way Midtjylland tried to measure everything. Everyone else in this book so far has entered soccer from the outside, beyond the confines of traditional thought; Sparv, though, became a convert from within. When a team signs you from out of nowhere and they tell you it's because of stats, then you're probably a little more likely to open your mind to whatever those stats have to say.

"In meetings, for example, we could see our expected-goals trend line, how we'd been performing for a period of time," he said. "And you can see that it wasn't only a coach's subjective opinion. It wouldn't be only the tape we were seeing from the previous game. We were also seeing statistics incorporated into that message. I thought that was really cool. For others, it didn't really make a difference, but I thought it was a good way of making their message clearer. It was this objective factor and not only what we were seeing with our eyes."

At Midtjylland, most of the data and technical jargon was hidden from the players. Deeper data and analyses were there for the players who wanted it, but only if they wanted it. Rather, the numbers just informed the guidance that was being given to the players. Most notably: Don't shoot from there!

"At some point we started talking a lot about taking shots from good positions instead of shooting from range because it doesn't statistically make sense," he said. "So we talked for a period of time about playing a pass because if your teammate is in a better position, the chance of scoring goes up. We were shown this chart as well and we could see where goals were scored from. So at least players had a picture in their head when they went out to train. And then maybe someone at the edge of the corner of the box is trying to take a shot and then he gets this image in his head, 'No, oh yeah, this is stupid shooting from here. I'm actually going to look for a pass instead.' At least it made me think when I saw it. Nowadays when I watch TV and somebody takes a shot from 35 meters, I always think to myself, 'That is not how we score.' I love these long-range efforts that actually end up with a goal. There's not a sweeter goal in the world, but it just doesn't make sense."

In the American sports vernacular, there exists this type of player who sacrifices his personal success for the greater good of the team: players who eschew individual stats in order to do the things that make their team more likely to win. At a loss for words, you'll hear an announcer say, "This guy? He's just a winner." In a sense, this is an indictment of the things we're counting. If a player is better off doing things that we're not counting—if other little actions and decisions have a bigger impact on the end result of a game—then we're counting the wrong things. The people who are employing analytical thinking in the right way are searching for their own version of the same thing: a way to quantify a player's true contribution to winning. When I asked Sparv how he tries to assess his performance, he gave the same kind of selfless answer you hear from so many athletes.

"I'm not so concerned about me having good stats after a game," he said. "I think when I was younger, I was more selfish, more looking after my own performance, and even if my team won, and I had a bad game, I was disappointed. Now my mood is the same as the team's mood: If we win, I'm happy. If we lose, I'm sad. So I don't look so much at my personal stats actually. It's more the team stats and how we're progressing as a team."

Of course, this was the same reason he was signed—by the most statistically fluent soccer club on the planet. If he's playing a lot of minutes and the team as a whole is playing well, then he's probably playing well, too, whether he realizes it or not. It's all still very theoretical, though. Might we ever figure out a way to isolate the things that Sparv does that make his teams better? He, at least, has an idea: "Maybe in the future we'll somehow be able to measure a person's organizational skills, or someone's communication skills."

* * *

Stefan Reinartz played the same position as Sergio Busquets. They're the same height, roughly the same weight. They were born within five months of each other, and they featured, respectively, for the two major international powers of the previous decade: Germany and Spain. But no, that's not the comparison Reinartz wants.

Rather, he thinks of himself more as the Barney Stinson of soccer. The, uh, who? On the CBS sitcom *How I Met Your Mother*, Neil Patrick Harris plays Stinson, a craven sex-fiend who makes his friends laugh and deals with unresolved childhood trauma by coming up with increasingly byzantine schemes for seducing unsuspecting women. When Reinartz, a dry, unnervingly measured and rational father of two, compared himself to the last fictional character I would've ever expected other than The Joker, I figured I'd misunderstood, or something was lost in translation. He spoke with a thick German accent, and thanks to the time difference between Los Angeles and Cologne, I'd woken up, walked over to my desk, popped open my computer, and started our conversation. I was feeling groggy from a bad night's sleep. I could've been hallucinating. Who knows.

But while Reinartz was playing for Bayer Leverkusen, one of the five biggest clubs in one of the five best soccer leagues in the world, he got invited to take part in a presentation at Cologne University. He was on a three-person panel with a journalist and a professor from the university. The professor had written a book that Reinartz says was called *The Truth About Soccer*. And what, exactly, was this truth about soccer? That stats were bullshit. The professor rambled on about how possession, pass-completion percentage, the number of sprints, and the other statistics commonly used in Germany had no correlation with winning soccer games. This was true, and Reinartz knew it, but he also thought the professor took it a step too far. This guy was basically saying that soccer *couldn't* be measured, that the game was too dynamic and too complex for it to be quantified in any useful manner.

"I said to him, 'Of course passing accuracy can't measure effectiveness. I can go into training tomorrow, play 100 passes to my goalkeeper—100 percent passing accuracy, 100 percent ball possession—but the goal is on the other end,'" Reinartz said. "So I asked him, 'Why don't you measure if somebody is breaking lines on the pitch?' Because it was not rocket science. It was quite easy."

To explain what he meant to the professor, Reinartz compared soccer to foosball or table soccer. There's a line of defenders, a line of midfielders, and a line of attackers. To score a goal, you typically have to move the ball past all three lines of players. On a full field, players were of course not limited to side-to-side movement; they also all had arms, their feet weren't fused together, they could dribble, and so on. But at its core, Reinartz saw soccer as not necessarily a fight for space but much more like an ancient military battle: There were lines of players arranged up and down the field, and in order to score a goal a team needed to find a way to bypass each of those lines without losing possession.

Perhaps because of the position he played, Reinartz was able to conceptualize the sport in his head so neatly. Attackers mainly see the game as a final-third puzzle: How do I get shots or create shots that will lead to a goal? And defenders would tend to be the opposite: How do I destroy the other team's chances of scoring a goal once they enter our defensive third? But for Reinartz, the game was all about getting the ball up to those selfish attackers and preventing the ball from ever getting near those overzealous defenders in the first place.

Reinartz raised this idea with the professor, who said that he didn't think that anyone had ever tried measuring such a thing. Reinartz suggested that the professor himself look into it, but he never did. Instead, he stuck to this line: "There will never be statistics in football that have a correlation to the end result because football is too complex." And so, Reinartz thought, "Challenge accepted, a little bit Barney Stinson style." The TV character commonly used this catchphrase whenever someone told him he would not, in fact, be able to get a particular woman to sleep with him. But Reinartz's goal wasn't quite as cliché. In fact, it was the opposite: The jock had become a nerd.

From there, Reinartz set out to figure out a way first to measure the number of players being bypassed in a game and then to see if it was just a complicated way of counting things or if it held any information about the way soccer works. He called his friend and fellow midfielder, Jens Hegeler, and they embarked on the project together. "We measured it by hand, action per action, and put it in Excel," he said. "It took us around 20 hours per game." The initial analysis found that the number of opponents bypassed and winning a game had a correlation coefficient between 0.3 and 0.4—a small but still statistically significant relationship. It wasn't the primary driver behind taking three points from a match, but it tended to help. However, when you looked only at the number of defenders bypassed—the last line of the opposition—then the correlation rose to as much as 0.6, meaning that teams with backlines that didn't get breached and attacks that broke past the opposition's final lines won their matches more often than not. If you focused just on games with a winner, the team with more bypassed opponents won 62 percent of the time, and that rose to as much as 79 percent with just defenders. Reinartz and Hegeler had created a statistic that both described what happened on a soccer field and helped explain the final score line, so now all they needed was a name. They landed on "packing" because they felt once a player was removed by a pass, he was "packed away," no longer able to influence the match until the ball changed hands.

One of the universal challenges that the advocates of statistical analysis have faced is figuring out how to get people to listen. Most of them are outsiders, whose unique vantage points are a double-edged sword. By being on the outside of the bubble, they're more inclined to think about soccer differently. But being on the outside also means that the people who play soccer and coach soccer and run soccer teams are less likely to listen to them. But this wasn't a problem for Reinartz. He developed the proof of concept in 2014, while he was still playing for Bayer Leverkusen. He didn't need to figure out how to get into the building; he was already there. He also had the benefit of playing for one of the few coaches who was interested in the fledgling world of statistics: Roger Schmidt, the same guy who'd picked Ted Knutson's brain and read Michael Caley's work. So, Reinartz brought the idea to Schmidt and Leverkusen's sporting director, Jonas Boldt. They were intrigued, Reinartz said, "because these are the first statistics that have something to do with football. Ball possession can be a metric for every game with a ball, and this was more of a football context." Leverkusen soon became the first client of Impect, the small company Reinartz, Hegeler, and their CEO, Lukas Keppler, created to sell their information.

Challenge accepted, challenge completed—except for one tiny problem. "It was quite funny," Reinartz said. "My own club judged me with my own statistics, and I could see why I was not playing. Unfortunately, the coach was right." After starting only nine games for Leverkusen across the 2014–15 season and selling them a new method of analysis, Reinartz left the club, played one more Bundesliga season with Eintracht Frankfurt, and then called it quits on his career at just 26. Injuries had hampered his early-career promise. Plus, he now had a data company to run.

Seven years later, Impect has 12 employees at its headquarters in Cologne and then another 100-plus doing data collection in the Philippines. (Impect developed tagging software, so the process no longer requires 20 hours of work per game.) German broadcaster ARD used packing data as part of its analysis during the European Championships in the summer of 2016. Then, Impect had a deal lined up for their data to be used by Fox in its coverage of the 2018 World Cup—only for the United States to fail to qualify and for Fox to scale back its investment in the event. After that minor debacle, the company decided to stop focusing as much on media work and instead dialed in on expanding their impact within clubs. Most of the top clubs in the Bundesliga signed on for access to the packing data. So, too, did Paris Saint-Germain and a number of other clubs outside of Germany.

Much of the appeal of packing comes from its simplicity: Move the ball beyond a player, and you get credit. There's no algorithm or anything requiring some degree of trust from the soccer person who's unsure whether it's worth their time. It allows clubs to assess their own performance, the performance of their players, and the performance of potential new players across this one specific aspect of play—and then they can decide how much value they want to ascribe to it. The simplicity of the idea has also allowed Impect to spin it off in a couple of directions. If you can measure it for passes, then you can measure it for dribbling, too. You can also look at incomplete passes; how many *teammates* did a player remove from the play by turning the ball over? And if you can measure how many times a player is taking an opponent out of the play, then you can also measure how many times a defensive player is taken out of the play by an opponent. This is especially useful in assessing the play of someone like Reinartz—a holding midfielder who sat in the space in front of his own back line.

There's a debate, both among traditional players and coaches *and* among the analytics community, about what it means to play good defense as a midfielder. In 2015, Premier League club Leicester City purchased a little—and little-known—midfielder from Caen in the French second division. Leicester had just been promoted to the Premier League a year prior, so the move either went unnoticed or was greeted with a "Why the hell is Leicester spending $10 million on N'Golo Kanté? Also, who the hell is N'Golo Kanté?" A year later, Leicester had won perhaps the most unlikely title in professional sports history, thanks to a strong defense and high-speed direct attack. While most modern teams play with three central midfielders in order to better control possession and clog up the most dangerous area of the field, Leicester got by with just two, which allowed them to create man advantages elsewhere on the field. The main reason it worked, according to Leicester's former head of recruitment Steve Walsh: "We play three in midfield. Danny Drinkwater in the middle, with Kanté either side." Kanté was everywhere for Leicester, and he racked up gaudy tackle and interception stats in the process. A year after moving to Leicester, he was sold to Chelsea for around $40 million. Chelsea, too, employed a two-man three-man midfield—the Serbian Nemanja Matić in the middle and Kanté either side—and they, too, won the Premier League title. In their first year without Kanté, Leicester dropped all the way down to 12th, while Chelsea went from 10th to first with him. It wasn't a perfect experiment, but even without controlling for all the other variables, it sure seemed like having N'Golo Kanté making tons of tackles and interceptions increased your team's probability of winning a title.

In basketball, the "steal" has a curiously powerful analytical impact. According to an analysis by Benjamin Morris for the website FiveThirtyEight, the marginal value of a steal was 9.1 points. "For example, a player who averages 16 points and two steals per game is predicted (assuming all else is equal) to have a similar impact on his team's success as one who averages 25 points but only one steal," Morris writes. "If these players were on different teams and were both injured at the same time, we would expect their teams to have similar decreases in performance (on average)." Why is that? It's unclear—but Morris suggests a combination of factors. A player who makes a steal both destroys an opposing possession and likely creates a high-probability fast-break possession for his own team. Steals could also be a proxy for softer skills—organization, positioning, communication, etc.—that affect the final score in harder-to-understand ways. In other words, players who make steals also tend to excel in these other areas, too. On top of that, Morris writes, "Think about all that occurs in a basketball game—no matter who is playing, there will be plenty of points, rebounds, and assists to go around. But some things only happen because somebody makes them happen. If you replaced a player with someone less skilled at that particular thing, it wouldn't just go to somebody else. It wouldn't occur at all. Steals are disproportionately those kinds of things."

While soccer can't quite be analyzed in the same way, the tackle or the interception has the same theoretical shape as the steal in basketball. To make a tackle or an interception, you usually have to make a decision to make a tackle or attempt to intercept a pass. And beyond that, a successful tackle or interception destroys a possession for your opponent and creates one for yourself. "There are players where it doesn't fit, but the simple ball winning numbers both seem to reflect a certain amount of value and reflect a certain amount of skill," Michael Caley said. "From what I've looked at and the studies people have done, there doesn't seem to be as much of a gap between defensive skills in the center of the pitch and the specific on-ball ball winning numbers as I expected there to be. Those two things seem to run together better than I thought." For Caley, the data matches what he thinks he's seen with his eyes, too: "Watching N'Golo Kanté's career, it just feels like he changes games with his defensive range in the middle of it."

However, Xabi Alonso doesn't agree. He played the same position in the same era as Sergio Busquets—often in the same lineup for the Spanish national team. Alonso first moved to Liverpool from the Basque club Real Sociedad before finishing up his career with successful stints at Spanish giants Real Madrid and German giants Bayern Munich. Alonso is one of the few players to play a central role for both José Mourinho and Pep Guardiola. He's seen the game from both sides of the argument and is one of the most thoughtful players of his generation. On the field, he was about as immobile as Busquets but stood out for his raking, precise, long-range passes. He rarely won the ball, but to him, that was a sign that he was doing something right. "I don't think tackling is a quality," he told the *Guardian*. "It is a *recurso*, something you have to resort to, not a characteristic of your game. . . . I can't get into my head that football development would educate tackling as a quality, something to learn, to teach, a characteristic of your play. How can that be a way of seeing the game? I just don't understand football in those terms. Tackling is a [last] resort, and you will need it, but it isn't a quality to aspire to, a definition." To Alonso, your positioning should prevent the opposition from ever bringing the ball near you in the first place.

Reinartz agrees. "If you're talking about holding midfielders, like you or Xabi Alonso or myself played, the name is holding because you try to hold your position to give your team stability," Reinartz said. "And stability is nothing else but not getting bypassed—if you manage to move in the right way, don't give the opponents spaces. We can measure this—how often is the defensive structure bypassed with you as the holding midfielder, and how often is it bypassed in the space you're defending? The defensive midfield zone in front of the back four—this is your responsibility, preventing the opponents from bypassing you there. From a football perspective, it's quite obvious and easy to understand. But for fans it may be too much."

However, Reinartz also agrees with Caley's assessment of Kanté. An interception by a defensive player also *removes* opponents from the play. It's another thing packing tracks, and Impect has found that the team that removes more opponents via interceptions from play wins 70 percent of the non-draw results. Perhaps it's just an argument, then, between two sides who are both right.

Reinartz believes that data beyond just packing can transform the way soccer clubs are run. He's a fan of xG: "Sometimes the media doesn't understand it or can't translate it—even though it is so easy. It's just goal chances. It's not just a 1, 0 thing but something in between." And he thinks, more than anything, that using data can save clubs time and prevent mistakes. "If you think about decisions in football, you tend to think about the diamond pick. You scouted an 18-year-old in South America, we use the data, we sign him, and then sell him for €50 million in two years. But generally, 99 percent of players, you have to 'kill them.' You have to filter them out, and data is the best filter. You can put a lot of red flags on players, and this filtering is a 'no' decision, but it is still a decision. Normally, it's scouting 10,000 players, and you kill 9,999 players, and this last one you sign. This is the normal process, and data is the best pre–decision maker."

However, Reinartz has also positioned himself as something of an insider *among* outsiders: a nerd who also played for the German national team. He took an idea he had about the way soccer works, quantified it, and then verified it by finding a correlation with winning. "We started with a football question that you can take to a sporting director. So, you are looking for a holding midfielder who has to give you stability and who has to break the next line? We created data based on these football questions. This is smart data in a football context. The other option, which is not good, is to collect a lot of data, everything you can count, and then you go to a sporting director and say, 'We have all the data you can imagine, what do you need?' It's a totally different language that doesn't reflect what your question is. We've translated football into data, and other companies try to translate data into football."

There's good and bad to what he's saying. Most data that's being collected has no connection to winning and often only a vague connection to what each player on the field is attempting to achieve. Most teams are trying to either move the ball beyond their opponents or prevent the same from being done to them, and Reinartz's data quantifies that. However, there is a problem with correlating *any* soccer data with winning. As Stefan Szymanski's work has shown, the best soccer teams are the teams that pay their players the most money. In other words, the best teams are the ones with the best players. Those teams don't have to play in the most efficient or optimal manner to win, so when working with correlations, it's unclear if you're measuring how the most talented teams play or if you're measuring the way of playing that—talent being equal—is more likely to lead to winning.

* * *

"I know it when I see it." These, famously, were the words of Supreme Court Justice Potter Stewart to describe obscenity during the 1964 case of *Jacobellis v. Ohio*. It's also, according to many of the people I've spoken to, how to describe a dangerous pass.

Watching a soccer game is an exercise in disappointment management. There's a moment in every established possession where the crowd is waiting for something to happen: They know that most movements don't lead to anything, but they also know that this movement could be one of the ones that does. There's a period of détente where the defense has its structure and is comfortable allowing the opposition to pass the ball sideways or backward. The attack, meanwhile, is seemingly content to make all the simple passes the defense allows. It could go on like this forever and ever, but then, all of a sudden, a player with the ball will decide it's time to change the state of the game and force a forward pass through traffic. If it's completed to the right location, you don't even really need to watch the game to know what happened. You can close your eyes and just hear it; the crowd will inhale all at once and their collective murmur will gradually rise a few decibels in anticipation of what might happen next.

The crowd is right, they know that *something* has been created, even if the possession, like most, still peters out before someone takes a shot. The crowd knows this because the crowd has been watching the match and the crowd understands the context of the play. However, this context disappears in the on-ball data. If the possession doesn't ultimately end in a shot, then these moments that briefly made the entire stadium stand at attention are lost to the numerical record.

This never really made sense to Karun Singh. He grew up in Delhi, India. Cricket was his first love, and his relationship with that sport will sound familiar to the average American baseball fan: He remembers being obsessed with the surface-level box-score stats that would appear on the TV screen and with the playing cards he collected. Around his ninth or tenth birthday, though, he started watching Arsène Wenger's Arsenal and quickly found himself hooked. This was the era when Arsenal moved the ball along the ground with mesmerizing synchronicity and speed. Then they had Thierry Henry and his effortless athleticism and virtuoso feet to finish off all the chances. So many beautiful moves were preserved in the historical record because Henry was there to finish them off.

Through high school and college, Singh had wondered if there might be a way to combine the data he loved from cricket with this new game that captured his imagination. In high school, he looked into it but couldn't find any data to make it worthwhile. He moved to the States to study computer science at Cornell and gravitated toward machine learning and specifically computer vision. He got a job with a small computer-vision startup in the San Francisco area that was eventually acquired by Facebook and spent some time there before leaving to work on the computer-science team at Grammarly, a company that created AI-powered grammatical correction software. On nights and weekends, Singh began digging more deeply into the world of soccer data.

After coming across a free dataset offered up by StatsBomb for the 2018 World Cup, Singh created what he thought was a better visualization of passing networks. You'll occasionally see them on a TV broadcast: 11 dots arranged on a field and connected by lines of varying thickness. The standard pass-map located each player on the field based on the average location of his touches, and then the thickness of the lines that connected each player with every other player was determined by the number of passes played between each pair. While they look neat and tidy, these images miss all kinds of context, including the effectiveness of the passes exchanged between players. By looking at pass patterns as one giant aggregate, you miss how teams might actually pass the ball in a given possession. So, Singh designed a new type of pass map that had multiple filters: one that showed which players exchanged the most dangerous passes, one that showed which players exchanged the *least* dangerous passes, one that showed which players exchanged the most sideways passes, and one that showed which players exchanged the most long passes. He wrote it all up in an impressively detailed, rhetorically sound blog post in which he analyzed Spain's loss to Russia in the 2018 World Cup: a game infamous for the fact that Spain completed 1,000 passes and controlled 78 percent of the possession. It was a modern, bordering-on-grotesque argument for the Reepian theory of soccer—and it also featured Sergio Busquets.

The new idea earned Singh some followers on Twitter, some nice notes, and one recurring question. Many of the people who read the entire post were interested in specifically how he was determining which passes in his pass-maps were the most dangerous. "I just wrote up something that felt intuitive to me, and I think it worked decently well, but I didn't quite realize that that on its own could be something valuable. I was just using it for the sole focus of highlighting dangerous combinations, and I just called it a day and moved on." While the pass-maps didn't change his life, they did give him his next idea.

He then spent about five months crafting the post in which he unveiled his dangerous-pass model. He came up with a catchy name: Expected Threat. He built a bunch of interactive visuals and took pains with his language, hoping that the idea would be comprehensible to someone with barely any knowledge of soccer analytics. And he sent out drafts to a bunch of people he'd met on the Internet—all for just the second blog post he'd ever written.

"In retrospect, that effort was probably worth it," Singh said. "I spent a lot of time getting the visuals right on that post and explanation, sent a lot of drafts to people. It was a whole process. I posted that in February 2019, and it had a pretty big reaction within the analytics community. That was actually a bit of a turning point. If that had not really gone anywhere, I may have called it a day since two things I had tried and put a lot of effort into didn't take off."

Instead, Expected Threat did take off. Singh got invited to speak to the analytics company Twenty3 in London. Laurie Shaw, a trained astrophysicist who now works for Manchester City as an artificial intelligence scientist, asked Singh to speak at a small analytics conference he'd organized while teaching at Harvard. In October of 2019, he presented his idea at StatsBomb's inaugural analytics conference. And then, right before the pandemic hit, he presented a separate research idea at the only soccer-analytics conference bigger than StatsBomb's: the Opta Pro Forum. After a bit of a lull during the first year of lockdown, Expected Threat broke through into the popular consciousness when it was written about by *The Athletic's* Tom Worville. In less than two years, Singh went from someone who'd never written a single word about soccer to someone who was getting berated on the Internet by know-nothing British soccer fans who didn't want numbers ruining their Saturday afternoons.

So, what is Expected Threat?

"I have a set of maybe 10 explanations I use for different audiences, but I think the simplest one is that based on where the ball is, we'll tell you how dangerous the possession situation is," Singh said. "At any position on the pitch, we want to quantify the probability of going on to score in that possession."

Expected Threat accomplished two things. First, it precisely quantified the value of every area on a soccer field. It divides the pitch into 150 squares: 15 long, 10 wide. Each square is valued in terms of how often a possession from that square has historically led to a goal within the next five actions a team attempts. Not a single location in a team's defensive half has a value north of 1 percent, while the highest-value areas, unsurprisingly, are the two boxes on the goal line and within the goal frame. However, neither of those values is greater than 41.3 percent, illustrating just how freaking hard it is to score a goal.

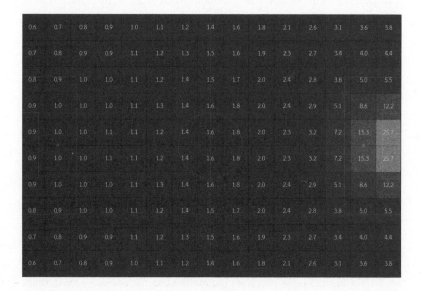

The second thing Expected Threat did was award players and teams values based on how they moved the ball around this map. If you passed the ball from a 1 percent zone to a 9 percent zone, then you were awarded an xT of 0.08

because you increased the likelihood of your team scoring a goal by 8 percent. "The reason any of this came about again is because I wanted to quantify who was making dangerous passes to whom," Singh said. "When you're watching a match you definitely know it, based on the context, but the event data itself doesn't tell you anything about that. Conventionally, the way people would do this is to look at assists as a proxy for threatening passes, but if you think a little bit about that, assists have so many problems with them. So the whole purpose was: Can we look at a pass in isolation, just based on its own merit? In football, you're trying to move the ball from location to location, and then eventually you're going to make a decision to shoot. But everything leading up to that is just ball movements. So any pass or any carry or movement of the ball can be defined by where it started and where it ended. Now if you have a sense of how dangerous each of those locations are, then you can simply subtract the two and find the difference."

This model of the world helps identify undervalued contributions from certain players in the attacking third and also, as Singh outlined in his initial post, provides a kind of automatic scouting insight to teams. By looking at all of a team's actions through this framework, you can determine from which areas they're increasing their Expected Threat the most. But despite widening the scope of value to as far as five moves in the past, there is one thing Expected Threat doesn't do: appreciate players like Sergio Busquets.

At that same StatsBomb conference that Singh spoke at, Thom Lawrence gave a talk in which he outlined his struggles trying to build a similar model to xT. Lawrence is the chief technology officer at StatsBomb and previously spent a year as a data analyst at Slavia Prague, winners of four of the previous six titles in the Czech first division. The talk is called "Some Things Aren't Shots: Comparative Approaches to Valuing Football," and it's a brilliant dissection of the problems that come with modeling a dynamic game with 22 players while doubling as an exercise in questioning everything we think we know about the sport. In it, Lawrence coins the term "The Valley of Meh" to describe how a model like his or Singh's perceives the midfield. In the defensive third, there are a lot of risks that the team in possession is taking because if they lose the ball, then they're more likely to concede a goal. In the attacking third, there is a ton of potential reward for a successful action but not much risk. And in the midfield? Well, there's a whole lotta nothing.

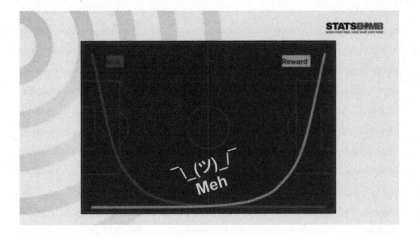

"Ultimately, the chance of scoring or conceding from the average passage of play is pretty small, and most individual actions, especially in the middle of the field, don't increase that chance very much," Lawrence said. "But, at the ends of the pitch: An attacker can turn, say, a 10 percent chance into a 40 percent chance with a single piece of skill (or indeed luck). A defender can lose the ball and turn an innocent situation into a dangerous opposition attack."

The model Lawrence tried to build, and the one Singh published, are colloquially known as expected-possession-value (EPV) models. In other words, how does every action on the field affect a team's probability of both scoring a goal and conceding a goal? Singh's is the simplest and most elegant of its kind; it looks just at where the ball is on the field and how that changes the probability. Other models account for the speed of the possession, the prior events in the possession, and the type of action: tackle, through ball, cross, carry, and so on. In theory, one of the biggest benefits of these models is their sheer computing power. They can sum up all of the actions a player attempts during the course of a match to determine a rough estimate of how he affected his team's chances of winning. An EPV model can strip out the biases coaches take into watching a match live or even on tape, and it can also remember more of what happened in a game since it's impossible for a coach to track and evaluate every action taken by all 22 players on a field across 90 minutes.

Once again, these are all just a fine-grained version of one of the ideas Richard Pollard was writing about 20-plus years ago when he didn't have access to any of this data or computing power. In fact, when StatsBomb released their official version of an EPV model in 2021, they even cited the paper Pollard wrote (and added Reep's name to) in 1997. One of the clear limitations of this type of model, though, is the same limitation that plagues all modern analysis: It doesn't take into account what's happening off the ball and can't reward players for creating space for their teammates or taking space away from their opponents. And so StatsBomb essentially includes this warning *in the name* of their model, which they've called on-ball value, or OBV. Their model passed the first hurdle of any good soccer model: Does it have Lionel Messi first? By OBV per 90 minutes, Messi has the two best seasons across Europe's top-five leagues since the 2016–17 season. However, among the 20 best seasons from 2016 through 2021, there's not a single midfielder listed. The same holds true for the top-15 players in the Premier League for the 2020–21 campaign: It's all attackers and then a couple of fullbacks, which quantified a growing tactical trend among top teams who have increasingly relied on their wing defenders to complete passes into the penalty area.

"That's a good indication that even if you go more complex and copy all the data they have, perhaps the hard reality is passes in midfield are not, in isolation, that valuable," Singh said. "There may be other reasons why they're tactically valuable but if you were to look at them just in isolation, they themselves are not contributing that significantly compared to that pass into the box or that pass into the final third."

I wonder if the ultimate achievement of Singh's work—and even of the more advanced possession-value models—is the codification of something obvious: It's better to have the ball near the other team's goal. The players who tend to drive value, when you watch the game with the eye of an EPV model, are the ones who move the ball into the penalty area and the ones who receive the ball in the penalty area.

"One thing I think is clear in the numbers when you're working with on-ball event data and looking at ball progression is the importance of the penalty area itself," Michael Caley said. "In a certain way that's highly intuitive: There are special rules about the penalty area and teams defend the penalty area in a different way. So I'm not surprised by it, but I am surprised by how much it stands out, how hard it is to wring other things from the ball progression data, compared to how easy it is to wring out, *wow, you moved the ball into the penalty area, you have done a feat.* There is something significant to being in the penalty area, and I think it shows you broke down a team's defensive shape in some way."

That might seem like it brings us all the way back around to Omar Chaudhuri's initial idea. Well, it does. And it doesn't. "From the player point of view, we need to understand that a dribble by an attacker that beats their man to get into the box might take the *exact same amount of talent* as a dribble farther back on the field, and that defender mistake might be relatively forgivable farther up the field," Thom Lawrence said. "And so you've got to be very careful with how you portion out the rewards here, because players can only demonstrate their skill in the roles and opportunities available. Now it's certainly true that in the middle of the field you're likely to have *more* opportunities in absolute terms, and perhaps in the aggregate they sometimes add up to the same as someone further up the field. But there are certainly some imbalances here that you should think about."

Maybe one day Singh will figure out how to properly model those imbalances. He's been approached by teams with job offers in the past, but those opportunities haven't appealed to him. The logistics would be a pain in the ass—he immigrated to the US from India and then would have to immigrate again to Europe—as would the daily problems people on the inside at clubs have to solve.

"A lot of my motivation starting out with analytics in the first place was kind of academic. From my perspective, what I want to see most is the field advance as a whole," he said. "I think one of the most effective ways to do that is remain an outsider, not be affiliated with a particular club or organization, which has a couple of benefits. First, of course, you get to open source your work, you get to share it more broadly, you get to share it at conferences, it's just more accessible. And second, I think if you're in that club or data company environment you're always going to be motivated by the problems at hand, whether it's business problems or the next game that you have to file a report for. Given my academic mindset or motivation toward the whole field, I feel pretty comfortable as an outsider. It gives me a broad view as well of the things people are doing across the board." He continued, "I'm not ruling out working for a club or organization at some point. It's on my bucket list to work for a club and see what that's like, but in the meantime, I've found peace with my current position. It allows me flexibility in terms of the ideas I want to explore. If I find something particularly interesting that isn't exactly motivated by what a coach is asking for, I can do that without anyone asking me questions. It has its disadvantages—I don't have as much context on the ground, I haven't worked directly with other practitioners, I don't know the best way to talk with them or work with them—but from an innovation perspective I like my current vantage point."

But hey, if Arsenal come calling, who knows?

* * *

Remember this Johan Cruyff quote? "It is statistically proven that players actually have the ball 3 minutes on average. . . . So, the most important thing is: what do you do during those 87 minutes when you do not have the ball. That is what determines whether you're a good player or not." It inspired one of the most important papers ever written about soccer.

That paper, cowritten by Luke Bornn and Javier Fernández of Barcelona, was titled "Wide Open Spaces: A Statistical Technique for Measuring Space Creation in Professional Soccer" and was presented at the MIT Sloan Sports Analytics Conference in 2018. Using GPS tracking data from a La Liga game between Barcelona and Villarreal, the authors created a dynamic model that is essentially a combination of Stefan Reinartz's and Singh's statistics. It awards a value to every area on the field throughout the game based on three factors: the location of the ball, the location of the other players, *and* proximity to the goal. So every area on the field has a sort of baseline value, but that value changes based on where the ball and the players on the field are at a given moment.

Bornn and Fernández were then able to calculate which players were able to both occupy the most valuable space and create the most valuable space for their teammates over the 90-minute match. In terms of space occupation, Lionel Messi had no peers. Another thing Messi is better than everyone else at: walking. "Much has been argued in recent years about several moments during matches where Messi walks through zones of the field," they write. "However, that walking behavior is not a detachment from the match but a conscious action to move through empty spaces of value and claim the control of valuable space, and ultimately the ball."

At its core, soccer is a battle for space—to create and then exploit the space near your opponent's goal and to destroy or limit access to the space near yours. Bayern Munich and Germany star Thomas Müller is known as the *raumdeuter*, or "space investigator." The gangly, barely coordinated attacker has no immediately obvious athletic ability or skill. He looks like an awkward, overeager fan who wandered onto the field and started playing, but he has an uncanny ability to pop up near the goalmouth without a defender anywhere in sight. His goals and assists tallies speak for themselves, but they don't explain what exactly makes him so effective. A better understanding of what spaces matter and who's best at both creating and finding those spaces seems sort of like the holy grail of this journey toward soccer enlightenment. However, only the richest clubs have access to the detailed data that Bornn and Fernández mined for their work.

In the paper, other star players, like Luis Suárez, Neymar, and Andrés Iniesta, all showed high levels of space generation and occupation, too. Suárez and Messi, best friends off the field, showed a particularly valuable on-field bond, too. "A special connection [between] Suárez-Messi is also shown for this game, where both were able to generate a high amount of space for each other," the authors write. However, there was one player who had a particularly comprehensive effect on the space created in the match. He was among Barcelona's leaders in space gained, he was near the top in space generated, and he was the only player on the team who received space from each one of his teammates at least once. He, as Bornn and Fernández write, "shows an incredible collaborative behavior by generating space almost anywhere around the field."

The space genius they're referring to? Sergio Busquets. And yet, there are still some nagging questions that pull at the strings of what seems like a tidy conclusion: How many other midfielders would look like savvy space operators if they got to play for Barcelona in Busquets's place? Even if Busquets really does have some unmatched ability to occupy open areas, is the marginal difference between him and the average midfielder really worth as much as the difference between a world-class player and a league-average contributor at any other position? And well, would anyone really care about Busquets if he wasn't surrounded by the greatest player ever and an army of world-class attackers and defenders?

Perhaps midfielders really don't matter. Not in the literal sense, but in the comparative sense—kind of like running backs in the NFL. There is absolutely a difference in skill between running backs across the NFL, but research has found the success of a running game is mainly determined by the offensive line and the blocking scheme. Over the past five years, countless high-profile, talented running backs have suffered season-ending injuries, only for a journeyman backup to replace them and for the team's offense to experience no drop-off. Could the same be true in soccer? A team would clearly suffer from a player with two blocks for feet touching the ball 90 times in a game and constantly turning the ball over. But those players don't reach the highest levels of the sport, and so maybe the difference between a league-average midfielder and the best in the world exists, as Lawrence described it, within "the margin of error" since most of their actions take place in an area of the field that barely has any effect on the likelihood of scoring or conceding a goal. He doesn't believe that, but the truth is that we still really don't know.

Beyond the tackles and interceptions, the broader defensive performances of midfielders aren't picked up by these models, but measuring defense is an elusive pursuit in all sports. Regarding the efforts to do so in basketball, Bornn told Zach Kram of The Ringer, "[We] had some of the brightest PhD students in computer science and statistics around [at Harvard], and for us, it was still a significant struggle, so I don't think it's something that's really easy to tackle." In the NFL, a team's defensive performance across most advanced metrics has very little correlation from year to year. I've heard it said that the best predictor of a football team's defensive performance is the quality of the offenses they play against. "I think there's a small appetite for me in looking more at the defensive side of the game," Karun Singh said, "which is something just as a theme within analytics we haven't been able to do all that successfully."

There's another thing that these models are missing. To view the game through this lens, you're implicitly assuming that every action on the field is aimed at optimizing a team's goal differential, but that simply isn't the case—specifically in the midfield. When a player gets on the ball in the midfield, he has to make a split-second decision, and the best players are making a cost-benefit analysis in their heads, but not quite in the way that these models view the game. They're not thinking, "What action can I take right now that will immediately increase our likelihood of scoring a goal?" Otherwise, they'd be bombing the ball forward—the worst version of Reep ball—at every opportunity. No, they're thinking, "What action can I take right now that will increase our likelihood of eventually winning—or in some cases, drawing —the game?"

"I think that begs a deeper question of what it is that defines the value of a player within a particular setup or within a particular situation," Singh said. "And there you may have metrics that are completely unrelated to whether they are going to go on to score. Maybe at some phases of the game you want to tire out the opposition that presses higher up the pitch by playing some passes that aren't particularly meaningful but they do increase that metric for you by decreasing the energy of the opposition. And maybe that gets at some inherent truth, maybe in midfield that balance is struck, and that's why we place so much emphasis on having good midfielders that have good control and can make that trade-off."

Perhaps the true value of the best midfielders, like Busquets, is that they have some innate ability to understand the tempo of the game. They know when the team as a whole is ready to push forward, and they also know when the team needs to sit back and regain its energy. These decisions may not lead directly to goals and may not show up in modeling of on-ball value, but over the long run—of a full match, a full season, a full career—they increase a team's likelihood of winning in ways we still can't quantify. Or, as Vicente del Bosque, former manager of the Spanish national team, put it, "If you watch the whole game, you won't see Busquets—but watch Busquets, and you will see the whole game."

CHAPTER NINE

THE MODERN MANAGER

It was either 1998 or 1999. Jesse Marsch doesn't remember the exact date, but he can't forget the conversation.

After growing up in Racine, Wisconsin, Marsch spent four years playing collegiate soccer at Princeton University from 1992 through 1995. This was the Wild West of American soccer. Across the country, youth participation was about to explode, and anyone with an English accent could get a job coaching kids on the weekend. In 1990, the men's national team qualified for its first World Cup in 40 years. Two years prior, FIFA had awarded the States with hosting duties for the 1994 edition of the tournament, but it came with a stipulation: You guys need to launch a professional league. The North American Soccer League, which famously featured the likes of Johan Cruyff and Pelé, had disbanded three years prior and peaked long before that. In 1993, US Soccer designated Major League Soccer as the country's sole first-division league, and MLS held its first season in 1996.

Marsch was drafted in the third round of Major League Soccer's inaugural collegiate draft by DC United. Led by Bruce Arena, DC won the first two MLS championships, but Marsch rarely played, starting just one match over his first two seasons as a pro. Then, in 1999, the league awarded an expansion team, the unfortunately named "Fire," to the city of Chicago. The Fire hired DC assistant coach Bob Bradley—who was Marsch's former college coach—to lead the team, and they soon traded a player and a second-round pick to acquire Marsch. In the Fire's inaugural season, Marsch started 25 games and the team won the MLS title. The Moneyball of the early MLS era, in other words, was to make sure Jesse Marsch was in your locker room.

And so here you had a 20-something professional athlete with an Ivy League degree, an infectious smile, and impeccable bone structure, who'd won the league title in every season the league had existed. He wasn't getting playing time, and he couldn't really complain because the team was winning without him on the field, but then he left, started playing, and his *new* team won it all. That said something about him, didn't it? Across the American professional soccer landscape around the turn of the century, few people knew more about winning than Jesse Marsch.

At the time, a friend of his was working for a startup that was attempting to do statistical analysis for basketball and football. "And he said to me, 'This is what we're doing in these sports. We're trying to figure out if it's possible to do these kinds of analytics in your sport. What do you think?'" Marsch said. "And I said, 'Our sport is too free-flowing and there are too many random acts and there are so many players on the pitch at one time and the space on the pitch is so big that the trends aren't as easy to track by the second, by the moment, by the action.' I said, 'If you're talking about set pieces, you could probably do some analysis there. But in terms of run of play and what it's like when it's 11v11, I'd find it very hard to find trends and statistical analysis.'"

Some 20 years later, after coaching against the likes of Guardiola, Klopp, Messi, and Mbappé in the Champions League, Marsch couldn't keep himself from laughing about it. "I mean," he said, "I got that entirely wrong."

* * *

If the previous chapters haven't yet convinced you that the vast majority of the soccer world doesn't know what it's doing, how's this? The only modern club to rise up from the depths of the lower leagues to the top of the European game is the one that doubles as a marketing vehicle for an energy drink that was originally created to help truck drivers in Thailand from falling asleep.

In 1984, an Austrian businessman named Dietrich Mateschitz founded Red Bull GmbH along with Chaleo Yoovidhya, the owner of a Thai pharmaceuticals company and creator of Krating Daeng, a non-carbonated energy drink that was typically sold to blue-collar workers. Mateschitz had been introduced to the drink on a trip to Thailand earlier in the decade, and it seemed to magically cure his jet lag. With a couple of tweaks to its ingredients and some better branding, he figured it would be a hit with his fellow white-collar workers across Europe and potentially beyond. He was right; 20-plus years later, both he and Yoovidhya were multi-billionaires, and Red Bull was the leader in an industry that was valued at more than $45 billion as of 2021.

Red Bull essentially created the energy-drink market—and stayed at the top of it—by throwing its name at everything that could remotely be related to "energy." As a person who has turned on a television before, you know that Red Bull supposedly "gives you wings." Those flickering pencil-sketch animations told you so. There's Red Bull Flugtag, a competition the company created where contestants try to create their own flying machines, most of which immediately flop off a pier and go crashing into the water. In 2012, they convinced Felix Baumgartner to jump out of a hot-air balloon from the edge of outer space. And they've managed to associate themselves—by sponsoring teams, athletes, and events—with just about every "extreme" sport there is. In 2012, in a rare interview given to *Fast Company*, Mateschitz was asked what Red Bull stands for. His response: "Let me answer this question in advertising terms: What Red Bull stands for is that it 'gives you wings . . .,' which means that it provides skills, abilities, power, etc. to achieve whatever you want to. It is an invitation as well as a request to be active, performance-oriented, alert, and to take challenges. When you work or study, do your very best. When you do sports, go for your limits. When you have fun or just relax, be aware of it and appreciate it." Even when you relax, do it to the extreme. The lines between Red Bull's product and Red Bull's advertising of its product have completely collapsed; even the guy who created the company can't tell the difference anymore.

Once Red Bull had become synonymous with extreme sports, the next step was to make the world's most popular sport synonymous with Red Bull. For more than 60 years, no one outside of Saxony, Germany, knew what SSV Markranstädt was. In fact, lots of people in Saxony probably hadn't even heard of the local football club. And why would they? Everyone in the region rooted for Dynamo Dresden. From its founding in 1953 through 1990, the East German powerhouse won eight titles in the pre-unification first division, and they very nearly tasted continental glory with a 1989 run to the UEFA Cup semifinals. Markranstädt, meanwhile, bounced around the lower regional leagues and was never a place for anyone serious about a career in the sport—until Red Bull came to town.

In 2009, Red Bull purchased the license of Markranstädt. German rules, however, forbid teams from being named after their sponsor, so they re-branded the team as "Rasenballsport Leipzig." ("Rasenballsport" means "lawn ball sports"—an almost embarrassingly literal name that no one uses and that, more importantly, can be abbreviated to "RB.") Within six years, RB Leipzig had vaulted all the way up from the fifth to the first division. And in their first year in the Bundesliga they finished, incredibly, in second place. Along the way, they drew the ire of fans of pretty much every team they passed by.

Unlike leagues in France, England, or Spain—all of which have attracted uber-wealthy investors from the Middle East and the United States—Germany has the 50+1 rule, which states that the majority of the voting rights in every club go to club members. Red Bull's takeover and subsequent transformation of Markranstädt was in direct opposition to the spirit of 50+1. Much like with the team name, Leipzig get around the law, rather than actually attempting to abide by it. At most clubs, memberships are relatively affordable, but Leipzig's membership costs around €1,000 a year, compared to the €60 it costs to be a member at Bayern Munich, one of the richest clubs in the world. On top of that, RBL reserves the right to reject any application for membership. As of 2014, the club had only 11 members, nearly all of whom worked for the Red Bull corporation. Bayern Munich, meanwhile, had more than 200,000 members. In the first round of the German Cup in 2016, Leipzig were drawn against Dynamo Dresden. During the match a Dresden supporter threw a severed bull's head onto the field in protest. Subtle.

But beyond the sponsorship and rule bending, the reason everyone hates them is that their teams are really freaking good. In a bizarre twist seemingly possible only during this exact moment of late-stage capitalism, the Austrian energy drink company bought this nothing of a club and turned it into one of the best teams in perhaps the best soccer-playing country in the world. Since being promoted to the Bundesliga, Leipzig have finished below third place only once. In 2020, they made it all the way to the semifinals of the Champions League before losing, 3–0, to Paris Saint-Germain. Without purely using brute-force spending on player talent like other clubs have, Leipzig have established themselves as one of the 10 or 15 best teams in the world. The money hasn't hurt, of course, but it's not the only explanation. So why, then, has an energy drink had so much sudden success in a sport people are still struggling to solve more than a century after it began?

Put simply, they have an identity. In 2012, Red Bull hired a man named Ralf Rangnick to be the head of football for RB Leipzig and Red Bull Salzburg, the other club purchased by the corporation. Eventually Rangnick, who would go on to become the interim manager at Manchester United in late 2021, was promoted to head of sport and development, which meant he also oversaw the work being done at Red Bull's two other clubs: the New York Red Bulls and Red Bull Bragantino in Brazil. Rangnick made his first waves in the German soccer scene when he appeared on a popular national television show called *Das aktuelle Sportstudio* in 1998. At the time, Rangnick was a coach at Ulm, a small club in the country's second division. He was on the program only for five minutes, but he set off a bomb aimed at the heart of German soccer, and its reverberations are still being felt today.

The Germans had popularized the use of a "sweeper," a spare defender who sat behind the three other defenders to prevent the opposition from breaking in behind. The role was perfected by "Der Kaiser" Franz Beckenbauer, the only German player to win the Ballon d'Or twice. In his brief appearance on TV, Rangnick explained why a flat back four—two fullbacks on either side of a pair of center backs—was a more efficient way to use space. This was heresy, and his comments were dismissed as the overintellectualized idle thoughts of a man who'd never played the game at the highest level. Rangnick's playing career had lasted about 10 years but he never reached one of Europe's top leagues. His critics mockingly referred to him as the "football professor."

While the back four would soon come to dominate European soccer, it wasn't Rangnick's most powerful idea. On *Das aktuelle Sportstudio*, he also shared his thoughts about the importance of pressing—the organized, proactive defensive scheme that aimed to win the ball back high up the field by swarming the opponent in a systematized, collective fashion. This wasn't necessarily heretical but it was revolutionary. If you watch a game from the late '90s or early 2000s, you'll notice how the ball often moves from one attacking third to the other uncontested, either by simple forward passes or by midfielders dribbling through acres of space. To Rangnick, this was a massive inefficiency. By denying these movements, teams could experience a twofold improvement: They'd concede fewer goals because they'd keep their opponent away from their own goal, and they'd score more often because they'd disorganize the opponent by winning the ball back closer to the opposition goal.

In 2006, Rangnick was named the manager of third-division TSG Hoffenheim, the proto-RB Leipzig: a soon-hated small club purchased by a billionaire with hopes of reaching the Bundesliga. At Hoffenheim, Rangnick came across research that suggested that goals are most often scored within eight seconds of winning the ball back from the opposition. This was sort of the final piece of information that Rangnick needed to fortify his philosophy. If most goals were scored from transitional moments, then the key to soccer was to master these moments and create as many of them as possible. The result was a refined kind of Reepianism: teams that swarmed the opposition high up the field, then quickly looked to play the ball forward through low-probability, high-reward passes. They didn't care if they lost the ball because they were so good at winning it back. "We are prepared to play risky passes, at the danger of them going astray, because that opens up the possibility to attack the second ball," he said.

Fully bought in to Rangnick's approach, Hoffenheim quickly ascended to the Bundesliga through a pair of successive promotions. Rangnick's most famous moment at Hoffenheim was a 4–1 thrashing of Jürgen Klopp's Borussia Dortmund, en route to a seventh-place finish in Hoffenheim's inaugural first-flight season. After the match, Klopp said, "That's the kind of football we want to play one day."

Lots of energy, lots of goals, always pushing forward? Unsurprisingly, that was a message an energy-drink company could get behind, so they hired Rangnick in 2012. Rangnick's way of playing also happened to exploit all of the inefficiencies in the way the market for soccer players worked. The constant running worked better with younger and therefore cheaper players. It also favored a kind of physical strength and high-speed intelligence that was perhaps a little bit easier to scout for than the subtle technical skill or tight-area decision-making that defined the likes of the great Barcelona teams. On top of that, Red Bull teams prioritized scoring goals, which certainly didn't hurt their players' transfer values. While the Rangnickian way of playing requires a collective commitment to running your face off and a tactical cohesion that protects against breakdowns, it also encouraged individuals to make spectacular plays: killer through balls, dangerous dribbles through traffic, aggressive tackles and interceptions. All of these things made Red Bull's young players look attractive to other clubs.

Essentially, Rangnick imposed a philosophy that allowed Leipzig and the other Red Bull clubs to win a lot of games *and* exploit the transfer market. Leipzig have spent $20 million on a player only 10 times, and four of those players were purchased from Red Bull Salzburg. (How these transfers work—how two teams with the same owner decide fair value for a transfer fee—is one of modern soccer's great mysteries.) To put that into context, the 100th-most-expensive transfer in Premier League history was Michael Essien's move from Lyon to Chelsea for $41.8 million—and that happened in 2005.

Now, it absolutely helps to be funded by a billion-dollar corporation. Leipzig might not outspend their current rivals for talent, but they certainly did that during their ascension through the lower leagues. Most other clubs also don't have the luxury of a global network of clubs, which both helps increase the organization's scouting reach and provides a kind of proving ground-cum-finishing school for talent. Players will frequently move from one Red Bull team to another, which limits the uncertainty inherent in a typical transfer. But the people I've spoken to within the Red Bull organization—even outsiders who have done work with Red Bull—all point to the top-down identity as the main driver behind the club's success. It makes it easier for scouts and analysts to know what to look for. Even if we haven't cracked the code for the best way to play soccer, Red Bull have found a pretty effective way to play, and so there are specific statistical indicators in team performance they can look at to make sure that they haven't lost their way. Amid the ever-expanding sea of datapoints, they have a better idea of what to look for. Same goes for player acquisition: Since the team prioritizes young players with a physically robust profile, that allows them to automatically cut down their player pool and focus their scouting on a much smaller group of players. Analysts who work for smaller clubs will often talk about how they think they've found a diamond in the rough somewhere in Africa or Eastern Europe—only to find out that he's already been gobbled up by the Red Bull network.

Then there's the coach. Red Bull teams are going to play the Red Bull way, no matter who's on the sidelines. "The playing style should be highly recognizable—so much so that, even on a bad day, you can still recognize the kind of football that the team wants to play," Rangnick said. This means the team theoretically won't change its team-building strategy based on the desires of the manager, which prevents a Tottenham-like situation where the manager and the players never quite match each other. For most clubs, hiring the wrong coach can be a catastrophic event that not only costs the club a lot of money but sets the organization back multiple years as not only the roster but the coaching staff has to once again be tailored to the philosophy and desires of the man in charge. At Red Bull, even if the coach changes, almost everything else remains in place.

It turns out, too, that the network of clubs can serve as something like a PhD in Progressive, Proactive Soccer Management. At the start of the 2021–22 season, former Red Bull coaches were managing all four Bundesliga clubs that had participated in the Champions League a season prior—and three more Red Bull disciples were coaching other Bundesliga teams. And then another one was getting his paychecks from a club in the Premier League. They've all been influenced by the Red Bull methods, but none of them embodied the organization's ethos more purely than the man who finally reached the sideline in Leipzig.

* * *

Jesse Marsch didn't know that he'd ever get this far. At least, he surely never imagined he'd be coaching in the Champions League against Neymar for a club owned by an energy drink. But while he was at Princeton, he realized he might make a decent coach one day.

"The first time I really thought about being a coach was in college," he said. "One of the things that professionals don't have and the university does is the natural progression of leadership within the team. When you're a freshman, you don't know anything, really. You're totally green. And by the time you're a senior, you're the boss. That four-year cycle promotes leadership. And obviously you learn from your coaches, but you learn more from the players who are older than you. And your vision of a senior when you're a freshman is of a man who has full control of his academics, his athletics, socially. They have four years of being at the university campus and learning from what the process and what the environment is. And by the time I was a senior, I really had full control of the team. Often there were days where Bob Bradley had something going on where I was almost coaching the team. At that point, I knew coaching could be something that would interest me. But at that time, I had my mind totally wrapped around becoming a professional player."

After about five mostly successful seasons in MLS, Marsch had a chance to move to a team in Europe. "I chose not to take it and to stay in MLS and sign a really shitty contract," he laughed. While he was still playing for the Fire, he took coaching courses offered by US Soccer, worked with some local youth teams, and served as a volunteer assistant at Northwestern. Although he continued playing in MLS for nine more seasons, his focus had already begun to shift elsewhere.

"I was a good leader as a player, always," he said. "That was my biggest strength: on-the-field communicating, having the right kind of mentality, pushing guys, understanding how to galvanize a group. I knew I would have to modify it a little bit as a coach because it's not quite the same when you're inside the team, but I felt pretty strongly in my last years as a player that my potential as a coach was going to be a lot higher than my potential as a player. Did that mean I'd ever be coaching in Europe, in Champions League, those kinds of things? I don't know if that was ever on my radar, but I felt strongly that I could be a good coach and achieve more than I was able to achieve as a player."

His connection to Bob Bradley proved fruitful once again, as his former college and professional coach was named the head coach of the US Men's National Team in 2006. Four years later, in early 2010, just a couple of months before the World Cup, Marsch retired from playing to take a job as Bradley's assistant. During his year-and-a-half with the USMNT, Marsch traveled across Europe to check in on the team members who were playing professionally abroad. "I did a lot of traveling to scout players, teams, and met a lot with club presidents, coaches," he said. "I got a taste of the way that things worked here and what kind of styles of play different coaches were employing."

This was all happening when Pep Guardiola's Barcelona were redefining what it meant to be a dominant soccer team: monopolizing possession to never-before-seen degrees and winning more than 75 percent of their matches. His 2010–11 team kept 72 percent of possession—the highest mark across the Big Five leagues in StatsPerform's database. (The four other teams to break 70 percent—Bayern Munich from 2013 through 2016 and Manchester City in 2017–18—were also managed by Guardiola.) However, with the US, Bradley emphasized the need for the team to be proficient in transition, the undefined moment when possession is up for grabs. Though the US wasn't anywhere near as talented as most of the club teams in Europe's biggest leagues, Marsch still felt like the game at the highest level was headed toward a transition-based revolution.

"The game was moving away from the Barcelona 'pass pass pass pass' and it was moving more into playing in transition, good at counter-pressing, and playing more intensively," he said. "I just feel like athletes were getting faster and stronger. Barcelona were unique to that group of players, to that country and that club. What drove me nuts about Barcelona's football is that I loved watching it and it was amazing, but there was a 10-year phase in football when everyone was trying to play Barcelona football and nobody had the quality of players and the technical ability and the intelligence on the pitch of what La Masia [Barcelona's academy] and what Barcelona had. So, it's always about trying to make sure that whatever style of play you want, it matches the types of players you have."

Marsch learned that the hard way when he was given his first head-coaching gig, as the manager for MLS's newest expansion side, the Montreal Impact. He lasted for one unspectacular season, as the side finished in seventh place in the Eastern Conference, two spots out of playoff qualification, and allowed six more goals than they scored. Soon after the season, the Impact announced that Marsch had left the club by "mutual consent." Why didn't it work? Well, it certainly didn't help that Marsch wanted to play a physical and fast game but was coaching a roster that featured four former Italian internationals with an average age of 34. However, he admits that was only part of the problem. "Some of it was based on me being young and not being so experienced with exactly what I wanted to be," he said. "A lot of it was trial and error. And a lot of it was that in Montreal I didn't have the player pool I wanted in order to play more aggressively and to play more in transition."

After Montreal, he went on what he calls "a trip around the world" with his family. He, his wife, and their three kids spent six months traveling across Europe and Asia on the cheap, seeing 33 different countries in the process. When they came back, Marsch spent two years as a volunteer assistant at his alma mater, where the coach, Jim Bardwell, allowed him to experiment with some of the fledgling ideas he hadn't quite refined while he was working at Montreal. "During that time, I had a lot of MLS interviews where I was the *second* guy," he said. "I had a lot of time to reflect on what I did well, what I didn't do well, what I wanted to be."

It all eventually started to come together when he found himself in New Jersey, sitting in a room with a bespectacled, silent German man, talking his way through yet another interview he thought he'd botched.

* * *

In November 2014, the New York Red Bulls were looking for a new coach. At the time, the late Gérard Houllier, former Liverpool manager, was Red Bull's head of global football. He'd come over to the States to help with the interview process and Ralf Rangnick, still technically just the sporting director for Red Bull's two European clubs, joined him. While Rangnick was somewhat well-known back in Germany, this was before either Red Bull side had begun to consistently qualify for the Champions League and before the top teams in the world had so clearly adopted his ideas. He wandered the Red Bull facilities without saying a word. People were freaked out. And so was Marsch, who'd been brought in as a potential managerial candidate.

"Ralf didn't speak for the first 45 minutes," he said. "Everyone there thought he didn't speak English. After 45 minutes of me speaking to Gérard Houllier, he started speaking to me in English and then we continued for an hour. I described it as 'an argument' and he described it as a 'high-level football conversation.' I thought there was no way I was getting the job, but in the end he wound up being a big part of the decision to hire me in New York and then to bring me to Europe." He added: "When I wound up getting the job, everyone said, 'Well, how do you communicate with Ralf since he doesn't speak English?' Ralf actually studied in England for two years and is a very intelligent person and speaks perfect English. But he didn't want to engage with people, he just wanted to watch from afar. And he did the same with me in my interview—until he realized that he liked what I was saying."

For Marsch, the interview wasn't just a hurdle that needed to be cleared for him to get back into coaching. It was a conversation that clarified many of the ideas he'd been circling around as he tried to figure out how he thought the game should be played.

"The first time I was really introduced to high-level pressing tactics was with Ralf Rangnick and with Red Bull Football," Marsch said. "When I met him, I think he liked the ideas I had and he liked the way that I thought. I talked a lot about defending and making sure that attacking players are close enough to defend and making sure that you're not stopping short. Winning balls, then playing forward and into transition. It fit, roughly, with the ideas that Ralf had, but then Ralf started introducing a lot more details to me about everything from pressing tactics to pressing behaviors to counter-pressing tactics and counter-pressing behaviors to transition tactics."

Four years before the conversation, Marsch felt like he'd started to see where the game might be headed. As in most sports, the pure athletic quality of the players was rapidly improving, thanks to massive advancements in both the size of the playing population and the science behind training and recovery techniques. He knew there had to be some way to leverage the changing player profile to create a new kind of dominance on the field. But it's one thing to have ideas about transitions, vertical passing, and winning the ball back; it's another to know how to implement them on a soccer field. For a press to work, not only do you need athletic players who are willing to run; you also need underlying tactics that teach the players when to press the ball, how to orient their bodies against the ball, how to position themselves in relation to their teammates, how to create chaos with cohesion. Without that coordination, the opponent will be able to find an easy pass to an open teammate or a simple dribble into space and suddenly they're bearing down on *your* goal. Marsch needed this knowledge, and Rangnick had spent more time thinking about these specific ideas than perhaps anyone else in the world.

In his first season with New York, the team won the Supporter's Shield, the trophy given to the club with the best regular-season record, and Marsch was named Coach of the Year. "The mentality of the players in New York was easily the best," he said. "They were relentless to do whatever it takes." Since then, the New York outpost has become the purest distillation of the Red Bull approach across the team's entire network. Without fail, the team seems to sit at the bottom of the MLS leaderboard for two stats every season: average age and pass-completion percentage. When I told this to someone who works for the club, he just said, "Not surprised."

After three seasons with the Red Bulls, Marsch signed on to be Rangnick's assistant at Leipzig. After finishing second in their inaugural season in the Bundesliga, they finished sixth the following season with a paltry plus-4 goal differential. And so Rangnick decided to take over as manager to help right the ship. With Marsch and Rangnick on the sideline, Leipzig finished third and improved their goal differential by 30 goals. Job complete, Rangnick stepped away and Marsch went on to become manager of Red Bull Salzburg.

With Salzburg, Marsch's teams dominated domestic play, but that wasn't anything new. They'd won the Austrian league title in all six of the seasons before he'd arrived, and he chalked up a lot of his team's league success to the massive talent advantage his side had in comparison to their opponents. However, under Marsch, Salzburg also qualified for the 2019 Champions League group stages—the first for the team since 1994. It was the first test of Marsch's methodologies against the best teams in the world—and he passed. Although Salzburg finished third and didn't advance out of the group, they quickly became the neutral fan's favorite team. In their opening match, they beat the defending Belgian champs Genk, 6–2, making Marsch the first American to both coach in and win a match in the Champions League group stages. And in the second game, they went to England to take on defending Champions League winners Liverpool. After going down 3–0 in the first half, they stormed back to tie the match 3–3 before conceding a late goal to lose 4–3.

The group stages were a coming-out party for a number of Salzburg players: Erling Haaland would quickly get snatched up by Borussia Dortmund and immediately become one of the best strikers in the world, while his partners in Salzburg's attacking trio, Takumi Minamino and Hwang Hee-chan, would eventually move to Liverpool and Leipzig, respectively. But the same was true for Marsch. Not only was the way his team played impossible to ignore—only the eventual finalists, Bayern Munich and PSG, scored more goals than Salzburg in the group stages—but so was he. He seemed to live and die with every shot. He sprinted down the sideline to celebrate the tying third goal in the match against Liverpool. And a video of him giving an impassioned halftime speech during the Liverpool match eventually went viral. Most of it was in German, but he occasionally slipped back into English when he needed to reach a higher emotional register. Apparently, there's a German word for everything—other than "get fucking stuck in."

* * *

Back in chapter 1, Luke Bornn posited that most managerial philosophies are the result of a random walk: A succession of events happen across a person's soccer lifetime, and they attempt to concoct some meaning from a collection of meaningless events. And while Marsch's way of playing is clearly more refined than that, it's still contingent on a succession of unlikely events. First, he goes to Princeton, a school that's not a soccer powerhouse by any means, where he just so happened to be coached by arguably the sharpest tactical mind in America and the future coach of the national team, Bob Bradley. Then Bob Bradley goes to DC United, who are coached by another future USMNT manager, Bruce Arena, and then the club drafts his former player. Then, Bradley gets named manager of MLS's first expansion team and he takes Marsch with him. And then when Marsch retires from playing, Bradley immediately makes him an assistant with the USMNT. And then after a couple of years in the wilderness, Marsch gets rejected by enough MLS clubs that he ends up in the Red Bull office, where he meets Ralf Rangnick, who essentially gives him a pair of glasses that clarify his vision for how he thinks soccer should be played. On top of that, Rangnick quickly becomes the most powerful and influential person at a global network of clubs owned by an energy-drink company that is constantly acquiring the kinds of players that will perfectly fit the way that Marsch will ultimately decide he wants to play.

When I asked Marsch how he thinks most coaches land on their preferred style, he pointed to another coincidence or connection: his personality.

"I've had coaches who coached the exact same way they played, and I had coaches that coached the polar opposite from the way they played. What would I say about myself? How it applies to soccer and what my personality is: I love scoring goals way more than I dislike giving them up. If we're winning 2–0, I'm always thinking about 3–0 and rarely thinking about protecting 2–0 or protecting it from going 2–1. And so when I started learning more and more about this style of play, it fit my personality perfectly—and my mentality. And now I'm 100 percent convinced by what my experiences are as a person and as a player and the combination of those things that this is the right way for *me* to coach the game," he said, laughing. "I've had assistant coaches along the way who aren't as aggressive as I am. You know, their personalities are a little bit more defensive or maybe they were defenders when they played and they're not always as comfortable with being as aggressive in this type of football. So, it didn't always fit right. Maybe this style of play wasn't always right for them because it wasn't really true to who they are."

It just so happens that Marsch's personality fits what Ted Knutson called "the highest expected value" way of playing. Coaches have been notoriously conservative across the history of all sports, frequently opting for the less risky approach even though it ultimately decreased their likelihood of winning games in the long run: punting, bunting, ignoring the 3-point line. In Marsch's second Champions League campaign, Salzburg conceded 17 goals in the group stages, more than all but one other team. (They also finished with the best expected-goal differential in a group with Bayern Munich and Atlético Madrid, the eventual German and Spanish champs, but soccer can be cruel like that.) After his two seasons with Salzburg, Marsch was hired to be the next manager at Leipzig. In his first Champions League game with his new club, they lost, 6–3, at Pep Guardiola's Manchester City. In his first league match against the nine-time defending champs Bayern Munich, Leipzig lost, 4–1. Against two of the best attacking teams in the world, most managers might've dialed back the aggression, packed more bodies into the defensive third, and tried to score with the occasional counterattack—but not Marsch. They kept pressing and pushing the ball forward despite the potential, then probability, then absolute certainty of an embarrassing-looking result.

The other reason Marsch stuck with his style is that he knows it works. He's seen the data, and the numbers bear it out.

"I've never met a coach or seen a coach that's used more statistics and data analysis than what I use," he said. "For me, it's incredibly important. Everything from our training methods to our loads in training to what we do in training to how we play to how we analyze the opponent to how we analyze ourselves to how we analyze phases of the game—it's all about statistics and then video analysis. Even here in Germany I've been shocked at how few coaches used real data analysis."

Red Bull has one of the most built-out data operations in world soccer. Recently, they started doing the thing that American franchises once did and more soccer clubs *should* do: hire bloggers who have unearthed new knowledge about the game. In February 2021, New York brought in Sam Goldberg, a former minor league baseball player and employee of the Chicago Cubs who wrote for the website American Soccer Analysis, as a data analyst. A few months later, Leipzig hired Tom Worville, from *The Athletic*, to take up the same role. Red Bull has invested more in data analysis than almost any other club in the world.

In the fall of 2021, Marsch employed that analytical power to dig his new club out of a rut. Under the previous manager, Julian Nagelsmann, Leipzig had moved away from pressing and forward passing to focus more on creative structures that enabled them to dominate possession. The summer before the season, Leipzig also sold their captain, Marcel Sabitzer (to Bayern Munich), and two of their center backs, Dayot Upamecano (also to Bayern) and Ibrahima Konaté (to Liverpool). As the team adjusted to a return to its roots and its new personnel, they lost their first three matches in the Champions League and three of their first four in the Bundesliga. They were unlucky to lose so many matches, but the underlying numbers also weren't up to snuff. They were creating the chaos. It just wasn't leading to many goal-scoring chances.

"We weren't being very effective in transitions," Marsch said. "After four or five games, we analyzed that in offensive transition we had the fewest passes of any team in the league and that the teams that were most successful in offensive transition had between three and four passes. We were averaging between one and two. So, what we then modified is that we told our players that maybe the first option is not always the best one but to make an extra pass in transition and allow for a second wave of players to join into the transition moment. And that was the way we thought we were gonna be able to create more concrete chances. And [in the seven or so games] since then, we scored five goals in transition."

If you've been paying attention so far, you're now thinking, "OK, but what about set pieces? This guy says he uses analytics more than any coach he knows? What about the free goals from free kicks?" Yeah, he's got those, too.

"When I was at Princeton between jobs, my best friend was Mitch Henderson, the basketball coach," he said. "And he always challenged me on set pieces in our sport because basketball is almost like one big set piece. And so he'd challenge me about everything from consistency to deceptions to variations. At first, I refuted a lot of what he said, and then I thought more carefully about it, and I started to apply a lot of the principles that he uses on inbound plays or pick-and-rolls or things like that for set pieces. That's sort of one of my things now: My teams are incredible at set pieces. In my last year at Salzburg, we were plus-29 in set pieces. I include penalties as well, but we were plus-29."

Marsch hasn't cracked the code for training set pieces without losing the attention of his players, so he tries everything. "I don't know the perfect way to train them," he said. "But my philosophy is 'not doing the same thing all the time.'" He tries to do whatever he can to get his players excited about the static, seemingly mundane part of the game. "I mean, I've done things like given homework to the team to come up with a specific corner kick or free kick or throw-in," he said. His teams also track the data for every moment when the ball is dead—corners, throw-ins, kick-offs, free kicks—to see if they're accomplishing what they want to accomplish from those moments.

Why care about data when most coaches still don't? "It's always about solutions," he said. "You're using everything available to you—with your players in the league you're in, in the culture you're in—to give your players solutions that make sense and help them be successful on the pitch."

After failing in Montreal, wandering the world, and missing out on job after job, he'd reached the top, coaching one of the best teams in the world in one of the best leagues in the world. More than that, he'd finally landed on what exactly he was as a coach. "I believe I'm very good against the ball, I believe I'm good in possession—that's definitely not my biggest strength—and I believe I'm very good at set pieces. And my teams play like that. You can see it. My teams are those things."

* * *

There's a Yiddish saying, "Man plans, God laughs." It's also the name of a Public Enemy album. While it wouldn't make an equally good record title, we could tweak that and say, "Man plans, soccer happens." Johan Cruyff, of course, had his own spin on the same idea, "toeval is logisch"—or "coincidence is logical." Even when you have the most fully defined organization in world soccer and the manager most fully formed by that organization, there's no guarantee it's going to work out. And it didn't. Marsch was ultimately fired by RB Leipzig less than halfway through his first season with the club.

Even Red Bull soccer isn't immune to institutional dysfunction, it turns out. Rangnick left Red Bull in 2020 to become the head of sports and development at Russian club Lokomotiv Moscow before being hired by Manchester United in November 2021 to take over as interim manager. Leipzig's sporting director, Markus Krösche, also left the club, in the summer of 2021, to take a similar position with Eintracht Frankfurt, and he wasn't replaced. For the entirety of Marsch's time in Leipzig, the team operated without a sporting director overseeing the short- and long-term status of the squad.

And that ties in with the second part of the story. Under the previous manager, Julian Nagelsmann, RB Leipzig had moved away from the core Red Bull ideas of pressing and vertical passing. They still pressed, but their pressing rate dipped significantly in both of Nagelsmann's seasons with the club. They also slowed down their play with the ball and broke defenses down with complex positional rotations rather than relentless swarming and risky passing. They'd emphasized the part of the game—possession—that Marsch admits isn't his strength.

So, while it seemed like Marsch was the perfect coach for Leipzig—the purest Red Bull man for Red Bull's best collection of talent—he had to come in and tell a bunch of players that had stopped running as much as they had in the past that, guess what, it's time to start running again.

"We wanted to return to the core philosophy, classic RB football, but the team were never 100 percent convinced about his match plans," Oliver Mintzlaff, Leipzig's CEO and the head of football at Red Bull, said after the club parted ways with Marsch. "There were always small moments in each game when we instinctively did things contrary to the way the coach wanted them," keeper Péter Gulácsi told *The Athletic*. Rarely will you hear a club openly admit that it wasn't the coach's fault.

Red Bull did the exact thing the Red Bull concept is supposed to avoid: hired a coach who didn't match his players, and bought players who didn't match their coach. Earlier, in November of 2021, it seemed like Marsch's team had turned a corner after a dominating-despite-the-score-line 2–1 win against second-place Borussia Dortmund, but after a two-week break for World Cup qualifying, Leipzig lost to Hoffenheim, 2–0, and it could've been way worse. Then Marsch tested positive for COVID-19 despite being vaccinated and had to enter a two-week quarantine. The team won its first match without him—5–0, against Belgium's Club Brugge in the Champions League—before dropping two more Bundesliga matches. With the team in 11th place, Marsch was informed that he'd been relieved of his duties while he was still quarantining. What a world.

While the results weren't there, Leipzig were sixth in goal differential and third in expected goal differential when Marsch was dismissed. It wasn't as good as recent seasons but it also wasn't as bad as it looked, either. Maybe it would've gotten better with some patience, maybe it was always doomed due to the front-office dissonance, or maybe it was only 14 games—too small a sample for any broad conclusions in a sport that we're still far away from figuring out. Despite a new blemish on his résumé, Marsch was hired by Premier League club Leeds United in February 2022. In a strange way, it might be a better fit than at the flagship Red Bull club, as Marsch replaced the Argentine Marcelo Bielsa, South America's own high priest of the high press. In his first partial season in England, Marsch oversaw an improvement across just about every conceivable metric—points, goals, and xG—as the team narrowly avoided relegation by winning their final match of the season and finishing in 17th.

From afar, and from the people I've spoken to within the game, it certainly seemed to me that Germany—with its progressive league structure and a national federation that completely revamped its approach to talent development after one bad tournament at Euro 2004—would be more receptive to an out-of-the-box thinker like Marsch than the money-rich-and-tradition-heavy soccer culture in England. He also went out of his way to learn German—even though English was the universal tongue for a fairly international roster—and often spoke it at press conferences. "I'm very thankful that I've invested so heavily in it, because it's helped me in so many more ways than just being the football coach of RB Leipzig or Red Bull Salzburg," he said. "It's helped me really have an enriched experience for being in Austria and Germany."

However, he took a deep breath before telling me that my theory might be only partially true.

"German culture is a rule-following culture. That's the best way to describe it. Clubs exist in a way where it's very clear what their identity is and it's very simple for the fans to follow, the coaches to follow, the club to follow, the players to follow. That's often called 'staying in your lane.' Germans like to stay in their lane," he said, before pausing. "I don't like to stay in my lane—at all."

CHAPTER TEN

POST-MONEYBALL

By now, we have something of a general outline of how a smart soccer club might operate. To start, they'd integrate analytics, data, knowledge-based decision-making, whatever you want to call it, into the top-down process of how the team functions on a daily basis. Data would be a part of every personnel and strategic decision the team made, rather than treated as some separate, alien voice in the conversation. Ideally, there would also be a common currency to assess decisions.

The team would also have a handle on just how random this silly game can be. This applies on both a macro and a micro scale. While results, of course, determine your place in the table and how much money everyone makes, everyone would also know that results themselves are not predictive of future results. And as such, our theoretical smart club would judge itself based on metrics that tend to predict future results. This club would make strategic and tactical decisions based on those metrics—even if, over a short period of time, those metrics were providing directly contradictory feedback to recent results. When assessing the performance of players—both in-house and elsewhere—the same thinking would apply. Goals and assists are noisy numbers, whereas expected goals and expected assists are much truer markers of player quality. A savvy club would then look to exploit any discrepancies between the surface level and the underlying data to bring a modicum of efficiency to the wildly inefficient transfer window.

More broadly, this club would decide on an identity and a style of play that, with the resources available, would make the club more likely to score more goals than the opposition. Most likely, this style would prioritize keeping the ball near the opposition goal and creating opportunities to move the ball quickly into the penalty area against an unsettled opposition. It would value risk-taking—pushing defenders high up the field, difficult forward passes—that might lead to embarrassing moments and the occasional lopsided results, but ultimately (hopefully) increase the team's chances of winning matches over the long run. By settling on an identity, said club could then cut down its list of potential players and coaches from an essentially unlimited worldwide pool to a much smaller group of individuals who fit the characteristics required to implement the style.

This team would also constantly practice set pieces and frequently develop new routines, inspired by both other clubs around the world and patterns seen in other "invasion"-type sports. And given the uncertainty of the value of everything that happens in the middle third of the field, the team wouldn't spend as much money as its competitors do on midfielders. It wouldn't ignore the midfield, but it would devote a bigger percentage of its resources to the players who occupy the areas on the field near both goals—the areas where it's easier to understand how individual actions affect the likelihood of a goal being scored or conceded.

Despite all of this, the team would be aware of the uncertainty of it all. "I have spent a lot of time in basketball and working in baseball," Luke Bornn said. "I have a very strong notion that you could run a baseball team or basketball team with a Robo GM. You'd probably need a human to talk to agents and so on, but for the most part, the player valuation could be done entirely with data. It's really unclear if the Robo GM is even possible in soccer. There's just way too much uncertainty and there's way too many other factors at play in terms of valuing players that it's just unclear to me whether that's even feasible. Now, that doesn't mean I necessarily think that the way that teams are evaluating players right now makes a ton of sense." Perhaps soccer isn't an unknowable game, but it's still a barely known game. There is so much more to be discovered and these ideas serve only to decrease the uncertainty of the myriad decisions a soccer team has to make; they're only bigger flashlights to carry through the darkness.

Among the 97 teams across Europe's five big leagues (excluding the ones owned by an energy-drink company), the vast majority aren't even trying to do any of this. They're inefficient operations without clear goals or decision-making processes: chasing the tail of their own results and making one short-term decision after another. However, a couple of clubs *have* at least tried to change the way they do things. Most of them failed or gave up or, quite simply, didn't know what they were doing. One of them, though, got just about everything right.

* * *

Things had not gone too well since Shad Khan bought Fulham FC. Already the owner of the NFL's Jacksonville Jaguars, the mustachioed Pakistan-born billionaire added the London-based club to his portfolio in 2013 for somewhere in the £150 to £200 million range. After Khan arrived, the club sold its American superstar Clint Dempsey to Tottenham, but perhaps more importantly, they removed the statue of Michael Jackson from outside its stadium, Craven Cottage. Previous owner Mohamed Al-Fayed claimed to be friends with the disgraced entertainer, and he had the statue commissioned in honor of Jackson's 2009 visit to the team's facility. After 13 campaigns in the English top flight, Fulham were relegated in Khan's first full season as owner. (Al-Fayed claimed it was punishment for removing the statue of his pop-star buddy.) It nearly got even worse from there, as the club plummeted all the way down to 17th in its first season in the Championship and then 20th the following year. (There are 24 teams in England's second division; 22nd and below gets relegated.) But then with the club on the verge of relegation into the English third tier—a disaster that would all but destroy Khan's investment—something changed.

First, the club sold its leading scorer, Ross McCormack, to fellow Championship side Aston Villa. Then they sent Kostas Mitroglou, a Greek international, over to Benfica, a team that plays in the Champions League nearly every season. And then they shipped Maarten Stekelenburg, the starting keeper for the Dutch national team, a man who played in a World Cup final, to Premier League side Everton. It seemed like a fire sale, except it wasn't. As replacements, in came 16 mostly unknown players from 14 different countries. And without McCormack, Fulham finished 18 points ahead of Aston Villa, all the way up in sixth place. The following season, Fulham were promoted to the Premier League. So, what happened? Shad's son, Tony, took over as the director of football and turned Fulham into a team that is, as he puts it, "almost completely run off stats."

"We got the team promoted, and some people were still complaining about [our approach]," he said. "Obviously the results improved dramatically. There's no disputing that. The changes we made were effective, and people were surprised that it was so effective. And I don't know why. It was pretty obvious this was a better Fulham team than we had in a while."

Pretty much every time I mentioned Khan's name to someone I spoke to for this book, I got the same reaction: a sheepish smile, followed by some muffled laughter, and a head shake. He never worked at Los Alamos, certainly does not have a PhD from Harvard, and has absolutely never written an academic paper before. He helped build out the Jaguars' analytics department, but he'd never run a team before Fulham, let alone worked in soccer. Our conversations—about soccer theory, the advantages and difficulties of employing analytics, what the future of the sport might look like—never quite reached the same levels as my conversations with the others I spoke to. Putting aside whether any of that matters at all—you can run a team effectively without a Harvard education or a visionary understanding of spatial dynamics—Khan has this job only because his dad owns the team. And it's not his only job, either. He's still working with the Jaguars, and in 2018, he also launched All Elite Wrestling, a wrestling promotion aimed at rivaling the WWE.

However, nepotism has provided Fulham with something most other clubs don't have: a data guy at the top of the ladder. Even if the data process isn't as nuanced or thoughtful as it could be, it's still better than what almost everyone else is doing, right? Well, kind of.

With the added revenue from the Premier League TV deal, Khan spent more than £100 million on 12 players in the summer of 2018, splashing more cash than all but two other English clubs over that span. Plenty of the new additions earned plaudits from the analytics community, including Ted Knutson, as the club acquired budding midfield stars André-Frank Zambo Anguissa and Jean Michaël Seri from France, along with Luciano Vietto, a promising Argentine attacker with impressive expected-goals numbers at Champions League clubs Sevilla and Atlético Madrid. That trio did a lot of the things that *could* be quantified. And I was bullish on their chances, too. Khan never went too deep with me about how the club weaponized data through their decision-making. But almost all of the players Fulham purchased in the summer of 2018 were the kinds of guys who jumped off the spreadsheet.

However, we all missed one important bit of context when Fulham were building their team: The Premier League . . . is not the Championship. In the second division, Fulham dominated possession with a proactive style undergirded by all the data that makes effective attackers easier to identify. But even with all the new additions, the squad was now going to be at a severe talent disadvantage compared to its opponents. They were no longer able to play the game on their terms, week in and week out. The exact philosophy that allowed them to achieve success in the Championship also set them up to fail. In the Premier League, Fulham completed more passes than any team outside of Manchester City, Liverpool, Tottenham, Chelsea, Manchester United, and Arsenal—a group known as the Big Six because of annual revenues that dwarf the rest of the league. Except, Fulham also allowed 81 goals in 38 matches—five more than any other side. They finished with the second-fewest points, and this wasn't just a case of bad luck, as their expected-goals differential was also the second-worst in the league. After one season up, Khan's team was relegated right back down. For Fulham, the things that won them soccer games had changed overnight—but then it changed again, and maybe it'll keep changing, year after year, forever and ever.

Khan told me that this was his biggest mistake since taking over the team. "You're playing much, much stronger competition in the Premier League than you are in the Championship," he said. "You're able to play more aggressively and you're rewarded for playing more aggressively in the Championship."

Back down in the Championship in 2019–20, they had a team that was better suited to win in the Championship, and they immediately earned promotion back up to the Premier League. And sure enough, back in the Premier League, they ended up in the same spot: relegated after one season. This time, though, it was at least a little different. They didn't spend big on data darlings and instead opted for a more reactive approach that saw them complete just the 10th-most passes in the league. "It is a lesson I learned," he said. "We did a better job defensively this last time around." They conceded 53 goals in 2020–21—fewer than seven other teams. The bigger problem was that they just couldn't score, as they found the back of the net only 27 times in 38 matches. They were still searching for the right balance, but the underlying process was much closer to being sound. They finished the season with the 14th-best xG differential in the league. If they play like that again—Fulham, of course, won the Championship in 2022—then they might not bounce back down the staircase.

Of course, next time they're up, they won't have the same roster that produced that performance, and they won't have the same manager, either. They're on their fourth coach since Khan was given the reins, and there's no real clear tactical through line with any of them: There was one with no first-division experience, another who's coached just about *every* first-division team, an interim-turned-permanent coach who'd never been a head coach at any level, and another one who didn't last for more than 60 games at any of his previous five jobs. There was a bizarre, public falling out with the club's associate director of football operations, Craig Kline, in 2017. In January of 2019, Khan told a supporter to "go to hell" after a 2–1 loss against Burnley. In 2020, after Khan apologized to fans on Twitter following a 3–0 loss to Aston Villa, Sky Sports pundit and former Liverpool defender Jamie Carragher called him a "clown" who should "keep his mouth shut and his head down." Directionless head-coaching chaos and useless off-field drama typically doesn't speak to a club with a clear long-term plan. At the same time, *most* clubs don't have long-term plans, and at least Fulham has a crazy rich guy making its decisions and backing them up, somehow, with data. Amid the inefficiencies of European soccer, that just might be enough to work. And according to Khan, it already *has* worked.

After that loss to Aston Villa—their third defeat in as many matches back up in the Premier League—a Fulham fan named Sophie Johnson sent a tweet to Khan, saying, "I expect no reply but I send this anyway, if you don't have the best interests of this club in you're [sic] heart, step aside and let someone who does, do the job properly. Our fans love this club dearly yet you seem to [sic] happy to let us become a yo-yo club for financial gains."

He actually did reply: "While absolutely nothing I can say would make up for tonight's performance, frankly we would've absolutely killed to be a yo-yo club when I took it over after finishing 20th in the Championship, Sophie."

* * *

At the other end of the spectrum from Fulham, Barcelona and Arsenal share a kind of spiritual lineage. Each club reached an unmatched level of dominance but also achieved an aesthetic ideal. Under Pep Guardiola, Barca took over La

Liga and won two Champions League titles in three years by elevating the ball to a spiritual object. Possession was a reverential state, and you did everything you could to remain there. Meanwhile, Arsène Wenger's Arsenal became the first and only team to ever go undefeated in the Premier League by eschewing brute British strength for a roster of foreigners who ripped England apart by passing the ball quickly along the ground. Both clubs prioritized a proactive style of play and individual technical skill. While the history of coaching across all the major sports is littered with conservative thinkers who briefly experienced success and eventually flamed out, these were the two clubs who, for the first 15 years of the century, proved that you could reach out and grab the trophy rather than waiting for it to come to you.

Another thing that Barcelona and Arsenal share: They hired two of the sharpest soccer minds in the world, didn't fully empower them, and then went into gradual decline.

Let's start in London, by way of Seattle. Despite an English father who couldn't care less about football, Sarah Rudd grew up with a passion for the game that exploded when she moved to New York City to attend Columbia University. Lazy Saturday mornings became "go to the bar and watch Arsenal" mornings. This was right around the time when Wenger and Thierry Henry were painting beautiful pictures together every weekend. Like so many Americans who became exposed to the Premier League around the turn of the century, Rudd found the allure of that era of Arsenal impossible to resist. After earning a degree in computer science and environmental studies, she moved to Chile for work. "It was just a whole different world where you could watch football all the time, play football all the time," she said. "It was just everywhere. And I loved it. So that's when I started thinking a little bit more about 'How can I get into this?'" Before answering that question, she moved back to Seattle to work as a software developer for Bing, Microsoft's search engine, where she did data mining and work on machine learning. "That was fine for a couple years," she said, "but then it started getting really bad. And I was like, 'I've got to get a job in football. I don't know how to do this, but I've got to figure it out.'"

Rudd assumed she had no skills that could be applied to working in the sports world, so she went to get her MBA from the University of Washington, thinking she might eventually land a gig with Nike or Adidas, both of whom have their American headquarters in the Pacific Northwest. Luckily, one of her professors at Columbia was Sunil Gulati, then-president of the United States Soccer Federation. He connected Rudd with Adrian Hanauer, a businessman who was also the managing partner for the Seattle Sounders, who, at the time, were a team in the United Soccer League, the second tier of the American soccer pyramid. "Adrian was kind of the first person in football who was like, 'Hey, this Moneyball thing, we've got to do this,'" Rudd said. "So that's honestly where the idea in my head came from. Things didn't work out with him in terms of timing." The Sounders were eventually awarded an expansion franchise by MLS, and Hanauer became the majority owner. They've won two league titles in 12 seasons, and in a funny little twist, Rudd's husband, Ravi Ramineni, was formerly the club's vice president of soccer research and analytics.

Inspired by her conversation with Hanauer, Rudd started looking into, as she put it, "how I could make Moneyball in soccer work." Like almost everyone else in this book, she started blogging, and she started scraping whatever bits and pieces of data she could find on the Internet. She went to the Sloan Sports Analytics Conference, where she heard that some company called StatDNA was holding a research competition and offering participants a real dataset to work with. The title of the idea Rudd came up with was "A Framework for Tactical Analysis and Individual Offensive Production Assessment in Soccer Using Markov Chains." Put more simply by Rudd herself, "I did a paper basically trying to quantify the value of a pass or any offensive action in soccer. And I won the research competition." This was essentially Expected Threat, eight years before Karun Singh wrote his blog post. Rudd created a Markov model, a chain system that predicts the probability of an event occurring based on the previous event that just happened, which determined how much each individual action increased or decreased a team's likelihood of scoring. StatDNA's CEO, Jaeson Rosenfeld, liked Rudd's work so much that he brought her to StatDNA full time. Within a year, Arsenal bought StatDNA to essentially function as the club's in-house analytics team. Not only was Rudd suddenly and literally working on "Moneyball for soccer" but she was doing it for her favorite team. "I think it's one of those things where it's be careful what you wish for because the highs are higher, but the lows are lower when it's your team," she said. "Why can't we just get back to the Champions League?"

Rudd and the rest of the StatDNA crew joined Arsenal in 2012. The Gunners hadn't finished outside of the top four since 1996. And since the

2015–16 season, when Arsenal finished second, they haven't made it back into the top four. Without all that sweet Champions League revenue, their spending power has steadily diminished and so has their performance. In 2016–17, their last season in the Champions League, they recorded the third-highest revenue of any English side. Come 2020–21, they'd dropped down to sixth. Their average finishing position in the table since they last played in the Champions League? Also sixth.

Of course, you buy the analytics company in order to break the link between revenue and results or to ensure that you keep performing at a level that doesn't lose you the Champions League revenue and then tank your results along the way. Or maybe you just buy the analytics company because you don't want anyone else to be able to use it.

Rudd described StatDNA as Arsenal having their own little StatsBomb inside the club: its own data provider and its own team of analysts. The club wasn't reliant on Opta coders to label big chances. They could collect the data however they wanted, massaging the process to smooth out errors, and answering their own questions rather than waiting for a provider to get back to them (and potentially share the results with their other clients). Each week, the analytics team worked on fine-tuning their models, assessing team and player performance, and identifying or analyzing potential players to sign. They were also responsible for preparing pre-match opposition analysis and a post-match review. This led to one particularly awkward moment in December 2020 when Arsenal had lost three straight matches. After a 2–1 defeat to Everton, manager Mikel Arteta told a reporter, "Last year we won against Everton with a 25 percent chance of winning, you win 3–2. Last weekend, it was a 67 percent chance of winning, any game in Premier League history, and a 9 percent chance of losing, and you lose. Three percent against Burnley and you lost. Seven percent against Spurs, and you lose."

Arteta didn't do a particularly good job of explaining what the hell he was talking about—you can probably imagine the reception it got in the British press—but he was actually just citing postgame win expectancy based on an in-house model built by Rudd and her team. "If I remember correctly, he got the general idea correct. I think there were some things he didn't get quite right," she said. "What we want to do in the post-match report is separate the result from the process and try to give the coaching staff insight into, well, how well did we play and were we reaching our objectives but then lost because we got unlucky? In the day-to-day grind, when the pressure is on, it's only natural to kind of over-react to results." But what if the model says the team isn't playing all that well despite a run of wins? "I'm not sure there's that many football managers in the world that are bold enough to change things when they're going well," she said.

Like others I spoke to, Rudd views the analytics advancement in soccer as a two-track path forward. On the one side, you have all the things we don't know about the sport and the things we might never know. Thanks to the deal for Premier League–wide tracking data, Arsenal's advanced analytical abilities and in-house models were applied to a much more comprehensive dataset that knew exactly where each player on the field was at a given moment and how they moved. Except, it seems that, for Rudd, the more she learned about the sport, the more questions she had. "When you're recruiting a player," she said, "you have to look at what's the quality of opposition that they're playing against? What's the system that they're playing in? What's being asked of them? Are they incapable of doing what you want, or just not being asked to do what you want? Who's the supporting cast around them? You can have a player with great vision, but nobody running in front of them. They're still going to have good numbers, but they're not going to have great numbers. You put them in a team with lots of people running, it'll be a lot better. Are they the main focus? Are they going to have two or three defenders on them the whole time or do they have somebody else creating space for them to operate in?"

When Rudd first started at Arsenal, she was convinced that she'd change the game by reimagining the field. Coaches and players always spoke about thirds: defensive, midfield, and attacking. "It felt a little bit arbitrary to me. I just wanted to look at if there's anything different that happens in the final third versus midfield third." If these delineations turned out to be ancient, subjective holdovers from a should-be-bygone era, you could try to deprogram your players and coaches from thinking this way and start occupying all new areas—quarters! eighths! sixteenths!—that your three-minded opponents wouldn't know how to handle. Instead, Rudd found out that teams divided the field in such a way for a reason. "I think when you're defending and when your backline gets near the penalty area, you stop retreating. And so that naturally just pushes everything to that kind of final-third boundary. Over years and years of watching football, people got it right."

That's not to say they got everything else right, too. Rudd said there was hesitancy at Arsenal to embrace the potential value of set pieces, although the club did eventually hire a set-piece coach in 2020 from forward-thinking Brentford. But when I asked her what she viewed as soccer's version of the 3-point shot or the walk—hidden-but-obvious analytical truths—she wasn't convinced that anything in particular could change the game in the same way. "I think this is one where football is probably just really different from baseball in that you're constantly having these tactical innovations and revolutions driven by the coaching staff, so a lot of those kinds of truths change really, really quickly," she said. "I think there's little things where it's teaching a fullback to come out and block the cross at all costs. And then you're kind of like, 'Let them cross from there. If they want to cross from there, that's fine.' Shooting from distance, I think that's another little one. There haven't been too many. Just recognizing the value of set pieces—even though teams aren't necessarily executing at the level that you would hope. I think teams are finally realizing that it's easy goals, if they can do it."

Which brings us to the second path toward analytical enlightenment: actually using the data to make decisions. Even if people like Rudd still haven't figured out How to Revolutionize the Game with One Cool Trick, the potential impact from all the marginal gains of integrating objective information into how the club operates is massive—and massively untapped. If baseball's full-scale adoption of data is a 10, Rudd rates the Premier League at a three or a four, which she said is an improvement from the beginning of the decade, when it would've been a one. "I think one of the big differences compared to baseball is managers have so much power and control," she said. "So there's going to be some, but very negligible, analytical impact in terms of tactics and team selection. But it's becoming ever increasing in terms of recruitment. And you can look at the transfer window. You can see who's listening to their analysts, who isn't, and when somebody went rogue and decided to just sign the player. I don't know if we'll ever get to the 10, to the level of baseball, but the needle is definitely moving."

Rudd worked at Arsenal at the tail end of the Wenger era and then for the first three years after it ended. Wenger was one of the most powerful managers in the world, and over his final few seasons it seemed like he'd been overtaken by a bunch of more modern managers and clubs. After finishing top four in his first 20 years with the club, the streak finally ended, but the team's performance has only declined since he left. Wenger, too, was more willing to listen to his in-house analytics team than most.

"With Arsène, there was a certain amount of work that we did," Rudd said. "And we kind of had free rein to work on problems. And then with the other coaching staffs coming in, there's a lot of reeducation that you have to do. So you spend a lot of time on that, but then they're going to have a whole different set of questions and a different style of working. And so you have to kind of adapt to that."

After years spent under the command of one of the true outliers in coaching history, across all sports, Arsenal have since had to operate like almost every other club: hiring and firing managers with regularity. Unai Emery, a Spanish coach who'd had lots of success with lesser teams but failed to win the French league with PSG, first replaced Wenger, but lasted only for a season and a half. He was replaced by Mikel Arteta, a former Arsenal player who'd never been a head coach at any level before but was Pep Guardiola's assistant at Manchester City. Neither one really seemed to fit within an already-existing infrastructure or clear vision for the club, but rather had everything changed to fit them and their vision.

"We're set up so that everything is flexible enough that if you change the profile of, let's say, a winger you want, we should be able to go and find that," Rudd said. "I think where it's difficult is that not everybody has a clear idea of what that profile is. And then it's constantly changing as well because you have to deal with the players you have on hand. And so maybe eventually, you want to play in a style and your wing will have this profile. But given who we have this year when we could only buy one or two players, that isn't going to work, and you have to be a little bit more pragmatic."

Rudd said the StatDNA group has had "some sort of say, whether it's just due diligence" on every signing that the club has made since 2012. If they were fully empowered and weaponized, though, they would've had a major say on every transfer. In 2020, Edu Gaspar, a former midfielder for the club and their current technical director (roughly equivalent to a GM in American sports), said publicly, "I want to work a lot more with StatDNA, which we have internally here at the club. It is very important." While he *did* explicitly acknowledge the importance of the club's in-house data team, he also implicitly acknowledged that he wasn't working much with them before.

In 2020, Jaeson Rosenfeld, the founder of StatDNA, left Arsenal to go work with his old boss, Wenger, who is now the head of global football development at FIFA. With that move, Rudd became the club's vice president of software and analytics, a role which she held for about a year before stepping down in the summer of 2021 and joining Blue Crow Analytics, a data consultancy that will also aid investors looking to buy soccer clubs. (Her husband also joined Blue Crow in early 2022.) "Working in different leagues, teams with different budgets, different ambitions—that's very attractive to me. I think with Arsenal, it was always top four, same goal every year. So it's nice to just have a different set of problems, a different set of parameters to play around with, and see what we can do."

Without having to service the specific needs of whoever's in power at Arsenal, perhaps Rudd will be empowered to push our collective knowledge of the game forward—toward something new that's way off beyond the horizon. "I think we're still a long ways away from really understanding what's the optimal way to play," she said. "And it's going to be the optimal way to play against *this* team. Very few teams are blessed to be able to just set up however they want and let the other team adapt to them."

* * *

One of those very few teams is Barcelona, or at least it used to be. The club motto, in Catalan, is *Mes Que Un Club*, "more than a club." But a better slogan might be *El Més Club*, "the *most* club." Barcelona, unlike Europe's other super-clubs, are still owned by their 140,000-plus members, or *socis*. Every couple of years, the *socis* vote for a club president, who along with the members of his board, function as the de facto owner of the club while they're in power. Most of the *socis* and board members are Catalan locals. They just also happen to control one of the three richest soccer clubs in the world.

The crude history of the club is that Barcelona have always stood in some kind of opposition: to Madrid, to Spain, to everyone else. The club became a symbol of the resistance when the fascist dictator Francisco Franco was in power from the mid-1930s to the mid-1970s. Romantically, Franco's favorite club was Real Madrid, another among the three richest clubs in the world and Barcelona's biggest rival.

When Johan Cruyff left Ajax for Barcelona toward the end of the Franco regime, he somewhat unwittingly became the vessel through which the club could channel its antiestablishment, collectivist identity. He smoked cigarettes and encouraged his teammates to float in and out of various roles on the field throughout the course of a match. When they won, it was beautiful. When they lost, it was tragic. When he returned to Barcelona as a manager, he further instilled the structure of the club with these ideals: that everyone on the field should be comfortable in any situation, that the pursuit of the ball—"There is only one ball, so you need to have it"—was to be valued above all else. And when his protégé and former player, Pep Guardiola, an avowed Catalan separatist, led Barcelona to its unprecedented dominance in the new century's second decade, the identity was reified. And who could argue with it? Barcelona wouldn't hesitate to tell you they were different, and throughout the 2010s, you just had to tune into a random La Liga game on a fall weekend to know that they weren't totally full of shit. In another strange kind of capitalist paradox, Barcelona's devotion to the local philosophical ideal made it appealing to fans around the world, which, along with the presence of the greatest soccer player of all time, turned this group of Catalan bureaucrats and club members into a global powerhouse. In 2019, they became the first club to record more than €800 million in annual revenue.

After Guardiola left, the club didn't quite hit the same heights until the arrival of Luis Enrique, a former Barca and Real Madrid player without much of a managerial résumé. When he took over, he had the audacity to suggest that maybe Barcelona didn't need so much of the ball. Messi was now joined by the slippery Brazilian superstar Neymar and perhaps the best attacker in the world not named Lionel or Cristiano, Luis Suárez. Enrique would frequently select a more defensive collection of players and encourage the team to play with more vertical pace, on the counterattack. The beauty of having those three players was that they could break down five or six defenders all by themselves, and Enrique didn't hesitate to pull on that strategic lever. However, it felt like a betrayal to some Barcelona fans and journalists, and although his team gave up just nine goals in the first half of his first season, the criticism of the team's style reached such a feverish level that in January of 2015, the team fired its sporting director, Andoni Zubizarreta. Five months later, Barcelona won the Champions League, La Liga, and the Copa del Rey (the Spanish League Cup). Many, including yours truly, consider this to be the greatest soccer team of all time.

Enrique left in 2017, and the club won two La Liga titles under another former Barca player, Ernesto Valverde. But they were humiliated in the Champions

League, blowing massive leads in the knockout rounds to Roma and Liverpool, and he was fired the following year. They haven't won a title since Valverde left. And while it seemed like the club had reached its nadir with an 8–2 loss to Bayern Munich in the quarterfinals of the Champions League in 2020, somehow it got even worse. The club mismanaged its finances so terribly that they couldn't keep Lionel Messi, the person who's most individually responsible for Barcelona's modern dominance and growth into an €800-million-a-year behemoth. They reported €1.35 billion in debt in the summer of 2021, which led to Messi giving a bizarre, tearful goodbye press conference, in which he suggested that he wanted to stay but the club simply didn't have the money to make it work.

Javier Fernández was around to see most of it happen. Born in Venezuela to Spanish parents from Galicia, Javi is no *soci*, but like Sarah Rudd, he knew he wanted to work in soccer, and with numbers. He got his bachelor's degree in computer engineering from Simón Bolívar University, a prestigious public college in Caracas. In 2014, he moved to Barcelona to get his master's and then his PhD in artificial intelligence from the Polytechnic University of Catalonia. As he developed his master's thesis, his professors tried to steer him away from focusing on football. "No one was really happy about the idea in the university, saying, 'Yeah, soccer is a sport, it's quite random. Could be nice, but no.'" Incredibly, Fernández's wife was getting her master's at the same school, and *her* professor told her class that he'd caught wind of a hush-hush opportunity that couldn't be shared outside of the classroom: Barcelona were looking for a student to come do their thesis with the club by working on some physical-performance data the club had collected from its players. She told her husband, and soon enough, Fernández was helping the club streamline and organize an Excel file filled with GPS-based data.

Fernández assumes that Barcelona figured they'd be getting some "geeky person" with technical know-how who could solve this one particular issue while wrapping up his thesis and then heading off to some tech company. But the club liked that Fernández actually knew soccer. His mentor and boss at Barcelona was Daniel Medina, who had been the team physician since 2006 but now was also overseeing the club's nascent sports science department, which was quite literally focused on the deployment of science in sports, which included what we colloquially consider sports analytics. Medina introduced Fernández to Bornn, who served as the latter's thesis advisor, and then he kept his protégé at the club beyond the completion of the academic work. Fernández served as Barcelona's lead data scientist from 2016 to 2018, then was promoted to head of sports analytics. Next time you're feeling overwhelmed, remember that Fernández got his PhD in artificial intelligence *while* he was leading the data-based efforts to prevent one of the biggest soccer clubs in the world from collapsing during a global pandemic.

Fernández's first year or so with the club was spent in rooms talking to coaches for the various teams throughout the organization. Before Fernández got there, video analysts would spend six or seven hours after each match logging the important details of the game. Using his technical skills, Fernández wanted to automate this process for the analysts so their time could be better spent elsewhere. But to do this, he and the coaches had to take a step back and essentially define the component parts of the sport that Barcelona had already conquered: "What is an attack? How do you define that? It was interesting because I learned the jargon, what was important, more advanced concepts like breaking the first line, breaking the second line. How are those lines dynamically formed? What is pitch control? Why do you think that player is better than the other? How do you think about positions? Are these really their positions? Why do we want Barcelona players to do first-touch, quick movements instead of the other things?" Once he got the answers, Fernández would create applications that would allow the analysts to easily go search for video of, say, a line-breaking pass or the start and end of an attack.

After a year of that, he moved into actually figuring out ways to assess how the team was playing—in a general sense and then in a "Barcelona-specific" sense. In other words, is the team doing things that will likely lead to the team winning more games in the future? And then, is Barcelona—and the players who play for Barcelona—doing the specific things that Barcelona wants from its players?

In particular, Fernández said that some of his most fruitful work came with the players themselves. In much the same way that players have begun to embrace data more quickly than the clubs that employ them in order to quantify their value and ask to be paid more money, some have embraced the insights analysts are able to provide about how they might improve their play. "One coach told me several times that if you can say something valuable that helps one player once, he's going to be [in] your debt forever," Fernández said. "If you can improve something in the way they are playing, they're really going to value that." After scoring in a 2–0 win against Chelsea, James Maddison, an attacking midfielder for Leicester City, name-checked the team's opposition scout, Jack Lyons: "Me, the gaffer, and Jack the analyst sat down—Jack will be buzzing that I've name-dropped him—and looked at where I could get more goals." Jack Grealish, another attacking midfielder who eventually moved from Aston Villa to Manchester City for an English-player-record $129.25 million, also mentioned his rising expected-assist totals as evidence of his improved performance.

While he was busy at work answering his Barcelona-specific problems, Fernández was able to take a high-level view of things through the work he did with his PhD. He linked up with Luke Bornn to write the paper about space occupation and how Messi is better at walking than everyone else. A year later, Bornn and Fernández, along with Dan Cervone, then the director of quantitative research with the Los Angeles Dodgers, built on that work using tracking data, and released their own expected-possession value model in another paper from the Sloan Conference: "Decomposing the Immeasurable Sport: A Deep Learning Expected Possession Value Framework for Soccer." With tracking data, this model advances way beyond the pleasing, intuitive simplicity of Singh's location-based Expected Threat. In a sense, this paper combines xT with Stefan Reinartz's concept of packing, valuing actions based both on where they happen on the field and in relation to where the players are on the field. In addition to potentially providing a finer-tuned value of what players are doing with the ball, this model allows for an analysis of what they're doing off it. Player positioning can be roughly valued by looking at both the likelihood that a pass would be completed to them and how much a completed pass would increase their team's chances of scoring. If you flip that concept inside out, it can also be used as a rough proxy for both decision-making and skill: What could a player do with the ball in a given situation, how likely is each one to succeed, and how much would each potentially successful action increase goal-scoring probability?

This paper is easily the most-advanced of its kind—possible only because of the brainpower behind it and the tracking data that's not widely available. One of the tricks that Fernández and Co. used to make the model more accurate was heresy for where he worked: Abolish possession. Most other EPV models defined the end of a possession when a team lost the ball or scored a goal, and then built their values out from there, but Fernández's model slightly twists the lens with which we normally view the game. It treats a possession as the entire stretch between a kick-off and a goal being scored, which taps a tenet that Richard Pollard was banging on about 50-plus years ago: Each team has a likelihood of scoring and conceding in a given moment, no matter who's actually in control of the ball. And from that follows a phrase that might get you banished from the city of Barcelona: Sometimes it's better to give the ball away.

"Many times, losing the ball can really provide value," Fernández said. "When we did this EPV framework, I thought it was an artifact or some issue with the data. But when the players were super-pressed and there's certain conditions happening, the model was basically saying that the best thing observed right now is to kick the ball really far away and press there, where you have lower risk. You will lose the ball farther away from your goal and there's an increased chance of recovering and scoring a goal rather than trying to keep the ball."

A congregant at the Church of Possession Play espousing the same values that got Charles Reep excommunicated? That couldn't have gone over well. "Yeah, it was definitely not the favorite type of feedback," Fernández said. "But if you drill with more specific situations, why can't we identify the value added by players without being so intense about what we consider is right and wrong?"

As it turns out, neither side is necessarily right. There are times where the model thinks the best move is to kick it long and try to regain possession far away from your own goal. And there are other times where, based on the positioning of a player's teammates and his opponents, a backward pass is the way to go. "You stop seeing the field as like a rectangular thing and start seeing it around the ball," Fernández said.

In the summer of 2021, Fernández left Barcelona to link up with Bornn (and Cervone) at Zelus. With Barcelona's ever-shifting leadership structure, the club is, in some ways, immune to a top-down adoption of analytics. Presidents are constantly changing, and a flashy signing will often look at lot better to *socis* than a special new model or a lesser-known talent with strong underlying numbers. With the cutting-edge work Fernández is doing, it's hard to imagine that the club would've signed a player like Antoine Griezmann, a 28-year-old attacker whose expected numbers had already begun to decline, if he had a larger influence. It's hard to imagine that they would've so badly botched the transition away from Neymar, too. In the sixth months that followed, Barcelona signed French winger Ousmane Dembélé from Borussia Dortmund and Brazilian attacker

Philippe Coutinho from Liverpool—for the third- and fourth-highest transfer fees of all time. They've combined for 36 non-penalty goals and 36 assists in four-plus seasons since arriving and Coutinho was eventually sold to Aston Villa for a massive loss. And it also seems unlikely that the club would've cut ties with Ernesto Valverde seemingly because of his Champions League mishaps. "Probably the most popular and random metric is winning the Champions League," Fernández said. "It's really difficult even when you have Pep Guardiola and Manchester City with all the money and great players and great playing style and everything perfect."

In a way, Barcelona's identity might ultimately have been its undoing. While under Guardiola the club *did* dominate the ball to a freakish degree, they also pressed high up the field and constantly turned their opponents over in the final third. They had a rare collection of players who were willing to both attempt and complete dangerous passes at a high clip. Midfielders like Xavi, Andrés Iniesta, and Sergio Busquets all had perfectly calibrated EPV models in their heads; they all seemed to know exactly when to attempt the exact pass that the situation called for. Then, the team was able to win the ball back when the passes didn't come off. Oh, and they also had the greatest soccer player of all time to turn all that possession into all those goals. Over time, it seems like the patient passing and the possession became the things that the club cared about—at the expense of the things, the high turnovers, the defense-splitting passes into the penalty area, that actually made Barcelona win all of those games. The generation of players who allowed them to play this specific style all aged out or moved on and the club decayed into a slow-moving sideways-passing team that kept waiting for Messi to do something amazing, even as he aged deeper into his 30s.

Despite all the resources you'd ever need to succeed—including at least one visionary who could create things to show you where it was going—the game simply left Barcelona behind.

* * *

While Fulham were yo-yoing back and forth between the first and second divisions and Barcelona and Arsenal were rapidly decaying, Liverpool were headed in only one direction. In the 2017–18 season, they reached the Champions League final, losing to Real Madrid 3–2 after a couple of spectacular errors from their keeper and an injury to their best player. In the 2018–19 season, they earned

97 points—then the third-highest tally in the history of the Premier League. Unfortunately for them, no. 2 was that same year's Manchester City, who edged them by one point, just two points shy of the record, which had been set by . . . Manchester City the previous season. However, Liverpool made up for the near miss by winning the Champions League for the sixth time with a 2–0 win over Tottenham. A year later, they won the Premier League for the first time, improbably improving by two points on the previous year's total. In 2022, they became the first English team to ever reach the final of the FA Cup, League Cup, and Champions League in the same season. They've cemented themselves as one of the three or four best clubs in the world—it took only two analytical revolutions to get there.

As owner of the Boston Red Sox, John Henry famously tried to hire Billy Beane away from the Oakland A's—only to be turned down. He instead had to settle for a kid named Theo Epstein, who would steward the franchise to Boston's first World Series in 86 years and then go on to break a 108-year drought with the Chicago Cubs. Baseball now conquered, Henry bought Liverpool in 2010 and immediately went looking for his new Epstein.

The man Henry hoped would bring Moneyball to soccer was Damien Comolli, a friend of Beane's. As Tottenham's director of football, Comolli had identified and signed future Real Madrid superstars Luka Modrić and Gareth Bale. At Liverpool, he immediately identified a handful of unconventional signings—including Andy Carroll, a gigantic, ponytailed center forward who played with the composure of an angry horse, and Charlie Adam, a young midfielder with the looks and athleticism of a middle-aged pirate—and seemed set to revamp the team in the image of his data. The Moneyball mandate seemed clear, as most of the players whom Comolli signed had led their previous teams in crosses. This approach, however, would later be refuted after extensive analyses revealed that crossing is an inefficient strategy with little upside and significant downside. Not all data, it turns out, is created equal, and Comolli lasted at Liverpool for only two seasons.

Comolli's legacy isn't one of destruction, though. He's currently working at Toulouse for Luke Bornn and Beane. At Liverpool, he sold the electric striker Fernando Torres to Chelsea for $64.35 million. It seemed like Liverpool were unwittingly strengthening one of their biggest rivals, but Torres was injury prone and already 27—young by societal standards, but already at the tail end of his soccer-playing prime. He scored just 20 Premier League goals for Chelsea in five seasons after netting 65 for Liverpool in four. Comolli also purchased a 24-year-old Uruguayan striker from Ajax for just $29.15 million. Luis Suárez would eventually produce the greatest individual attacking season in Premier League history—1.31 non-penalty goals+assists per 90 minutes—before moving on to Barcelona for $89.89 million. And then there's Jordan Henderson, the 21-year-old from Sunderland whom Sir Alex Ferguson had dismissed because he didn't like the way he walked. The $19.8 million Liverpool paid for Henderson seemed a bit rich for a guy who'd scored just three goals and assisted four in the previous season. But Henderson went on to become the club captain and has since made more than 300 appearances for Liverpool.

Just as important, though, were the two men Comolli brought to work *under* him: Michael Edwards and Ian Graham. Edwards became the club's sporting director in 2016, while Graham is the director of research. Edwards left the club after the 2021–22 season, but Graham remains. Together, they created the most analytically sound elite club in Europe.

Without the funding of an oligarch or a petrol state or the old money of Manchester United, Liverpool needed to figure out a way to break the chain between wages and performance. They'd been knocked off their perch by Ferguson's United, and although they'd won more first-division titles than any club other than their rivals in Manchester, they hadn't won one since the Premier League was formed. They remained constant top-four finishers and won the Champions League in 2005, but the rise of Manchester City and Chelsea eventually crowded them out of that competition, too. In the first five seasons of Henry's ownership, they finished in the top four only once and averaged a table finish of sixth. Then, in consecutive summers they signed attackers Roberto Firmino from Hoffenheim, Sadio Mané from Southampton, and Mohamed Salah from Roma for less than a combined $150 million. At their peaks, some estimates put their combined values north of $580 million. As of May 2022, they'd combined for 279 goals and 121 assists for Liverpool. For the second half of the 2010s, they were easily the most prolific attacking trio in the world.

"This is something I've said about Liverpool for a while," Michael Caley said. "You can hire all the genius PhDs that you want, but there's still no better thing than identifying a forward who is underperforming their expected goals over several seasons and has elite numbers."

Firmino and Mané had both underperformed their xG numbers in the season before Liverpool signed them. Caley conducted an analysis that removed all strikers and all players at the 10 richest clubs, and he found that Firmino, Mané, and Salah were all toward the top of the list for xG+xA per 90 minutes. Salah, who hadn't underperformed, had the best xG+xA performance in the *entire* sample of players Caley looked at. He was seemingly undervalued by the market because he'd been signed and then discarded by Chelsea, which created doubts about his ability to perform in England. Eventually, Liverpool added a fourth member to its attacking corps by acquiring Diogo Jota from Wolverhampton. He might've been the most extreme version of the approach: underperforming both his xG and his xA numbers the season before Liverpool signed him.

A similar process was applied to their manager. While most research does suggest that coaches don't make a huge long-term difference to results, it's clear that there's at least a select group at the very top who do. Despite a massive resource disadvantage to Bayern Munich and a constantly churning roster that saw the club sell its best young players to richer clubs, Jürgen Klopp guided Borussia Dortmund to a pair of Bundesliga titles in 2010–11 and 2011–12 with a Rangnickian pressing approach that he referred to as "heavy metal football." (Bayern has won every title since.) However, in 2014–15 Dortmund found themselves in the relegation zone midway through the season. They climbed up to 7th by the end of the year, but it seemed like Klopp's demands had worn the team out. He and the team mutually parted ways.

Well, maybe if you watched the games. Unswayed by observational biases, all Ian Graham saw was a team that, according to various expected-goal models, should've finished in second, just like they had in the previous two seasons. After a slow start to the 2015–16 season, Liverpool decided to part ways with Brendan Rodgers, by all measures a competent manager who nearly led them to a title in 2013–14, in order to replace him with someone they felt was one of the few coaches who could truly and tangibly add points to your end-of-season total: Jürgen Klopp.

Like most managers, Klopp didn't rely on any data at Dortmund. However, he met with Graham during the interview process at Liverpool. Prior to the meeting, Graham, who has a PhD in theoretical physics from Cambridge University, gathered data from a few matches where Dortmund were particularly unlucky not to win. He told Klopp about them, to which the German responded: "Ah, you saw that game. It was crazy. We killed them. You saw it!" Graham told him that, no, he hadn't ever seen the game. He could tell just from the data. This seemed to create a bond between the coach and the data department that just doesn't exist in many clubs. "The department there in the back of the building?" Klopp told the *New York Times Magazine*. "They're the reason I'm here."

That relationship proved most important in 2017, when Klopp reportedly wanted the club to sign young German attacker Julian Brandt from his old club. The front office, however, preferred Salah—and they eventually won out. Brandt has scored 10 goals and logged 11 assists over the course of his Dortmund career. Salah scored 32 goals and assisted 10—in his first *season* with Liverpool.

With the front three scoring goals for fun and Klopp transforming the team into a pressing machine, Liverpool reestablished themselves as a Champions League side with Champions League revenues. But they still conceded too many goals and too many high-quality shots on the defensive end. Early in 2017–18, they were embarrassed against Manchester City and Tottenham by a combined score of 9–1. However, the club's mastery of the transfer market provided a multi-directional benefit. The front three had rendered one of the club's other stars, a Brazilian midfield-attacker hybrid named Philippe Coutinho, surplus to requirements. Barcelona had just sold Neymar to PSG. They had $200-plus million to spend—and everyone knew it. The unbalanced incentives—Barcelona needed to replace a superstar, Liverpool didn't need their superstar—led to Coutinho being sold to Barcelona for €135 million, still the fourth-most-expensive transfer of all time.

With the added money, Liverpool spent big to solve their biggest problem. First, they broke the transfer record for a defender (€84.5 million) in order to acquire Virgil van Dijk, a smooth, towering Dutch center back from Southampton who was equally adept at winning balls in the air and covering lots of ground. Then, the same summer Chelsea blew €80 million on Kepa, Liverpool acquired Alisson from Roma for €72.5 million. In his last season in Italy, the Brazilian keeper saved 10.8 goals above average, according to StatsBomb, which was the third-best mark in all of Europe. The thinking was pretty clear: Van Dijk would prevent Liverpool from giving up some of those big chances in the first place. And whenever the ball did still get through, Alisson would be there to stop it.

In addition to those main moves, Liverpool have pushed just about every tiny edge along the way, too. Each season, they're among the leaders in Europe for goals scored on set pieces. They hired Thomas Grønnemark, the throw-in coach from Midtjylland. They've frequently purchased players from relegated teams, capitalizing on the desire of those sides to cut costs and the fact that abject team-level performance can obscure impressive individual outputs. They acquired left back Andy Robertson from relegated Hull City for just $9.9 million, and he quickly became one of the best fullbacks in the world. How'd they identify him? Graham told Stephen Dubner of *Freakonomics* that the Scotsman's stats had popped on his expected-possession-value model. "We tried to put everything into one currency," he explained. "We try to take whatever action a player does on a pitch—whether it's a pass or a shot or a tackle if you're a defender—and ask the question, 'What was this team's chance of scoring a goal before this action happened?' And then, 'What was this team's chance of scoring a goal after that action happened?' And we call that 'goal probability added,' which is a really catchy name." "Goal-probability added" is just Liverpool's in-house version of expected-possession value.

As for the question of midfield, Liverpool have mainly ignored it. For the majority of Klopp's tenure, midfielders have served the unspectacular purpose of maintaining team shape, not losing the ball, and covering for other players. Rather than attempting to ring value out of the mystery in the middle of the field, they've shifted the creative passing responsibility to Robertson and fellow fullback Trent Alexander-Arnold, who have combined for 90 assists over their first five full seasons with the team.

Despite all of that, their success required a bunch of luck, too. At the 2021 StatsBomb Conference, Graham gave a talk where he summed up his theory of player recruitment. He said there were six ways a transfer might fail: The player isn't as good as you thought, the player doesn't fit your style, the player is played out of position, the manager doesn't like the player, the player has injury/personal problems, or a player already on the roster ends up being better. Even if you're 90 percent sure of success in each of those areas, Graham said, that means a given transfer has only a 53 percent chance ($0.9 \times 0.9 \times 0.9 \times 0.9 \times 0.9$) of working out.

Alexander-Arnold was a youth prospect who grew up in Liverpool and blossomed into the best attacking fullback in the world before his 21st birthday.

What are the chances that this specific player just happened to be living in Liverpool? No one considered van Dijk as one of the best defenders in the world when Liverpool bought him; everyone thinks that way now. While Salah was a savvy signing, he's been better than anyone could've reasonably imagined. He has a legitimate claim as the best player in the world, post–Lionel Messi. Now, maybe those outcomes were more likely to happen at Liverpool than at other clubs because of the structure of their decision-making and because of a coach like Klopp, but nothing could've ensured that any one of the three players would reach their 99th-percentile outcomes of their potentials—and that happened to all three.

"I tend to think that the media, historically, has drastically overrepresented the impact of analytics within clubs. Maybe this was on your end, hopefully I can call you out. Hopefully, I'm implicitly calling out your writing here," Bornn said, laughing. "But you would think that Liverpool is run by a Robo GM and their success has been won by statistical models. Of course, that's some small piece of all these decisions, but that's certainly how it's portrayed, which is wildly wrong."

Whatever the true driver of the uptick in performance, the success, in turn, has driven Liverpool's revenues, as they've climbed from 12th in the money league rankings in 2013 to fifth in 2020. In the summer of 2021, much to the chagrin of many fans, the club signed only one player: 22-year-old center back Ibrahima Konaté from RB Leipzig. Instead, they spent most of their money re-signing seven key members of the current roster to lucrative, long-term salaries. Even they know that they can't break the chain forever.

* * *

The Higgs boson is a once-theoretical particle that scientists believed constituted the Higgs, a sort of cosmic mush that all other particles move through. Physicists needed a way to explain how particles got their mass, so they came up with the Higgs to suggest that mass itself came from how various particles moved through the Higgs. Mass-less particles moved through it without any resistance, the theory suggested, whereas other particles experienced varying degrees of drag, depending on their mass. In 2012, at CERN, the European Organization for Nuclear Research, in Switzerland, a group of scientists finally discovered proof of the existence of the Higgs boson using the Large Hadron Collider, a machine that smashes protons together at just below the speed of light at a rate of more than a billion times per second. In 2013, the two leading researchers, François Englert and Peter Higgs, were awarded the Nobel Prize in Physics.

While getting his PhD in particle physics from Harvard, a Texan named Will Spearman spent two years at CERN, working on the massive team of scientists trying to discover the Higgs boson. His thesis attempted to determine the mass and the width of the particle that Stephen Hawking once said would never be discovered, let alone measured.

Now, Spearman works as a data analyst at Liverpool. Before joining the club, he'd built a model that employed physics-based techniques to determine the likelihood of a goal being scored within the next 15 seconds, based on the movement characteristics of the players on the field and the ball itself. The title for the paper was "Beyond Expected Goals," and it was featured, along with several other papers we've covered, at the MIT Sloan Sports Analytics Conference in 2018. One of Spearman's remits at Liverpool is to imagine something totally new, to try to answer the question: Is there a different and better way to play soccer? In 2020, Spearman and the rest of Liverpool's data staff coauthored a paper with some members of Google's artificial-intelligence team, DeepMind. At DeepMind, they created a program that first taught itself how to play chess and then demolished the world's most advanced chess engine. The paper posits a number of ways that things like machine learning and artificial intelligence could shine more light into the darkness still shrouding things like player value, player decision-making, and tactical strategy.

Other advancements might not require the same kind of computing power and know-how—and some might be possible without expensive tracking cameras being installed at every stadium around the world. Bornn, Beane, and RedBird's Toulouse won Ligue 2 on the second try, breaking the record for goals scored in a single season. Soon after that, the same group became the majority owners of seven-time winners of the Champions League, AC Milan. Paul Power now works for SkillCorner, a French company that has developed technology that can generate relatively accurate tracking data from broadcast video. While broadcast feeds rarely show the positioning of all 22 players, the SkillCorner model uses a technique called "ghosting" to predict where the off-screen players are based on where they were in similar situations during matches for which full tracking data is available. This data can be recorded for any league that's on TV, it's cheaper, and it's available to anyone who wants it. StatsBomb, meanwhile, have expanded their freeze-frame technology to every action that happens on the field. The computer vision is no longer limited to shots only, so whenever a coder logs a pass or a tackle the computer now takes a snapshot of what the field looks like. Both approaches create the possibility of a much larger dataset of contextualized actions, expanding the width of the flashlight.

Yet while the likes of Liverpool have already moved on to asking deeper questions about the fundamental nature of the sport—sometimes out in public—almost everyone else is still working on just making something like expected goals a common currency across their clubs.

"[F]or a long time, credibility in decision-making primarily depended on human specialists such as managers, retired players, and scouts, all of them with track records and experience in professional football, in part due to cultural reasons," Liverpool's data team and the AI experts from Google wrote, after listing off all of the things that make the game difficult to measure from a scientific perspective. "As a result of these various factors, the potential influence and gains of predictive analytics on the football game have also been less obvious, with sports analytics as a game-changing phenomenon not realized until recent years."

If it's not obvious by now, there is still much to learn about the Beautiful Game, and what little we have already learned isn't being used nearly enough.

Baseball, basketball, and football are all wildly different from the games they were 20 years ago. The search for wins, however, has had little time for entertainment value. The NFL has certainly seen its product improve with the rise of passing and aggressive play-calling. But while the NBA has become a higher-scoring league, the sport can sometimes feel like it's hurtling toward a kind of uniformity in which every team is searching out the same shots and winners are increasingly determined by the raw chance of who hit more threes on a given night. Baseball, meanwhile, has all but eliminated its in-game diversity, as the ball rarely enters the field of play and home runs, walks, and strikeouts monopolize the action. Perhaps due to an ambient awareness of xG in the Premier League, the average distance from the goal on a given shot has declined in each of the past five seasons. There are slightly fewer long-range lightning bolts ending up in the upper corner, and there are also slightly fewer off-target rockets that end up in the stands.

The game has changed ever so slightly even without most clubs adopting a more analytical approach. But as more teams slowly start to mimic Liverpool's approach and pin their strategies on something tangible, soccer is soon going to seem drastically different than it did just the other day.

And what if the likes of Spearman and Bornn and Knutson ultimately find out that the other stuff—the stuff that makes up the majority of each match—*really* doesn't matter? Could the sport devolve into something wholly less elegant than it is in its current form, with each team launching long passes toward the other penalty area, scrambling for loose balls, and hoping to win free kicks? Could the Red Bull influence make the game even more physical and crowd out the inexplicable space geniuses like Sergio Busquets and Cesc Fàbregas who manage to keep the game surprising? Could scripted moves from open play take scoring a goal from something of a minor miracle to the rote result of a pre-planned routine?

Or might the search for a better way to play transform soccer into a game that values more and more risk-taking, encouraging the spectacular pass rather than the simple one and forcing defensive managers to push more bodies forward? The goal-scoring rate in European soccer has remained constant for more than half a century. Doesn't that seem due for a disruption?

I have some theories. Set pieces aren't going anywhere, and neither is pressing, nor the primacy of the penalty area. Barring a drastic rule change, wherever the game goes, it's hard to imagine that its new forms won't all feature lots of running, goals from free kicks, and passes pumped into an 18-yard box. The logic behind each one is as airtight as "three points is more than two" or that a home run is better than a single. But beyond that, who knows? Despite all the brainpower and sheer computing force being thrown at the problem today, there's still a dazzling possibility sitting at the heart of all this, something that's been true since William McGregor decided that, yeah, maybe we should start scheduling some of these games, huh? It's been true no matter what methods various thinkers, innovators, philosophizers, taskmasters, and visionaries have used to determine their own theories of the sport. My dad knew it, too: Soccer never stops changing—from decade to decade, season to season, game to game, minute to minute. Once you think you've figured out the answer, someone else, inevitably, will find a better way to ask the question.

ACKNOWLEDGMENTS

It should be obvious, but I never could have written this book without my dad, Michael O'Hanlon. By taking the long view, he found a pathway for his son to lead a fulfilling life of soccer in America. I wouldn't think the way I do—about soccer, about life—if it weren't for him and his endless empathy. Also: shoutout to my mother, Janet O'Hanlon, for the genes. She earned a gymnastics scholarship to the University of Florida and then, somehow, raised my younger twin brothers while she was in law school (where she graduated as valedictorian). There's none of this without you two.

The others who pushed me to do this: Nick Jackson is the best boss I ever had, and he convinced me to leave Brooklyn for Santa Fe for Santa Barbara. Chris Ryan is the guy who hired me out of magazine-editorship and encouraged me to write weirdly and creatively and differently about this sport. Eileen Hutchinson, you're the one who knew this is what I wanted to do before I even did. Kevin Lincoln is the best friend/editor/hype-man anyone could ever ask for. My guys Franco Bacigalupo and Tom Van Grinvsen kept me sane while I was writing this thing. My editors at ESPN, James Tyler and James Martin, gave me the space to finish the project. And then there are the coaches—Nick Iadanza, Mike Gallaher, and Ted Priestly—who made me stick with a sport that can so often seem so stupid.

To my agent, Howard Yoon: you encouraged me to think way bigger about this book, and your immediate belief in my capabilities and my ideas was the final push I needed to start a new career. I've never done this before, and you guided this thing from a kernel of a thought to a full-blown proposal that somebody wanted to buy. And thank you to Carl Bromley, who first convinced the two of us that we should chat.

To my editors, Connor Leonard and Jamison Stoltz—and everyone else at Abrams: you jumped on this project right away, and most importantly, you wanted me to do it my way. You showed a ton of faith in a first-time book writer and didn't suggest that I just write the whole thing about Liverpool or Lionel Messi. Thanks for understanding the ideas, pushing me in all the right directions, and saving me from myself.

To my transcribers Kate Mooney, Hannah Steinkopf-Frank, and Sumit Som: I hope the ability to both recognize and spell the world "Midtjylland" will come in handy again at some point.

All of the characters who have appeared in this book—and plenty who didn't—were so gracious with their time and showed immense patience with my constant questioning over the existential nature of the sport. Luke Bornn and Paul Power, in particular, were always up for a chat, and the two of them have shaped my thinking about the way soccer works—and could work and should work—more than anyone else. It's not easy for an American to convince people within European soccer to talk; thanks to everyone who did. Thanks, too, to A. J. Swoboda and James Yorke for all the conversations over the years. You're both the best.

And lastly, to everyone who has ever read my work and in particular to the Infinitos (you know who you are): I had no idea how much interest there would be in my kind of writing about soccer when I first set off on my own, and you all convinced me to keep going with it. Without all of you thoughtful readers, this writing doesn't mean anything.

SOURCES

Each chapter contains original reporting from interviews I conducted for this project with the book's primary—and secondary—characters. I relied on a number of other sources, however, to piece everything together: This narrative wouldn't have been possible without all the reporting of other journalists and researchers over the last fifty-plus years. I've also relied on some past reporting I've done in my career covering professional soccer.

Here is a partial list of the many sources I consulted to assemble the book.

Introduction

Farrey, Tom. "How France Really Won the World Cup." Aspen Institute, October 9, 2018. https://www.aspeninstitute.org/blog-posts/how-france-really-won-the-world -cup/.

Ford, Paul R., and A. Mark Williams. "No Relative Age Effect in the Birth Dates of Award-Winning Athletes in Male Professional Team Sports." *Research Quarterly for Exercise and Sport* 82, no. 3 (2011): 570–73. doi 10.1080/02701367.2011.10599790.

Musch, Jochen, and Roy Hay. "The Relative Age Effect in Soccer: Cross-Cultural Evidence for a Systematic Discrimination against Children Born Late in the Competition Year." *Sociology of Sport Journal* 16, no. 11 (1999): 54–64. https://doi .org/10.1123/ssj.16.1.54.

Norton, Kevin, and Tim Olds. "Morphological Evolution of Athletes Over the 20th Century." *Sports Medicine* 31, no. 11 (2001): 763–83. https://doi.org/10.2165/00007256–200131110–00001.

Pulisic, Christian. "1,834 Days." The Players' Tribune, November 23, 2017. https://www.theplayerstribune.com/articles/christian-pulisic-usmnt-world-cup.

Sokolove, Michael. "How a Soccer Star Is Made." *New York Times Magazine*, June 2, 2010. https://www.nytimes.com/2010/06/06/magazine/06Soccer-t.html.

Yagüe, José M., Alfonso de la Rubia, Joaquín Sánchez-Molina, Sergio Maroto-Izquierdo, and Olga Molinero. "The Relative Age Effect in the 10 Best Leagues of Male Professional Football of the Union of European Football Associations (UEFA)." *Journal of Sports Science and Medicine* 17, no. 3 (2018): 409–16. https://www.jssm.org/volume17/iss3/cap/jssm-17–409.pdf.

Chapter 1

Caley, Michael. "Want to Have a Long Career in Soccer? Play in Goal or Central Defence." ESPN, March 29, 2017. https://www.espn.com/soccer/blog/tactics-and-analysis/67/post/3056495/soccer-age-curves-show-goalkeepers-and-central-defenders-peak-latest.

Doyle, Paul. "The Day in 1982 When the World Wept for Algeria." *Guardian*, June 12, 2010. https://www.theguardian.com/football/2010/jun/13/1982-world-cup-algeria.

Frelund, Cynthia, and Matt "Money" Smith. "Super Bowl LII Recap with Eagles HC Doug Pederson." *NFL: Game Theory and Money* (podcast), February 8, 2018. https://podcast.app/nfl-game-theory-and-money-p367060/.

Galeano, Eduardo. *Soccer in Sun and Shadow*. Translated by Mark Fried. London and New York: Verso, 1998.

Hay, Phil. "How Prozone Sparked a Football Analytics Boom." *Athletic*, November 16, 2020. https://theathletic.com/2193722/2020/11/16/prozone-analytics-ramm-mylvaganam-analysis-premier-league/.

Herring, Chris. "The Odds of the Rockets Missing That Many Threes? 1 in 72,000." FiveThirtyEight, May 29, 2018. https://fivethirtyeight.com/features/the-odds-of -the-rockets-missing-that-many-3s-1-in-72000/.

Hunt, Joshua. "The Shame of Gijón." *New Yorker*, June 24, 2014. https://www .newyorker.com/sports/sporting-scene/the-shame-of-gijn.

Lewis, Michael. *Moneyball*. New York: W. W. Norton, 2003.

Serrano, Adam. "Bruce Arena Provided a Vintage Bruce Quote When Describing the Use of Analytics in Soccer." Los Angeles Galaxy, July 23, 2016. https://www .lagalaxy.com/news/bruce-arena-provided-vintage-bruce-quote-when-describing -use-analytics-soccer.

Smyth, Rob. "World Cup Stunning Moments: West Germany 1–0 Austria in 1982." *Guardian*, March 20, 2018. https://www.theguardian.com/football/blog/2014 /feb/25/world-cup-25-stunning-moments-no3-germany-austria-1982-rob-smyth.

Vecsey, George. "When West Germany and Austria Danced a Vienna Waltz." *Pittsburgh Post-Gazette*, June 29, 1982.

Chapter 2

Caley, Michael. "Premier League Projections and New Expected Goals." *Cartilage Free Captain* (blog), SB Nation, October 19, 2015. https://cartilagefreecaptain .sbnation.com/2015/10/19/9295905/premier-league-projections-and-new -expected-goals.

Craggs, Tommy. "My Uncomfortable Encounter with an Angry Joe Morgan." *Deadspin*, November 9, 2010. https://deadspin.com/my-uncomfortable-encounter -with-an-angry-joe-morgan-5685456.

Grayson, James. "Another Post About TSR." *James' Blog*, July 15, 2012. https:/ /jameswgrayson.wordpress.com/2012/07/15/another-post-about-tsr/.

"Joe Morgan Pulls a Joe Morgan." *Fire Joe Morgan*, May 18, 2005. http://www .firejoemorgan.com/2005/05/joe-morgan-pulls-joe-morgan.html.

McKenzie, Bob. "The Real Story of How Corsi Got Its Name." TSN, October 6, 2014. https://www.tsn.ca/mckenzie-the-real-story-of-how-corsi-got-its-name-1.100011.

[Pugsley, Benjamin]. "Analysis: Total Shots vs Shots on Target." *Bitter and Blue* (blog), SB Nation, January 11, 2013. https://bitterandblue.sbnation.com/2013/1/11 /3857360/analysis-shots-vs-shots-on-target.

Skinner, Gerald K., and Guy H. Freeman. "Soccer Matches as Experiments: How Often Does the 'Best' Team Win?" *Journal of Applied Statistics* 36, no. 10 (2009): 1087–95. doi: 10.1080/02664760802715922.

Slowinski, Piper. "Linear Weights." FanGraphs, February 5, 2010. https://library .fangraphs.com/principles/linear-weights/.

Chapter 3

Kwiatkowski, Marek. "Quantifying Finishing Skill." StatsBomb, July 13, 2017. https://statsbomb.com/articles/soccer/quantifying-finishing-skill/.

Walton, David. "Brendan Rodgers Opens up on What Vakoun Issouf Bayo Will Bring to Celtic." *67 Hail Hail*, [2019]. https://www.67hailhail.com/news/brendan -rodgers-opens-vakoun-issouf-bayo-will-bring-celtic/?grva_cmp_open=1.

Chapter 4

Dell'Osso, Filippo, and Stefan Szymanski. "Who Are the Champions? (An Analysis of Football Architecture)." *Business Strategy Review*, June 1991. https://doi .org/10.1111/j.1467–8616.1991.tb00155.x.

Elberse, Anita. "Ferguson's Formula." *Harvard Business Review*, October 2013. https://hbr.org/2013/10/fergusons-formula.

Robinson, Joshua, and Jonathan Clegg. *The Club: How the English Premier League Became the Wildest, Richest, Most Disruptive Force in Sports.* New York: Houghton Mifflin Harcourt, 2018.

Szymanski, Stefan. "Why Is Manchester United So Successful?" *Business Strategy Review*, January 6, 2003. https://doi.org/10.1111/1467–8616.00082.

Szymanski, Stefan, and Andrew Zimbalist. *National Pastime: How Americans Play Baseball and the Rest of the World Plays Soccer*. Washington, DC: Brookings Institution Press, 2005.

Whitwell, Laurie, Adam Crafton, Matt Slater, and Oliver Kay. "This Is Ed Woodward." *Athletic*, October 11, 2019. https://theathletic.com/1282731/2021/04/20/1282731/.

Winner, Davis. *Those Feet: A Sensual History of English Football*. London: Bloomsbury, 2005.

Chapter 5

Djazmi, Mani. "Rudi Gutendorf: The Colourful Life of a 'Footballing Missionary.'" BBC, March 2, 2013. https://www.bbc.com/sport/football/21636939.

Sykes, Joe, and Neil Paine. "How One Man's Bad Math Helped Ruin Decades of English Soccer." FiveThirtyEight, October 27, 2016. https://fivethirtyeight.com/features/how-one-mans-bad-math-helped-ruin-decades-of-english-soccer/.

Thompson, Mark. "Analytics Is Older Than You Think: (Re)introducing Charles Reep." *Get Goalside*, May 13, 2021. https://getgoalsideanalytics.com/c/36315087.analytics-is-older-than-you-think.

Wilson, Jonathan. *Inverting the Pyramid: The History of Soccer Tactics*. New York: Nation Books, 2013.

Winner, Davis. *Those Feet: A Sensual History of English Football*. London: Bloomsbury, 2005.

Chapter 6

De Hoog, Michiel. "How Data, Not People, Call the Shots in Denmark." *Correspondent*, March 24, 2015. https://thecorrespondent.com/2607/how-data-not-people-call-the-shots-in-denmark/230219386155-d2948861.

Horncastle, James. "Allegri's 'Natural' Style Won Him Six Serie A Titles Since 2010. What's Next for a Coach Who Doesn't Own a Laptop?" ESPN, December 19, 2019.

https://www.espn.com/soccer/italian-serie-a/story/4015457/allegris-natural -style-won-him-six-serie-a-titles-since-2010-whats-next-for-a-coach-who-doesnt -own-a-laptop.

Ingle, Sean. "How Midtjylland Took the Analytical Route towards the Champions League." *Guardian*, July 27, 2015. https://www.theguardian.com/football/2015 /jul/27/how-fc-midtjylland-analytical-route-champions-league-brentford -matthew-benham.

———. "'What We Do Isn't Rocket Science': How Midtjylland Started Football's Data Revolution." *Guardian*, October 25, 2020. https://www.theguardian.com /football/2020/oct/25/what-we-do-isnt-rocket-science-how-fc-midtjylland -started-footballs-data-revolution.

Power, Paul, Jennifer Hobbs, Hector Ruiz, Xinyu Wei, and Patrick Lucey. "Myth-busting Set-Pieces in Soccer." MIT Sloan Sports Analytics Conference, 2018. https://www.statsperform.com/resource/exploiting-inefficiencies-at-set-pieces-sloan/

Chapter 7

Chotiner, Isaac. "Jalen Rose Has a Problem with Basketball Analytics." *New Yorker*, June 6, 2019. https://www.newyorker.com/news/q-and-a/jalen-rose-has-a -problem-with-basketball-analytics.

Dukić, Darko. "Most World Cup Talent Are Born in France (Data Analysis)." Run-Repeat, August 6, 2021. https://runrepeat.com/most-football-talent-france.

Jahromi, Neima. "The Twenty-Five-Year Journey of Magic: The Gathering." *New Yorker*, August 28, 2018. https://www.newyorker.com/culture/culture-desk/the -twenty-five-year-journey-of-magic-the-gathering.

Kuper, Simon, and Stefan Szymanski. *Soccernomics: Why England Loses; Why Spain, Germany, and Brazil Win; and Why the US, Japan, Australia, and even Iraq Are Destined to Become the Kings of the World's Most Popular Sport.* New York: Nation Books, 2018.

Sawchik, Travis. *Big Data Baseball.* New York: Flatiron Books, 2015.

Trainor, Colin. "Defensive Metrics: Measuring the Intensity of a High Press." StatsBomb, July 30, 2014. https://statsbomb.com/articles/soccer/defensive -metrics-measuring-the-intensity-of-a-high-press/.

Worville, Tom. "Inside De Bruyne's Data Report: Sancho Comparison and Impact of Playmaker's Possible City Exit Crucial to New Deal." *Athletic*, April 12, 2021. https://theathletic.com/2509349/2021/04/12/inside-de-bruynes-data-report -sancho-comparison-and-impact-of-playmakers-possible-city-exit-crucial-to-new -deal/.

Yam, Derrick. "Chelsea's Rebound Date: Kepa Arrizabalaga." StatsBomb, August 16, 2018. https://statsbomb.com/articles/soccer/chelseas-rebound-date -kepa-arrizabalaga/.

Chapter 8

Cox, Michael. *Zonal Marking: From Ajax to Zidane, the Making of Modern Soccer.* New York: Bold Type Books, 2019.

Fernández, Javier, and Luke Bornn. "Wide Open Spaces: A Statistical Technique for Measuring Space Creation in Professional Soccer." MIT Sloan Sports Analytics Conference, 2018. http://www.lukebornn.com/papers/fernandez_ssac_2018.pdf

Honigstein, Raphael. "Stefan Reinartz's Path from Player to Analyst Helps Us Understand Passing." ESPN, July 21, 2016. https://www.espn.com/soccer /german-bundesliga/10/blog/post/2915634/stefan-reinartz-new-metric -packing-helps-us-understand-effective-passing.

De Hoog, Michiel. "How Data, Not People, Call the Shots in Denmark." *Correspondent*, March 24, 2015. https://thecorrespondent.com/2607/how-data-not-people -call-the-shots-in-denmark/230219386155-d2948861.

Kram, Zach. "If You Thought Playing NBA Defense Was Hard, Try Quantifying It." The Ringer, May 11, 2021. https://www.theringer.com/nba/2021/5/11/22423517 /nba-defense-analytics-nikola-jokic.

Lawrence, Thom. "Some Things Aren't Shots: Comparative Approaches to Valuing Football." StatsBomb Innovation in Football Conference, October 11, 2019. https:/ /www.youtube.com/watch?v=5j-Ij5_3Cs8

Lowe, Sid. "I'm a Romantic, Says Xavi, Heartbeat of Barcelona and Spain." *Guardian*, February 11, 2011. https://www.theguardian.com/football/2011/feb/11/xavi-barcelona-spain-interview

———. "Xabi Alonso: 'Spain Benefited from Players Going to England.'" *Guardian*, November 11, 2011. https://www.theguardian.com/football/2011/nov/11/xabi-alonso-spain-england-interview.

Morris, Benjamin. "The Hidden Value of the NBA Steal." FiveThirtyEight, March 25, 2014. https://fivethirtyeight.com/features/the-hidden-value-of-the-nba-steal/.

Singh, Karun. "Introducing Expected Threat (xT)." [February 2019]. Website of Karun Singh. https://karun.in/blog/expected-threat.html.

Slowinski, Piper. "Positional Adjustment." FanGraphs, February 26, 2010. https://library.fangraphs.com/misc/war/positional-adjustment/.

Chapter 9

Hamilton, Tom. "Ralf Rangnick on RB Leipzig's Success and Being the Godfather of Gegenpressing." ESPN, October 28, 2020. https://www.espn.com/soccer/german-bundesliga/story/4218884/ralf-rangnick-on-rb-leipzigs-success-and-being-the-godfather-of-gegenpressing.

Hodson, Tony. "My Epiphany: Ralf Rangnick," n.d. The Coaches' Voice. https://www.coachesvoice.com/ralf-rangnick-rb-leipzig-and-bundesliga/.

———. "The Three Cs: Ralf Rangnick," n.d. The Coaches' Voice. https://www.coachesvoice.com/ralf-rangnick-red-bull-salzburg-jurgen-klopp-rb-leipzig/.

Iezzi, Teressa. "Red Bull CEO Dietrich Mateschitz on Brand as Media Company." *Fast Company*, February 17, 2012. https://www.fastcompany.com/1679907/red-bull-ceo-dietrich-mateschitz-on-brand-as-media-company.

Lyttleton, Ben. *Edge: Leadership Secrets from Football's Top Thinkers*. London: HarperCollins, 2017.

Olterman, Philip. "How RB Leipzig Became the Most Hated Club in German Football." *Guardian*, September 8, 2016. https://www.theguardian.com/football/2016/sep/08/why-rb-leipzig-has-become-the-most-hated-club-in-german-football.

Smyth, Rory. "The Oracle Is Speaking Again. Who Will Listen This Time?" *New York Times*, December 8, 2020. https://www.nytimes.com/2020/12/08/sports /soccer/man-united-RB-leipzig-ralf-rangnick.html?searchResultPosition=1.

Wahl, Grant, "Jesse Marsch Is the Closest Thing to a Real-Life Ted Lasso." *Fútbol with Grant Wahl*, August 25, 2021. https://grantwahl.substack.com/p/jesse -marsch-is-the-closest-thing?s=r.

Chapter 10

Dubner, Stephen J. "Can Britain Get Its 'Great' Back?" *Freakonomics Radio*, October 19, 2019. https://freakonomics.com/podcast/can-britain-get-its-great -back-ep-393/.

Fernández, Javier, Luke Bornn, and Daviel Cervone. "Decomposing the Immeasurable Sport: A Deep Learning Expected Possession Value Framework for Soccer." MIT Sloan Sports Analytics Conference, 2019. https://www .sloansportsconference.com/research-papers/decomposing-the-immeasurable -sport-a-deep-learning-expected-possession-value-framework-for-soccer.

Hughes, Simon. "Meet William Spearman, Liverpool's Secret Weapon." *The Athletic*, September 9, 2020. https://theathletic.com/2041669/2020/09/09/meet -william-spearman-liverpools-secret-weapon-15-seconds/.

Kuper, Simon. *The Barcelona Complex: Lionel Messi and the Making—and Unmaking—of the World's Greatest Soccer Club.* New York: Penguin Press, 2021.

Rudd, Sarah. "A Framework for Tactical Analysis and Individual Offensive Production Assessment in Soccer Using Markov Chains." New England Symposium on Statistics in Sports, 2011. http://nessis.org/nessis11/rudd.pdf.

Schoenfeld, Bruce. "How Data (and Some Breathtaking Soccer) Brought Liverpool to the Cusp of Glory." *New York*

INDEX

Note: Page references in *italics* refer to figures.

.